Autobiography of Allen Jay
(1831–1910)

**Edited with a Foreword
by Joshua Brown**

Copyright 1910, 1909, 1908 The John C. Winston Co.
First Edition 1910 The John C. Winston Co.

Published by Friends United Press,
101 Quaker Hill Dr., Richmond, Indiana 47374
First Edition 2010

All rights reserved. No part of this book may be reproduced, transmitted, or printed in any form or by any means, electronic, mechanical, photocopying, recording, or otherwise, without prior permission from Friends United Press.

Cover photographs appeared in the original edition of *Autobiography of Allen Jay* and depict Allen Jay himself and West Branch Quarterly Meetinghouse where Allen Jay had a conversion experience at the age of thirteen.

Library of Congress Cataloging-in-Publication Data

Jay, Allen.
 Autobiography of Allen Jay : 1831–1910 / edited with a foreword by Joshua Brown. — 1st ed.
   p. cm.
 Previously published: [S.l.] : John C. Winston Co., 1910.
 Includes index.
 ISBN 978-0-944350-75-1 (pbk.)
 1. Jay, Allen. 2. Quakers—United States—Biography. I. Brown, Joshua, 1956- II. Title.
 BX7795.J38A3 2010
 289.6092--dc22
 [B]
                                    2010003058

Contents

Introduction by Thomas Hamm v
Editor's Foreword by Joshua Brown xi
Foreword to the Original Edition xix

Chapters

1. Ancestry and Family 1
2. Early Influences: School and Meeting 7
3. The Millerites and Spiritualists 17
4. Old Randolph Meeting 23
5. The Work of my Father and Others in the Ministry 31
6. Origin and Influence of West Branch Quarterly Meeting 39
7. Moving to Indiana 47
8. Early Married Life 55
9. Beginnings in the Ministry 63
10. The Draft During the Civil War 75
11. The Setting Up of Western Yearly Meeting 79
12. The Era of Separation 83
13. Reflections on Separation 91
14. How Nathan Hunt Delayed Separation in North Carolina ... 97
15. Visits to North Carolina and Baltimore Meetings 103
16. Visiting Friends in North Carolina and Tennessee 115
17. The Call to the Work of the Baltimore Association 121
18. Conditions in Carolina at the Close of the Civil War ... 127
19. Work and Leaders of the Baltimore Association 141

20. Duties as Superintendent for the Baltimore Association 155
21. Some of the Teachers and Ministers.................................... 165
22. Revival Work in North Carolina.. 173
23. Final Work of the Baltimore Association 185
24. Preparations for a Visit to Great Britain............................. 191
25. Among Friends in Ireland... 195
26. At London Yearly Meeting... 201
27. Acquaintance with John Bright 207
28. Some Prominent English Friends...................................... 215
29. With Friends in Norway... 219
30. Religious Service in England and Scotland 231
31. With Stanley Pumphrey in America 237
32. The American Friends Board of Foreign Missions............. 243
33. Albert K. Smiley and the Providence School..................... 255
34. Earlham College Past and Present..................................... 265
35. The Founding of Earlham College.................................... 269
36. Educational and Religious Influence of Earlham 279
37. Filling Various Offices at Earlham 285
38. Origin of the Five Years' Meeting 295
39. The Origin of the Bible Institute 303
40. The Opening of California Yearly Meeting 307
41. Winter in Alabama and Florida.. 311
42. Marriage and Visit to England and Ireland....................... 323
43. Helping Guilford, Earlham, and Whittier Colleges 329
44. From North Carolina to Puget Sound 341
45. The Five Years' Meeting of 1907....................................... 347

Appendices

In Memory of Allen Jay..353
Memorial Minute...357
Dr. Nereus Mendenhall and Delphina Mendenhall 367
Timeline of Events in the Life of Allen Jay 379
Index..383

Introduction
by Thomas Hamm

Allen Jay was one of the most remarkable Friends of the nineteenth century, indeed, perhaps one of the most remarkable Friends who ever lived. His life was full of paradoxes. Born with a cleft palate, he became one of the most admired and successful Quaker preachers of his time. A native of the Ohio frontier, he became widely traveled and admired around the globe. A peacemaker by nature, he nevertheless did not shrink from controversy when he saw a principle involved. Firmly committed to what he understood as historic Quakerism, he nevertheless helped lead perhaps the most dramatic, even revolutionary, change that it has ever experienced. And in the midst of controversy, he managed to retain the respect, even love, of almost everyone with whom he came into contact.

Jay was a child of the "Great Migration" of American Friends from the South into the Ohio Valley in the first quarter of the nineteenth century. His ancestry included several streams of Friends. Most were rooted in the Delaware Valley, whence many Friends moved south, into Virginia and the Carolinas, between 1730 and 1775. But one of his grandmothers came of Nantucket Quaker stock, and as an infant Jay sat on the lap of his great-great-grandfather Paul Macy. Jay's marriage to Martha Sleeper joined him to another stream of Quaker migration, Friends from upstate New York who moved into Ohio and Indiana. His own life would be migratory. Born in Ohio, he reached adulthood in Grant County, Indiana, then moved west to Tippecanoe County, Indiana, when he married. After the Civil War, he would go south to become a central figure in the rebirth of North Carolina Quakerism in the 1860s and 1870s. He would then head north, to New England for a few years in Rhode Island before he returned to Indiana, this time to Richmond, where he spent the last three decades of his life.

Three things stand out, I think, about Allen Jay's life. He was first and foremost a minister. Much of this autobiography is devoted to his life and travels in the ministry. He was at the center of an upheaval in American Quakerism, what is usually referred to as the "Great Revival" of the last third of the nineteenth century. Jay tells how a generation of young Friends in the 1850s and 1860s, mostly better educated than their forebears and more open to influences from outside of Quakerism, began to advocate innovations that would pare away what they saw as archaic constraints that hampered Quaker outreach and growth, such as rules against marrying out of meeting. They also tried to give young Friends more active roles in the lives of their meetings. Jay's account of the young people's prayer meeting at Indiana Yearly Meeting in 1860 is an excellent example. Jay sees such currents as first waves of revival.

In the 1870s, however, the revival took a more radical turn, largely because of the influence of other ministers who had been swept up in the larger Holiness revival of the period 1850–1880. This was a broad, vibrant movement that cut across denominational lines. Mainly Wesleyan in origin, it brought all of the features of Protestant revivalism—extreme emotionalism, altar calls, music, and finally pastoral ministry—into the Gurneyite yearly meetings, which at the time accounted for at least three quarters of the Friends in North America. The movement brought new life and growth to every yearly meeting it touched, from New England to the West Coast, but it proved controversial. Separations took place in Indiana, Western, Iowa, Kansas, New York, and ultimately North Carolina yearly meetings, as more conservative Friends found the changes too radical and dramatic.

Jay's response to the revival is instructive. He was in North Carolina when it reached its height, and under his influence the revival there took a relatively moderate course that delayed a separation until after 1900. On the one hand, he used revival methods, and delighted in seeing Friends converted, or "born again." On the other hand, he was careful not to push meetings farther than conservative Friends were willing to go. The alienation of older Quakers and the fire and brimstone preaching in which revival ministers like David B. Updegraff of Ohio Yearly Meeting seemingly delighted, held no appeal for Jay. "No doubt it is right to preach at times of the terrors of the law," Jay wrote to his wife Martha in 1875, "but there is so much danger of getting a little of self in with it—wishing to bring everybody to our idea of what is right—that I often think it is safer for me to leave the judging with my Heavenly Father."

This closely relates to the second important aspect of Jay's life, his talent as a force for moderation and conciliation. Jay lived in an era of separation and division among Friends. He was born only a few years after the Hicksite Separation, but he has almost nothing to say about it. It is possible that he reached adulthood without ever encountering a Hicksite Friend, at least not before he went to Richmond to attend Friends Boarding School—now Earlham College—in 1852, since there were almost none in the Quaker settlements at West Branch and in Grant County, Indiana, where he grew up. But he has much to say about the second wave of separations that split Orthodox Friends into Gurneyite and Wilburite, or Conservative bodies, from the 1840s to the 1870s. He consistently mourns these splits as a loss for Friends, arguing that the yearly meetings affected would have been stronger had they retained the more conservative Friends who departed. His inclination is always to see blame on both sides.

By the 1890s, new tensions were affecting the Gurneyite bodies of Friends that the "Great Revival" had transformed. A group of young Friends, mainly associated with the Quaker colleges, cautiously at first, then more aggressively, introduced critical Bible study and modernist theology to their schools and yearly meetings. The most prominent was Rufus Jones (1863–1948), a long-time professor at Haverford College who in 1894 became editor of *The American Friend*, which originally published Jay's autobiographical sketches in article form.

Equally controversial was Elbert Russell (1871–1951), Earlham's Bible professor from 1895 to 1915. Jay acknowledges Russell's assistance with the autobiography. By Russell's account, written many years later, his persuasion was crucial in bringing the temperamentally modest Jay to record his life. Many Friends, strongly evangelical if not fundamentalist in their views, saw these modernists as threatening the authority of the Bible and the truths of the Christian religion and tried to push them out of their academic and yearly meeting posts.

Jay says little directly about this controversy, but from his correspondence with his family and with Rufus Jones and accounts left by Russell we know that he quietly defended the young liberals. His own theology remained thoroughly evangelical, but he saw not heterodoxy but deep Christian Quaker commitment in the modernists. Jay's references to this controversy are usually oblique, but clear when one understands their context. For example, in the last chapter he recommends reading the published proceedings of the 1907 Five Years Meeting. Russell had read a paper, "A Ministry for the Present Day," that was a forthright affirmation of modernist Quakerism, one which critics tried to exclude from the published version. They failed, and everyone would have understood Jay's implicit affirmation at the time. Clearer is his account of Oregon Yearly Meeting in 1906. Fundamentalist influences were strong there, but Jay felt led "to deal plainly and to bear my testimony against a spirit of judging and fault-finding."

Finally, Jay was a builder and strengthener of institutions. He spent roughly the first half of his life as a farmer, the vocation of most Quakers in the United States before 1900, before discovering other talents that would take him off the land. Perhaps his greatest achievement was nurturing the rebuilding of North Carolina Quakerism after the Civil War, an accomplishment in which he took understandable pride that comes through clearly in his writing. It is an accomplishment that is still remembered around High Point, where one of the neighborhoods is called Allen Jay. He would doubtless have been pleased by an Allen Jay High School, and probably bemused by the

Allen Jay Baptist Church. But he would have certainly disapproved of the Allen Jay Package Liquor Store!

Jay's experience in North Carolina determined the course of the second half of his life, which was largely devoted to academic administration and fundraising. And few nineteenth-century Friends were his peers as fund-raisers. Jay's lifetime saw the establishment of a system of Quaker higher education in the United States. By 1900, it was a given that the widely scattered yearly meetings of Friends in the south and west would each have a college to serve their young people. These institutions were uniformly poorly endowed. Earlham would be the focus of Jay's labors. During his association with the college it saw the number of buildings increase from one to five, including a library that was praised as the best in the state of Indiana. Particularly endearing to me were Jay's efforts to raise the money for Earlham to acquire in 1905 the library of Joseph Elkinton of Philadelphia, undoubtedly the best collection of Quaker books in private hands in North America at the time. Guilford, Whittier, Pacific (now George Fox), and William Penn would also benefit from his fund-raising talents.

When Jay died in 1910, Rufus Jones called him "the most deeply loved Friend of our generation." These pages, with their restraint, humility, and insight, explain why.

Thomas Hamm
Richmond, Indiana
2008

Editor's Foreword

I first discovered the *Autobiography of Allen Jay* in the early 1980s on a shelf full of books which were due to be discarded from the library of the Friends meeting where I was serving as pastoral minister at the time. Something about the book drew my eye. I took it down, blew the dust off it, and started to read.

What I discovered was the story of a Friend whose life encompassed nearly every major development and change in the Quaker world of the 1800s. Allen Jay was born shortly after the Orthodox/Hicksite separation. As a boy, he worked on the Underground Railroad. He moved with his family in a covered wagon from Ohio to the newly-opened territory in Indiana. He grew up in an unprogrammed meeting, and was a witness and active participant in the growth of the new style of programmed worship.

He was recorded as a Friends minister, and traveled extensively in traditional Quaker fashion with a minute from his meeting, visiting families, encouraging isolated Friends, and holding "opportunities" in places where there was no organized Quaker activity. Later in life, he sympathized with the younger evangelical Friends, who brought many innovations into Quaker worship, including revivals. He was a bridge between the old Quakerism and the new, encouraging growth and innovation, but cautioning against the rapid changes which alienated Friends who were dear to him.

Allen Jay suffered for his faith during the American Civil War, and nearly had his livestock and farm equipment auctioned off when he refused to hand over payment to commute his draft notice. After the Civil War, he spent eight years working with the Baltimore Association to rebuild schools and local meetings in the shattered Quaker communities of the South.

Allen Jay was born with a cleft palate, and he was always self-conscious about his speech impediment. He became widely known as an inspiring public speaker, but speaking was always difficult for him. His real strength was in personal ministry with individuals, families, and small groups. His faith and his genuine love for people, his complete lack of jealousy and guile, and his willingness to work tirelessly on behalf of Quaker concerns, drew people to him like a magnet.

He was deeply interested in education, and spent more than thirty years in association with Earlham College, which owes Allen Jay a tremendous debt for his vision, energy, and fund-raising ability. As superintendent of the college (what would now be the dean of students) he liberalized many of the college's policies, and helped Earlham change from a provincial boarding school for farmers' children into a modern liberal arts college. He also rescued Guilford College from bankruptcy, and was instrumental in raising funds for several other schools and colleges.

He worked for many years with Indiana Yearly Meeting to start and build up new local meetings. Almost ninety percent of the surviving local meetings of Indiana Yearly Meeting were founded during his lifetime. Many of the small rural congregations have merged or been laid down, but others are still full of life today.

Allen Jay was a central figure in the closely-connected group who worked to unite the Orthodox yearly meetings in America into a larger cooperative body. The Richmond Declaration of Faith of 1887 was dictated in his living room. He was one of the main organizers of the American Friends Board of Foreign Missions and later of the Five Years Meeting, which have since merged into Friends United Meeting.

One of the interesting things to notice about Allen Jay is what he *doesn't* talk about. He doesn't mention many important events in the 1800s. For example, although he talks about the Civil War and how it affected Friends, he never mentions any of the wars in Europe (the Crimean War, the Indian Mutiny, the unification of Italy, or the Franco-Prussian War). The Spanish-American War is only mentioned because it opened the mission field for Friends in Cuba.

Allen Jay belonged firmly to the Orthodox Quaker tradition. During most of his life, Orthodox and Hicksite Friends were not on speaking terms with each other. In his *Autobiography*, he delicately refrains from mentioning the important Hicksite Friends of his generation, though he records a few contacts. On the other hand, his *Autobiography* is a virtual "Who's Who" of the Orthodox Quaker world. He was intimately acquainted with nearly every Orthodox minister, missionary, and leader in the U.S., and became close friends with many of the leading Quakers in Great Britain and Ireland.

The 1800s were a time of enormous change in America. The Industrial Revolution was in full swing. Most American Quakers, however, still lived in small towns and on farms. Railroads, steam ships, telegraph, telephone, gas, and electric lights and radio were all invented during his lifetime, but he only mentions them in passing. The Panic of 1837 is mentioned as a cause of delay in the starting of Earlham; other financial crises are hardly mentioned at all. The rise of the robber barons, the industrial unrest, and the violent strikes that tore the country apart are not part of his story.

Although Allen Jay was eager for Friends to move in an evangelical direction, and led many revivals himself, he clearly had reservations about the "machinery" of large-scale evangelism. He never mentions the evangelists who were transforming American religion in the late 1800s—Charles G. Finney, Dwight L. Moody, and their many imitators.

Perhaps most interesting of all, Allen Jay never mentions the revolutionary scientific ideas which he certainly must have heard about, especially Darwin's theory of evolution. Joseph Moore, who led the Baltimore Association work before Allen Jay and was president of Earlham, was an early champion of evolution. Several Quaker ministers who were Allen Jay's younger contemporaries, notably Luke Woodard, wrote violently against evolution. The controversy rocked Indiana Yearly Meeting for three generations, but Allen Jay never even mentions it.

In the same way, he hardly mentions the controversy over modern biblical studies. Elbert Russell, who came to Earlham as a student in 1890 and joined the faculty in 1895, was one of the most controversial Quaker figures of his generation. Russell introduced modern biblical studies to Earlham, and became the first pastor of West Richmond Friends Meeting, which Allen Jay joined. Allen Jay *must* have known in some detail about these and many more controversial issues, but he never mentions them. Why?

Part of the answer is probably generational; by the turn of the century, Allen Jay was over seventy years old, and he may not have wanted to wear himself out in intellectual and spiritual battles like these. Part of the answer also probably has to do with Allen Jay's background. He grew up on a farm, worked as a young man mainly in rural areas, and taught in small schools. He visited large cities in later life, but he never lived in one for any length of time. His world view never seems to have been affected by the enormous waves of immigration, or by the growth of new industry and technology. His view of industrial relations is indicated by his accounts of the Quaker "success stories" of the British cocoa makers, Rowntree and Cadbury.

He was horrified by the violence of the American Civil War, and was actively involved in some of the earliest organized Quaker peace work, but the basic underpinnings of his thought were spiritual and practical, rather than scholarly and political. The American Friends Service Committee was still years in the future. The wholesale re-evaluation of the peace testimony which was called forth by the First World War took place a decade after Allen Jay's death.

On various social issues which involved Friends in the 1800s, Allen Jay is something of an enigma. He was active in the Underground

Railroad, but he barely mentions Quakers' extensive work with former slaves. He strongly approved the temperance movement, but he doesn't seem to have been directly involved in it. He highlights the role of women in Quaker business meetings and mentions dozens of female Quaker ministers, but he never mentions the role Quakers played during his lifetime in the struggles for women's rights and suffrage.

If there is one theme which rings through the entire *Autobiography*, it is Allen Jay's hatred of the spirit of separation. Friends today need to listen, because that same spirit surfaces in every generation and threatens to destroy us again. In my favorite passage in the entire book, Allen Jay asks: "Has a separation ever caused more people to hear the Gospel? Ever enlarged the Church? Ever shown to the world more of the gentleness and meekness of Christ? Has a separation ever caused the world to exclaim, 'Behold how these Christians love one another?'"

Allen Jay's *Autobiography* originally appeared in serial form in the periodical, *The American Friend,* in 1908 and 1909, and was revised and rewritten before being published in book form. In editing the book for today's reader, I have tried to stay faithful to the original text. One chapter about North Carolina Quakers Dr. Nereus Mendenhall and Delphina Mendenhall has been moved to an appendix, since it breaks up the main narrative of the book. Also in appendices are a moving account of the last forty-eight hours of his life and the lengthy memorial minute which was not available at the time the first edition was printed.

I have tried to preserve the spelling and punctuation of the original edition of the *Autobiography*, because it adds to the "flavor" of the book and reminds us of the difference a hundred years has made. On the other hand, I have broken up some of the lengthy paragraphs of the original, to make the book easier to read.

I have left unchanged Allen Jay's use of the traditional Quaker "plain language." In many conversations he records with family and friends, he says "thee" instead of "you" for individual persons, as was common until the early twentieth century. On the other hand, he frequently uses both plain language and regular English in referring to dates—sometimes he will say "First Month," other times he will say "January." I have kept Allen Jay's mixed dating, not just out of a sense of faithfulness to the original edition, but also because it shows again how Allen Jay lived through an important transitional period.

Allen Jay made many allusions to Bible verses and hymns, which I have identified for today's readers who may not be as familiar with them. I have added notes throughout the text to identify Friends and others whose names were everyday names in Allen Jay's time but who are less well-known to us today. I have also prepared a brief timeline of events in Allen Jay's life.

I owe special thanks to Thomas Hamm, Professor of History and Archivist at the Friends Collection at Earlham College, who has written a splendid introduction to this book. Hamm was also very helpful with many research questions along the way. John Punshon, now retired from the faculty of the Earlham School of Religion, was helpful in highlighting many of the British and Irish connections made by Allen Jay. Gwen Erickson, Librarian and Archivist at Guilford College, provided some very helpful material about Mary Mendenhall Hobbs' contribution to the *Autobiography*. Many other Friends have assisted with various bits of information.

I am grateful to the Communications and Publications Committee of Indiana Yearly Meeting for their financial help in publishing this book. West Richmond Friends Meeting in Richmond, Indiana, where I currently serve as pastoral minister, has generously given me time to work on this project and provided financial assistance for its production; Allen Jay was one of the founding members of our meeting. During Allen Jay's lifetime, our meeting met on the Earlham College campus. Shortly after his death, we moved to temporary quarters in a converted farmhouse owned by the family of his second wife, Naomi Harrison Jay. In 1916, our present meetinghouse was built. The bronze plaque in the front entrance way reads:

EDITOR'S FOREWORD

> Allen Jay
> 1831–1910
> In appreciation of his faith and
> vision this building is erected
> by loving Friends as a
> memorial

One-hundred years after his death, Allen Jay deserves fresh appreciation from Friends and from those studying Friends. Commentaries and summaries are important, but primary sources like this are essential for a full understanding of any period. If you want to understand Quakerism in the 1600s, you have to read *The Journal of George Fox*. If you want to understand Friends in the 1700s, you have to read *The Journal of John Woolman*. And if you want to understand the complex challenges and changes faced by Friends in the 1800s, you have to read *Autobiography of Allen Jay*.

Joshua Brown
Richmond, Indiana
August, 2009

Foreword to Original Edition

Having now entered my seventy-ninth year, and looking back, I am prepared to say, "The hand of my God has been good upon me."[1] My friends and the Church have been pleased to call me to fill some active positions during the past fifty years in the Church of which I was born a member. Having seen many changes and having labored in various positions in the Church in connection with others who were trying to build up the Redeemer's kingdom in the earth, it has seemed to many of my friends that I ought to leave an account of the part I have taken in the work, of the changes that the Church has passed through during these years, and perhaps a little sketch of some of those whom I have met during this time.

Therefore, with the hope that it may be of interest to some who are younger and desirous to do the Master's will, I have consented with much reluctance to undertake this service in my declining years. My greatest reason for hesitation is the fact that I have taken an active part in the work in which I have been engaged, and therefore I feel that the pronoun "I" may appear too prominent in what I may have to say. I hope to avoid that as much as possible and to be able in all I have to say to give the glory to my Heavenly Father, who called me from following the plow to enter His vineyard, and later, in a more public way, to build up His kingdom.

The matter in this volume has been written at odd moments, amid many other claims upon my time. The account lays no claim to

---

[1] Nehemiah 2:18

literary attainment, and if there is any appearance of anything of that kind it is due to my faithful stenographer, Ruthanna Simms,[2] who has done her part so well, and to the kind assistance of Professor Elbert Russell,[3] both of whom have tried to eliminate the mistakes and put the narrative in proper shape for the publishers.

I wish to express my thanks to my dear uncle and aunt, Eli and Mahalah Jay, for their help in furnishing facts and correct dates, and to John and Charles Thomas, of Baltimore, Maryland, for their assistance in obtaining access to the records relating to the Baltimore Association work. In a special manner, also, I owe much to my dear friend Mary Mendenhall Hobbs,[4] who has so greatly helped with her pen and with words of encouragement.

To all of these and to others who by letters and words of encouragement from this country and on the other side of the sea have aided me, my heart goes out in tender love. With this feeling to all and for the Church, I now commit my account to the reader, praying that God may bless it for good.

Allen Jay
Richmond, Indiana
1909

---

[2] Ruthanna Simms (1880–1974) is best known for her service from 1920–53 as executive secretary of the Associated Committee of Friends on Indian Affairs (ACFIA).

[3] Elbert Russell (1871–1951), was professor of Biblical Literature at Earlham College at the time Allen Jay wrote his *Autobiography*. Russell authored *The History of Quakerism* (Richmond, IN: Friends United Press, 1979, reprint of the original 1942 edition) which remains one of the standard resources today.

[4] Mary Mendenhall Hobbs (1852–1930), Quaker minister and close friend of the Jays, was married to Lewis Lyndon Hobbs (1849–1932) who served as president of Guilford College from 1888–1915. She contributed several sections to Allen Jay's *Autobiography*.

CHAPTER 1

Ancestry and Family

I was born near the southern line of Miami County, Ohio. My father, Isaac Jay (1811–1880) was born at the same place, and my mother, Rhoda (Cooper) Jay (1813–1894), was born about seven miles farther south and six miles north of Dayton, Ohio. Their parents were pioneers in the settlement of the Miami Valley, in southwestern Ohio, in the opening years of the last century.

My father was the son of Walter Denny Jay (1786–1865) and Mary (Macy) Jay (1787–1868). My Grandfather Jay was born in Newberry County, South Carolina, the son of John Jay (1752–1829) and Elizabeth (Pugh) Jay (1755–1821). Both of his parents were born in Frederick County, Virginia, from whence they emigrated to South Carolina about 1770 and were married at Bush River Meeting of Friends, Third month 4, 1773. They had eleven children, seven sons and four daughters, born in South Carolina in the years 1773 to 1795. The family removed from South Carolina to Ohio in 1803, settling at first at Waynesville, Warren County, Ohio, and five years later in Miami County, Ohio. All their eleven children married and had families, and the average ages of nine of them, the dates of whose deaths are known, is over sixty years.

My great-grandfather, John Jay, was the son of William and Mary (Vestal) Jay. Mary Vestal was the daughter of William and Elizabeth (Mercer) Vestal. The Vestal family were Friends at Newark Monthly Meeting, Pennsylvania, from whence, about 1730, they removed and settled in the new colony of Friends, formed about that time, near Winchester, Virginia. There William Jay and Mary Vestal were married, about 1743. They were parents of eight children, five sons and three daughters, born in the years 1744 to 1765. Little is known of this William Jay and nothing with certainty of his ancestry. He was probably born in Maryland, and died in Virginia before the emigration of the family from Virginia to South Carolina, shortly before the Revolutionary War. The mother, Mary (Vestal) Jay, after living more than thirty years in South Carolina, came to Ohio in 1805, where she lived several years.

My great-grandmother, Elizabeth (Pugh) Jay, was the daughter of Thomas Pugh (born 1731) and Ann (Wright) Pugh (born 1725), both natives of Pennsylvania. They went with their family from Hopewell Monthly Meeting, Virginia, to Bush River, South Carolina, in 1769 but returned to Virginia in 1777. Ann Pugh was an approved minister in the Society of Friends, and after their return from South Carolina, she made two visits, with a certificate from Hopewell Monthly Meeting, to Friends in North and South Carolina, returning from the last in 1798. Her husband, Thomas Pugh, accompanied her on her first visit, in 1784. He was the son of Jesse and Alice (Malin) Pugh, both of whom were born in Pennsylvania in 1711 and removed to Frederick County, Virginia, about 1750. Jesse Pugh was the grandson of Ellis Pugh, who was born in Wales, 1656, and emigrated with his family to Pennsylvania in 1687, where he died in 1718. Ellis Pugh was a minister in the Society of Friends, both in his native land and in Pennsylvania, preaching in the Welsh language.

My grandmother, Mary (Macy) Jay, was born in Guilford County, North Carolina. She was the daughter of Thomas Macy (1765–1833) and Anna (Sweet) Macy (1768–1840). They were both born in Nantucket Island and taken to North Carolina in childhood, about 1773, by their parents. There they married at Deep River Meeting of Friends, in the early part of the year 1787, and in 1797 removed to East Tennessee. In 1807 they came to Miami County, Ohio. They had twelve children, ten of whom married and had good-sized families, the other two dying in childhood. The average of the ages of nine of these, the dates of whose deaths are known, is over seventy years.

Thomas Macy was the son of Paul Macy (1740–1832) and Bethiah Macy (1744–1810), both born in Nantucket, where they married in 1761, Bethiah dying in North Carolina and Paul in Miami County, Ohio. Both were of the fifth generation of the Macy family in America, Paul being the grandson of the second Thomas Macy (1687–1759), who was the grandson of Thomas Macy (1608–1682), the immigrant. Bethiah Macy was the granddaughter of the second John Macy (1675–1751), the grandson of Thomas Macy, the immigrant, who was born in Wiltshire, England.

The latter came to America some time between 1635 and 1640, and settled at Salisbury, now Amesbury, Massachusetts, where he lived till 1659, when he settled in the Island of Nantucket, the first white family to locate there in the midst of 3,000 Indians. He left Amesbury to avoid the persecution that fell upon him because he had permitted William Robinson and Marmaduke Stevenson to lodge in his house. These dear Friends were arrested in Boston a few days later, tried and condemned and hung on what is now Boston Common, because of their faithfulness in preaching the Gospel.

I was born the year before my great-great-grandfather, Paul Macy, died, and, according to my mother, had the honor of being held in his arms in my first year. It is now three-hundred years since the birth of my distinguished ancestor, Thomas Macy, and the following four lives cover these three-hundred years, with an overlapping of eighteen years: Thomas Macy, 1608 to 1682; his grandson, John Macy, 1675 to 1751; [my] great-great-grandfather, Paul Macy, 1740 to 1832, and myself, Allen Jay, 1831 to 1908 [present].

My grandmother, Mary (Macy) Jay, embraces in her ancestral lines the most of the family names of the early settlers of Nantucket Island. Of these, the following ten may be given: Austin, Barnard, Bunker, Coffin, Coleman, Folger, Gardiner, Macy, Starbuck, and Worth, and by intermarriages she was related to almost all the other families found in Nantucket history.

My mother, Rhoda (Cooper) Jay, was the daughter of Isaac Cooper (1774–1825) and Elizabeth (Kennedy) Cooper (1782–1859). Isaac and Elizabeth (Kennedy) Cooper came to Ohio from Georgia, where they were probably married. The Cooper family came South from Pennsylvania, but when we do not know. The records of the South Carolina and Georgia Meetings of Friends show that several of the name Cooper belonged to them at different times. Isaac Cooper was the son of Isaac and Prudence Cooper, and Elizabeth Kennedy was the daughter of John and Esther Kennedy.

I was the oldest of five children. My brother, Milton Jay, became a useful man, practiced medicine for forty years, was rather a noted surgeon, and at his death was the chief surgeon of the Rock Island Railroad system. He died three years ago in Chicago. Brother Walter Denny Jay grew up a useful, Christian man, a farmer, and died at Marion, Indiana, about thirty years ago. Brother Abijah died in Marion, Indiana, May 18, 1909. He was at one time County Commissioner of Grant County. For a number of years he was connected with the public school work and helped to secure the Marion Carnegie Library. Sister Mary Jay Baldwin, the youngest of the family, has been a minister in our Society for a number of years, and still lives at Marion, Indiana.

I feel that I owe much to my ancestors and to the Church which has done so much for me. My grandparents were persons of marked character, especially my Grandfather Jay. As an illustration of his character, I will give the following incidents: He settled on a farm in the woods of Miami County, Ohio. It was customary in that new country for the farmers to go into the green woods and kill the green timber by cutting a circle around a tree and then leaving it until it was dead. This was called "deadening."

During the winter season they would cut down these dead trees, cut them off or burn them off at a suitable length to roll into log heaps. Then, in the spring of the year, the neighbors would unite and go to one farmer's house, taking their oxen, log chains, and axes, and spend one, two, or three days, as the number of acres might require, in rolling and piling these logs into heaps to be burned. Then they would go to the next neighbor and spend the time in the same way. Sometimes the women would go, also, and have quiltings at the same time.

One spring, when they had gone the rounds, they went to my grandfather's—the last one, he being the youngest married person in the neighborhood. When they went to work they soon found out that grandfather had not provided the whiskey which was thought to be necessary in those days at barn raisings and log rollings. By night the murmuring had increased, so that his father told him it would be necessary for him to comply with the custom or the neighbors would not come back to help him finish. In the evening, when the time came to quit work, he got on top of a large stump, and, calling the men around him, delivered the following speech: "Neighbors, I have helped you roll your logs all through the spring, and have not tasted your liquor, and now, if you cannot help roll my logs without liquor to drink, you can go home." There was no liquor brought, but the logs were all rolled. So far as I know, this was the first temperance speech ever made in that part of Ohio.

Soon after my marriage, my wife and I settled on a farm on the Wea Plains, near the High Gap, about eight miles southwest of Lafayette [Indiana]. There being a good orchard on the farm, I took a load of winter apples to the city to sell one day. When I stopped my wagon near a bank in the city, the president of the bank, who was called Judge Barbee, came out and looked at them. He asked me how many there were and the price. Being satisfied, he went in and got his hat, came out and got on the wagon and we drove out to his house. We commenced measuring them out and his hired man carried them into the cellar.

Pretty soon he asked me where the apples were raised and what my name was. When I told him, he looked at me and said: "Are you any relation to 'old Uncle Denny Jay,' of Miami County, Ohio?" When I told him that I was his eldest grandchild, he lay down the half-bushel and said, "We will not measure another apple. I will take your word as to the number of bushels." When I reminded him that a great many good grandfathers had dishonest grandsons, the reply was, "You cannot afford to lie if you are his grandson. I have done several thousand dollars' worth of business with your grandfather and we never had a scratch of a pen between us. I would trust his word for any sum."

This reminds me of the saying of George Fox, "Then the lives of Friends began to preach." It would be hard to compose a sentence more significant to a thinking Christian to-day than this expression of George Fox. It reminds us of the saying, "Thy life speaks so loud I cannot hear thy words."

CHAPTER 2

Early Influences: School and Meeting

Having given a rather full genealogy of my ancestors, especially on my grandfather and grandmother Jay's side, I now proceed to give some account of my life and work in connection with the Church in which I have labored more or less for over fifty years.

The educational advantages that surrounded my early childhood were those common to the new country of that day. There were no public schools, but Friends very early had schools started under their control. Here again I was blessed in having a father who took more interest in education than many persons did. He himself, though not much of a scholar, was chosen to teach two or three terms in the log school-house in the neighborhood. It was built of logs on the plan of that day, with openings cut out on one side and paper pasted over them for window lights. Holes were bored in the logs and a broad board fastened on for a writing desk. When the time came for writing, we sat on a high bench with our faces to the wall so that the light from these primitive windows might fall upon our paper.

One incident in my early life showed my father's interest in the education of his children. I had just commenced going to school. When I awoke one morning my mother told me that I could not go to school that day, as it had been snowing during the night and I was too little to walk through the snow to the school-house and father could not spare the time to take me. I began to fret and cry, because I wanted to go.

Father was busy out in the barn threshing wheat, in the way that many farmers did in those days. The wheat was laid down with the heads together in a circle around the barn floor, and then the horses were turned on to it and made to walk around while the farmer with his fork kept it stirred up until the wheat was all threshed out.

While I was pleading with my mother to let me go, my father pulled the string, raised the door latch and said, "Where is Allen?" Mother replied, "He is here fussing because he cannot go to school." Father simply said, "It is time for him to go. Where is his dinner?" When mother handed it to him, he got down on the porch and told me to put my arms around his neck. He then put his hands behind him to hold me up, carried me half a mile to the school-house, set me down on the door step, and said, "Be a good boy and wait until I come after thee to-night." Many times in life I have been thankful that I had a father who thought enough of his boy to stop his work and carry him to school on his back.

> Many times in life I have been thankful that I had a father who thought enough of his boy to stop his work and carry him to school on his back.

The same example of faithfulness in the attendance of meetings for worship and discipline, on the part of my parents, was a training that I appreciate. It has been a strength to me through life. Some of my earliest recollections are of being taken to meeting with the other children and made to sit quietly through the meetings, many of which were held in silence. Some of these meetings wherein there was not a word spoken are impressed upon my memory to this day. I can remember that while sitting in stillness I was often impressed with the desire to be a good boy.

This stillness was sometimes broken by vocal prayer, during which the congregation rose, pulled off their hats, and turned their backs to the one who was engaged in vocal prayer. We were also expected to bow our heads, and, when he was through, to sit down with as little noise as possible. I have wondered sometimes whether, if more of this reverence were manifested to-day in time of vocal prayer, we might not find it beneficial.[1]

When the minister rose to address the meeting, there was attention given to what he said that is lacking to-day in many places when the sermon is preached. While there was not so much doctrine preached, the message was directed to the hearts of the hearers and they were impressed with the fact that we were called to live pure and honest lives, and above all, that God sees us at all times. While much of this ministry was directed to the observance of outward things, yet we were forcibly reminded that God expected us to obey the teaching of His Spirit and to live honest and upright lives.

Let us not speak lightly of the ministry of our forefathers. Some of us, as we look back to the lives of those who were brought up under their ministry, are ready to believe that they were God-fearing men and women. They were the salt of the community where they lived and leaders for good among their fellow-men. Their word was as good as a bond.

When I was about ten years old my parents moved from Mill Creek Meeting, where I was born, to Randolph Meeting, located some six miles north of Dayton, Ohio, and settled in the old home where my mother was brought up and lived until she was married. Here the course of my life continued to flow on in the channels common to a farmer's boy in that day. My father was a hard-working man. We children were taught to labor and do all kinds of work incident to a farmer's life. My mother was in poor health and it fell to my lot as the oldest child to assist in the washing each week. It was an unwritten law that this had to be done on Second-day morning. For some two or

---

[1] This practice of turning their backs on the speaker during prayer was meant to emphasize that the worshipers were not listening to the individual, who was a fallible human being and who might become puffed up or arrogant if attention was focused on them personally. Instead, they were listening to the message, which was given by the Holy Spirit. They took off their hats as a sign of respect for the message, not for the person who delivered it.

three years I did the most of it myself, putting the clothes through the washing, and boiling, bluing, starching, and hanging them out without any assistance, but I cannot say that I ever enjoyed it, although it was the understanding that when it was done I was to have the remainder of the day to fish, hunt, go swimming, or do whatever I desired.

Life went on in this way, divided between working on the farm in the summer and going to school in the winter. Our school-house was near the meeting-house. When the meeting hour came on Fifth-day, we all went in a body to the meeting. Here, again, I believe our fathers were right in mingling religion with education, or, in other words, in educating the heart along with the intellect. Sometimes, after there had been a long silence, some one would rise and speak so long that we were made to fear that the time for our games of base, town-ball, or bull-pen would be cut short. It was a practical lesson in patience. Perhaps we did not always let it do its perfect work.

Be that as it may, years afterwards, in another State, when my father sent me away from home to attend an academy, where there was a Friends Meeting about three-quarters of a mile from the school-house, I had so fixed in my mind the importance of going to meeting in the middle of the week that when the hour came for the Fourth-day meeting, I arranged with the principal that I might rise from my seat and go out and attend the meeting. It made me appear a little like a speckled bird [Jeremiah 12:9] among my schoolmates, yet in walking through the woods, going and coming, the sense of doing right was often a comfort. Years afterwards, one of that number who had grown to be a man said that my example in this had first led him to consider the subject of religion.

Conversion

About the thirteenth year of my age there occurred a scene in my life which stands out more vividly than any other in the history of my attendance on West Branch Quarterly Meeting, the quarter to which we belonged. It was during the consideration of the "State of Society," as it was called, when they read the "Queries and Answers," and the condition of the Church was brought in review before the meeting. A Friend arose with a concern on his mind for some one who was present. With his face turned towards the far corner of the house, where I sat among the young people, he entreated that we should yield our hearts to the tender visitation of God's love. He went on with his loving message, pointing us to the Spirit of God that would lead us in the way of truth and righteousness. The messenger has long since passed away, but his message is not forgotten.

The meeting closed and I rode home on horseback in company with other young people, but did not enjoy the laughing and foolishness of the crowd. After supper I went out into the orchard and sat down to pray. I wanted to kneel down and offer prayer, but my training was such that I felt that none but those called to public prayer should kneel down. After sitting in silence a while, I rose to go to the house, but the burden was so great that I returned and ventured to kneel, thereby hoping to find peace. Now I was impressed that I should open my mouth and speak out the burden of my soul. But here again my education was such that I was afraid to speak words unless called to public ministry. We had been told that we could pray as well by thinking as by speaking. I rose and started to the house again. The burden was so great that I went back and fell on my knees and broke out in vocal expression, confessing my sins and asking God to forgive. Joy came to my soul. Sweet peace filled my heart.

After waiting a while to wipe away the tears of joy, I went into the house, trying to hide my feelings. But a mother's loving heart and watchful eye perceived that something had come over her boy. When the time came to go to bed, she put her hand on my shoulder and simply remarked that we had had a good meeting that day and she hoped I would rest well. Dear mother wanted to say more, but her training, like that of most Friends of that time, was to repress all religious conversation. I have often wondered what would have been the result had she taken me to her embrace and told me what the change was—that I had been converted and that God had heard my petition. I doubt not she prayed for me, and if she had spoken to me it might have saved me days of darkness and doubt in coming years.

In reviewing this blessed experience I am often impressed with the fact of how little theology there was mixed with the preaching of those dear Friends compared with the hair-splitting doctrines and controversies we hear in some places in our Church to-day. But after threescore and ten years, having seen the results of the ministry of that day, which directed our thoughts to the Spirit of God and urged us to listen to His voice as He called us to follow Him, and comparing it with the dogmatic and superficial teaching of some of the present day, who point us to their own experience in spiritual things, I am ready to say that our fathers' ministry produced men and women of ability and Christian character which I sometimes fear are not produced by the methods of the modern revivalist. They were men and women who were the salt of the earth, who walked the earth in the fear of the Lord and kept themselves unspotted from the world.

Family Worship

Soon after these occurrences, another took place which strengthened my religious life. My father had a hard spell of sickness which lasted several weeks. I heard the doctor say to my mother one evening while leaving, "I fear your husband will not get well." When I stood by the bed that night, before retiring, father said to me, "Be a good boy, and help mother all thee can." It was not customary in those days, in that community, even among Christians, to have family worship. However, I heard my father say to mother, "If I get well, we will have religious services in the house."

Two or three weeks later, one night, mother brought a rocking-chair, placed a bed-quilt over it, and pillows upon it, and then, going to the bed, helped my father out and led him to the chair. She brought the Bible, and while we children sat around father read a few verses from it. Then he asked mother to help him down on his knees. She knelt by his side and held him while he offered vocal prayer. I have seen many beautiful paintings that have cost large sums of money, but no picture is more vivid and beautiful in my memory than that of mother holding father while he prayed. I do not remember much of that prayer, but the words, "God bless Allen and make him a good boy," have followed me over land and sea. I pity the child who has never heard his father pray.

> I have seen many beautiful paintings that have cost large sums of money, but no picture is more vivid and beautiful in my memory than that of mother holding father while he prayed.

I would not convey the idea that because the Friends of that day did not read the Bible in family worship, that they never read the Bible. Many of them read it much. Many of us can call to mind how grandfather and grandmother read the Bible, with a solemn tone, similar to that in which many of the ministers of that day delivered their messages, and their old Bibles lying upon the shelf to-day are well worn with much use.

It may appear strange that my father was often found fault with for introducing family worship into our house. Some Friends were uneasy, fearing it might result in reading the Bible formally and having formal worship. One dear Friend, whose name I will not mention, traveling on a religious visit, stopped with us over night. When father brought out the Bible and remarked that it was our custom to read before going to bed, he made the remark, "I suppose it will not hurt me to sit and listen to it." The next day, at quarterly meeting, he preached, but it did me no good. I did not want to hear him, for I knew what it had cost my father to introduce this practice in his family.

Visiting Friends

The hospitality of Friends in those days was something to look back to with pleasure. Our home was on the direct line between Miami and West Branch quarterly meetings. We always expected a number of Friends the night before quarterly meeting from Center and Miami, as well as Friends traveling in the ministry. Among these I recall the names of Thomas Evans, Joseph Doan, Asher Brown, Samuel Steddom, Abram Taylor, Joseph Taylor (who afterwards founded Bryn Mawr College), and many others.

Very often with these would be a company of Friends from other yearly meetings, such as Joseph D. Hoag, John and Elizabeth Meader, and Benjamin Seebohm. These were days that we looked forward to with interest. Everywhere was activity, in the house and outside, getting ready to welcome the company. It was a feature in my home life that had much to do with shaping it for the Church. I have known as many as thirty visitors to stay all night at my father's. We boys learned to sleep on the floor, giving up our beds to others. The young people among the visitors shared the floor with us.

After supper I enjoyed sitting in the corner and listening to the conversation about the Church and its work, interspersed with anecdotes about noted Friends, especially about the ministers and their work and travels. It was very instructive. It was a history of the past that had been handed down from one generation to another. The Friends who could tell the most stories and create the most laughter were our heroes, especially if they noticed us and laid their hands upon our heads or asked us how old we were, or some other commonplace questions. We never thought of getting sleepy, but as it grew late, someone would suggest that it was near bedtime. Then the Bible was brought out, father would read a portion of Scripture, and we dropped into silence. After a little perhaps some one or two might engage in vocal prayer, and perhaps another might feel called to express a word in the line of the ministry, in the way of encouragement and advice, and sometimes a word might be spoken directly to us children. This was called a "religious opportunity before going to bed." Let no one be surprised that these occasions live in the memory of those of us who are growing old.

The Underground Railroad

Sometimes the discussions would develop a difference of opinion on some subject claiming the attention of the Church. There were sometimes two or three beds in one room, and one night two Friends who slept in the bed near where my brother and I were sleeping kept up a long conversation on the subject of the "Underground Railroad," and the practice that some Friends engaged in of helping the runaway slaves to reach a place of safety.

To my young Friends, who may not understand the Underground Railroad of that day, it may be explained that it was a system of helping runaway slaves from one "station" to another, generally at night, until they reached Canada or some other place of safety. My father's house was one of the stations on this "railroad," and while these dear Friends were discussing the propriety of engaging in this work, one of them feeling that it was hardly the right thing to do, while the other upheld the practice, my mind was actively engaged in thinking; for a few days before this our family physician, who was an Abolitionist, had ridden up to the gate, called my father out and told him that there was a runaway slave out in the woods nearby, and that he was being pursued by his master and others. I heard the conversation and understood its meaning, though I was young.

He rode off and my father turned to me and said, "I am going out back of the house to work. If any negro comes to the gate thee can take him down in the cornfield and hide him under that big walnut tree, but thee is not to tell me or anyone else." As the corn was very tall in the bottom, no one could see him. In a little while the poor man came, with his bleeding feet and ragged clothes, looking around and showing that he was very much frightened. I went to him and told him I would hide him.

At first he was afraid of me and asked me if I was Mr. Jay's son, and when I told him I was he followed me. I took him down to the walnut tree and told him to remain there until I came after him. He said, "I am hungry. I want a drink." I told him I would look after that. When I got back to the house mother was in the kitchen fixing up a dinner in a basket. I knew what that meant without asking any questions. Pretty soon she simply said to me, "Allen, if thee knows anybody who thee thinks is hungry, thee might take this basket to him." I started out with it and a jug of milk and went to the cornfield. The poor man heard me coming through the corn, and, not knowing whether I was friend or foe, had his pistol ready to shoot when I drew in sight. The moment he saw me he commenced smiling. I left my load with him with the promise that perhaps I would come after him about dark.

During the afternoon, the men who were pursuing him came up to the gate and called. They asked my father if he had seen a "nigger" going by. He truthfully said he had not. I kept out of sight. They threatened to search the house. Father told them they were welcome to do so, provided they had the proper authority. After talking roughly for a while, they rode off in a hurry.

That evening, just as it was growing dark, my father hitched up "Old Jack" to the buggy and tied him in the barnyard. He then came into the house and asked me how I would like to go to my grandfather's. Understanding what he meant, I told him I would be very willing to go. He added, "If thee knows of anybody thee thinks ought to go, thee had better take him along." I went out and closed the door and soon had the negro in the buggy with me.

The poor fellow could see that I felt a little afraid to be with him alone, and asked me if I were not. When I did not give a positive answer, he said, "If you are afraid of me, I will let you carry the pistol." After we had got started he said, "If anyone comes to take me, you must stop and give me the pistol. I will get out and you drive on, for I do not want you to be hurt. I am never going to be taken back. They may kill me, but I intend to kill one first."

As I looked at the poor man and saw his condition, for he had shown me his lacerated back that had been cut by the whip, I did not tell him that it was wrong to shoot. Neither did I stop to give him a lecture on peace principles.

About ten o'clock we reached my grandfather's. I went to the door and told him what was up. He understood the situation. He at once called my uncle, Levi Jay, and in about thirty minutes each one was on a horse on their way to Mercer County, where there was a large settlement of negroes, which was another important station. We learned afterwards that he reached Canada safely.

CHAPTER 3

The Millerites and Spiritualists

As I have already said, at this time I was very much interested in religious subjects and was ready to listen to all I might hear on religious doctrine. My experiences ought to be a lesson to parents to be careful about whom they employ, who will be associated with their children.

My father had a hired man on the farm with whom I had to work. It was at the time of the Millerite excitement in regard to the end of the world and the second coming of our Lord Jesus Christ.[2] This was in 1843. He was in the habit of attending their meetings of nights, became convinced of their doctrine, and believed that they had predicted the exact time of His personal coming. He was able to quote their interpretation of the Scriptures in the language of their ministers. He told me that some of their members were preparing their white robes in order that they might be ready to meet the Lord in the air at His coming. I became deeply impressed and desirous that I might also be ready.

---

[2] The Millerites were followers of William Miller (1782-1849), who predicted the end of the world in 1843 based on interpretations and calculations he had made from the Bible. He strongly influenced the Adventist movement, Charles Taze Russell, and the Jehovah's Witnesses.

When the morning of the day came, on which they had prophesied that He would come at twelve o'clock, I felt little like eating breakfast. After we had finished eating, father, who was going away from home that day, pointed to the woodpile and told me he wanted me to chop and pile up that wood while he was gone. He noticed that there was something the matter and asked me if I was sick. I answered, "No." But mother, who understood something of her boy's feelings, followed him into the room and told him what she believed was the matter. He came to me and told me that he hoped I would not be uneasy, for he remembered several times having been set for the ending of the world since he was a boy, and that, in his opinion, I had better chop the wood, for he thought we should need it next winter to burn.

He went away and I went to the woodpile, but had no heart for the work, for I felt if all things were coming to an end at noon we would not need the wood and I had better be thinking about something else. For me it was a serious time. I shall never forget my feelings. I could not work. Near twelve o'clock I sat down on a log, waiting to hear the old-fashioned family clock strike the hour. When it began, I looked up, looked all around, and after waiting a few minutes and seeing no change, my mind was relieved, and that afternoon I chopped wood with a lighter heart than I ever had before, and by night had it all piled up nicely.

That wood was burned up more than threescore years ago, and now sometimes when I hear people telling that the time is near at hand when He is coming, I think that the Church had better go on chopping wood and remember that our Saviour said: "No man knoweth the time; no, not even the Son of Man."[3]

As a further illustration of the influence that may be exerted upon children by those who in the employ of their parents, I will mention another instance in my religious experience which made a deep and solemn impression upon my mind. I can never look back to it without thankfulness that I was delivered from temptation. It was at the time

---

[3] See Matthew 24:36; Mark 13:32.

when what they called spirit rappings were being introduced, and a person who claimed to be a spiritual medium and to converse with those who were dead persuaded me secretly to meet with a few of that class and to take part in their exercises.[4]

To be sure, my parents knew nothing of it. Neither did they know that I was furnished with books and pamphlets on this subject and literature that discarded the Bible and endeavored to point out the inconsistency of its teaching. For nearly two years I was more or less under this influence. I look back to it as a time of spiritual darkness. I lost the freshness of my religious experience and no longer enjoyed our religious meetings. But all this time there was a fearful feeling that made me uneasy and restless.

One First-day I had been lying upon my bed during the afternoon, reading some of this literature. As it began to grow too dark to read I laid down the paper, and as I did so the thought came to me, "Perhaps there is a reality in the religion of the Lord Jesus Christ, and the Bible may be true, and what I have been reading may be false." This impression came upon me with such force that I buried my face in the pillow and exclaimed, "Oh Lord, I want to know the truth. I don't want to be deceived. Show me what is right."

I lay still for a little while, and do not know to this day whether I fell asleep or not, but this I do know, that all at once it came to me that I was standing in an open plain, with nothing in sight but the earth beneath and sky above. As I stood there, it appeared to me, a large building rose in front of me. It was so large that the ends were lost to sight, and so high that the top appeared to be hidden in a cloud of glory.

---

[4] The Spiritualist movement began in upstate New York in the late 1840s. The "spirit rappings" refer to the activities of two sisters, Kate and Margaret Fox, who claimed that spirits communicated with them during séances or trance sessions by rapping on the table. The Fox sisters received a good deal of attention from some Quakers. They soon attracted many imitators, some of whom were outright frauds. In 1888, Margaret acknowledged that the rappings were a fraud, and that she had produced the sounds by cracking her toe joints.

As I stood listening to the music that I heard coming through the clouds from the top of the building, one more beautiful than any I had ever seen, like unto the Son of Man, approached me and said, "My child, what art thou doing?" I told him I was listening to the music that came from the top of yonder building. He said, "Eye hath not seen nor ear heard what the Lord hath for those who reach that place."[5]

I said, "I am going up there." He then pointed to the only door there was in the whole building. It was narrow and was overshadowed by cherubim. I went with all the intense purpose with which a young Christian ever starts on his Christian journey. No sooner had I started up the stairs than the doors began to open upon the right and upon the left, and from each door someone was calling me to come in. I kept on, but went more and more slowly until I stopped, with one foot on the next step. A voice at my left hand said, "Where are you going?" I told him I was going out on top of the building. He replied that we were all going to the same place and that there were innumerable rooms in this great building, and much to be seen and learned and enjoyed upon the way, and at his earnest persuasion I entered into the room, which I found was devoted to historical research; but I soon grew tired of his portrayal of the beauty and elevating effect to be found in his department and said I wanted to go back.

Immediately another door opened a little further away, and someone beckoned me in there. This room was devoted to geological research, and here again the occupant endeavored to interest me in the history and formation of the world, but I soon grew tired and said I wanted to go back. Then another door opened further off and I was invited to another room, where I was told I would be sure to be satisfied. This, I believe, was given over to theological discussions and religious controversy.

I soon tired of that and was starting to return when another opened, and I entered a room of pleasure and beauty and was shown the happiness there was in worldly entertainments; but, as before, I

---

[5] See 1 Corinthians 2:9.

was tired and sick and turned my face to go back when another room opened and another voice called me. This room was just as unsatisfactory as the others, and the same was continued until I had passed through six or seven rooms. I became utterly tired and overwhelmed with sorrow that I had ever left the straight stairway that led up to the top, and I exclaimed, "What shall I do and where shall I go?" as I discovered that the doors through which I had passed had all been locked when I entered.

All at once where I was became darkness. I tried to find the door by going around and feeling on the walls. The walls were iron, the ceiling overhead was iron, and the floor was iron. In despair, I fell on my face and exclaimed, "I am lost; I am lost." Words would fail to describe my feelings at that moment. I can never think of them without a shudder. As I lay weeping, I heard a gentle noise. I raised my eyes and there stood one like unto the Son of Man, with tears on his cheeks. He stooped and placed his hand upon my head and said, "Arise, follow me."

I arose and followed Him. He took me back through every room that I had passed through, and as he approached the doors opened of themselves. He took me down to the door where I had started from, laid his hand upon my head, and said, "Now follow thou me." I remember well, as he started up the steps, I watched his feet and endeavored to put mine in his footsteps as we went up.[6] Soon after we started the doors began to open on either side as before. I remember putting my fingers in my ears that I might not hear the voices. When we reached the top he took me in his arms and said to the redeemed, as they gathered round him in praise, "Another soul has been redeemed," and presented me to them.

The joy was so great that I was roused from my dream or vision, whichever it may have been, and found myself weeping for joy. I lay

---

[6] Possibly a reference to 1 Peter 2:21; also possibly a reference to the devotional book, *In His Steps*, by Charles M. Sheldon, which was first printed in 1896 and which was very popular in evangelical circles.

quiet for a moment, feeling that this was a revelation to me in answer to my prayer. I rose from my bed, took the spiritualistic papers to the fireplace, and burned them up. The books that I had borrowed I returned to their owners as soon as possible and announced to the man who had influenced me to attend their circles that I should do so no more. I have hesitated to write down this experience for fear it might seem to make too much of dreams and visions.[7] But I feel that, however it is to be explained, that dream was the means by which I was led back to walk in His footsteps who said, "I am the Way, the Truth, and the Life."[8]

---

[7] Colossians 2:18

[8] John 14:6

CHAPTER 4

Old Randolph Meeting

Perhaps a description of the meeting where I spent my boyhood days may be interesting to some of my young readers. Like many of the country meetings seventy-five years ago, it was located at the side of the road in a grove. This we find was the case in most of the yearly meetings, and especially was this true in the South. Often these meeting-houses were so hidden that you would not see them until you came very near, or would be revealed to you by seeing the horses tied to the trees or to a swinging limb overhead.

The hiding of the meeting-houses may have resulted from the fact that the early Friends in England, on account of persecution, built back from the streets so that they were hidden by high walls or other buildings. In some places they would pass through a gate; in other places under a covered archway into an open court to reach the meeting-house.

In some instances in our country this building of our meeting-houses in secluded places has resulted in some feeling when it has been proposed to move the location to a more central place where more people could reach the house with less travel. It should be the rule, in locating a house for worship, to build it where the greatest number can reach it with the least travel.⁹ God will meet where two or three are met in His name.¹⁰

Our little brick meeting-house at Randolph, like many others, was built in a grove, with many trees on all sides of it. One particularly large beech tree, filled with nuts nearly every season, I especially remember. A large oak tree had been cut down in front of the house, and the body of the tree had never been cut up. There we boys gathered and talked over things pertaining to our neighborhood and other things that interested us until "meeting set."

We had no First-day school in those days, as most Friends in that part of Ohio did not. The "setting of meeting" was indicated by the older Friends going into the meeting-house, taking the little children with them and seating them by their sides. We older children arranged ourselves as we saw proper, but we, too, were under the watchful eyes of our parents. Inside the house were rows of seats, which, in our meeting-house, were better than some others, because they had backs to the benches, though our feet did not reach the floor until we got to be big boys.

There were three seats facing the body of the meeting. The first and second were called "facing seats," the upper one the "top seat." The top seat had the ministers and sometimes some of the elders sitting upon it. The next two were filled with older Friends, whose lives had been such that they were deemed worthy to occupy them. The inside of the house was divided by a partition called "shutters." The women sat on one side of this partition and the men on the other.

About the usual length of time for meetings for worship was occupied with the "shutters open," on days for business meetings, during which words in the ministry, in exhortation, or vocal prayer, were sometimes heard. Then the Friend who sat head of the meeting

---

[9] Elbert Russell, at the twenty-fifth anniversary of the founding of West Richmond Friends Meeting in 1934, remarked: "Allen Jay said he had never known of a Friends meetinghouse being built, repaired, or moved without a fuss." (from the manuscript copy of the twenty-fifth anniversary program)

[10] Matthew 18:20

would rise and say that if "Friends' minds were easy," he thought the shutters might be closed and we might proceed with the business of the meeting.

Ours was a "Preparative Meeting" only, a meeting so called because it was intended to prepare and get in shape business to be forwarded to the monthly meeting and other matters of a local character pertaining to our special meeting. The closing of the shutters in our particular meeting-house was not always easy. Sometimes the rope would get off of the pulley or a rope at one end would break. In such cases as this we boys would have to wait for an older person to come and help. When this was all done the clerk proceeded with the business by reading the minutes of last meeting.

Often there was business in common to both men's and women's meetings, which was carried from one clerk's table to that of the other by "messengers"—a man representing our side and a woman the women's side. To us of the present day the question naturally arises: why did they not transact the business together, without separating one sex from the other? To those who have studied the religious history of the times, when George Fox was "moved," as he says, "by the Lord, to establish women's meetings of business," the wonder is rather that he gave them the privilege of holding meetings and looking after the interests of the Church as far as he did.[11]

John Bright said to me at one time, when we were standing on a hill where George Fox had once preached to a great multitude, "He was the greatest reformer the world has ever seen since the days of the apostles. He saw more clearly what the spirit of the Gospel would lead to than any other of the so-called reformers. He not only saw that the Gospel would do away with war, slavery, [and] oaths, but that it would also give freedom of conscience and establish religious liberty.

---

[11] Women's meetings for business were set up in the very first generation of Friends, but were often limited in their scope to the care of prisoners and those "suffering for truth." Ireland set up a women's yearly meeting as early as 1679, and most American yearly meetings had women's yearly meetings, but London did not do so until 1784.

In doing this, woman would be liberated from her spiritual bondage and would be given a part in preaching the Gospel of Christ."

While at first their meetings for business were confined mostly to looking after the interests of the women of the Church, relieving their sufferings, and having an oversight of the sick and those in prison, their influence soon began to grow. They held their meetings at the same time that men Friends held theirs; much business grew up in common and they appointed committees which worked jointly in carrying forward the work of the Church, until now they are recognized as being an important branch of the Church, and no one would think of giving them a minor position. The future historian will see the "hand of the Lord" in the establishing of the women's meetings, as George Fox believed.

Not only have Friends been blessed, but the world has derived a benefit from this training which our women received. It was nothing unusual on boards of charity, hospital boards, boards of homes for the friendless, and W.C.T.U.[12] meetings, to hear the expression, "You Quaker women have been trained and you know how to lead the meetings of these organizations better than we do."

But above and beyond all that, the ministry of our women Friends has been so fruitful of results that the women of other churches have felt the call to preach the Gospel of Christ. Some have already entered the open door and others are waiting for the door to open. Sooner or later, all the churches will have to acknowledge that the Lord "pours out His spirit on the daughters as well as the sons."[13]

The method of conducting our business meetings was different from that of any other organization. At times a subject would be discussed for some time, and then the clerk would read his minute, giving, as he believed, the "sense of the meeting" or "the weight of the discussion." Sometimes this judgment would be on the side of the minority and against the majority who had spoken. Generally unity

---

[12] W.C.T.U.—the Women's Christian Temperance Union, founded in 1873.
[13] See Acts 2:17-18; Joel 2:28-32.

was expressed with the minute the clerk had read. Often it was felt that the clerk had been favored to go beyond the words that had been spoken and to reach a decision in harmony with the mind of Truth.

At other times the clerk's minute would read something like this: "The way does not open to proceed in the matter." In such cases the matter would be dropped or laid over for future consideration. This manner of settling the questions that came before our meetings for business generally proved more satisfactory than the modern plan where voting has been substituted in the place of it, where spiritual matters are decided by numbers rather than by spiritual experience and mature judgment.[14] After a pretty wide observation, I am inclined to the belief that the decisions thus arrived at were more harmonious and tended more to the unity of the Church than the voting system. There was no room for pulling and scheming, and it rarely left anything bitter and unpleasant as the result. It made a Friends meeting for business different from that of any other religious organization.

The late Charles Spurgeon, after attending London Yearly Meeting a few years before he died, remarked something like this: "It is the most solemn and deliberate body in the transaction of its business that I have ever been permitted to attend. Its decisions are arrived at more harmoniously and with less discussion and friction than I have ever witnessed in other religious organizations."[15]

It must be admitted that it required a spiritually-minded clerk, one who could sink himself out of sight and get the judgment of others

---

[14] It may come as a shock to today's readers to learn that some Quaker meetings in the late nineteenth century made decisions by voting, rather than by uniting in the sense of the meeting. This was especially true in the 1902 business sessions of Five Years Meeting, where we have a stenographic record of the entire proceedings. Business was introduced in the form of motions, which were discussed and carried just as in any organization using Roberts' Rules of Order.

[15] The source for this wonderful quote is unknown. Charles M. Spurgeon (1834-1894) was one of the most famous English Baptist preachers of the nineteenth century, first at the New Park Street Chapel and later at the Metropolitan Temple. Spurgeon was very familiar with Quakerism, and delivered a cordial and thought-provoking lecture on George Fox at Devonshire House, the headquarters of London Yearly Meeting, in 1866, which was printed and widely read by Friends.

rather than his own. A clerk in those days was more than a presiding officer. While I would not join the ranks of those who say, "Why were former days better than these latter days?" for I do not think such is the case, yet there are some things in which I think we might take lessons from the Friends of seventy-five years ago, especially here in the West. Their example and influence in attending their meetings for worship and discipline, especially in the middle of the week, should be a lesson to us.

The country was new, the roads were bad, at some times in the year almost impossible. Carriages were few, especially in the new districts. Often the big farm wagon was used, and while the parents sat on chairs or a board across the top of the wagon bed, the children were piled in straw thrown in the bottom of the bed and rolled about as the wheels ran over roots, logs, jolted over the corduroy bridges, or sank in mud up to the axle. Others went on horseback, the wife riding behind the husband, if they did not have a horse apiece. Often the mother would be seen with a baby in her lap and an older child behind holding on to her. The father, with his share of the children, would be on another horse.

They would ride up to the side of the "uppenblock" and dismount. This block was so named, in familiar Western phrase. It was generally made by sawing off a log about three feet in diameter and about three and one-half feet long. It was then stood up on its end. Two steps were cut in the side so you could step up on top. Or a wide, thick board, ten or twelve feet long, would be placed with one end on top of the block and the other on the ground. Then pieces were nailed about one foot apart, and with a hand-rail or a fence on one side, the women and children could reach the top of the block, which enabled them to get on and off the horse's back without much effort.

My last mail has brought me a letter from J. D. M.,[16] a friend of mine, telling of his memory of those days. His word picture is so clear that I venture to insert a little of it here:

---

[16] J.D.M.—John D. Miles, Quaker agent for the Kickapoo Indians.

As thou knows, I am a birthright member of the Friends Church, and, although my parents were always considered liberal and progressive Friends, yet we boys were required to comb our hair straight down on the forehead and wear a plain coat, with straight stand-up collars, and say "thee" and "thou," and to stop all kinds of work on Fourth-day and go to meeting. Sometimes mother would have one of us children on her lap on the horse, with two behind, and father would have an equal number on his horse. This was our automobile in those days. We had to go one mile and a half to the old meeting-house. We were certainly taught to live up to the law in those early days, but I would not say that there were not good Christians in the Society of Friends; on the other hand, I believe that their Christianity would compare favorably with that of to-day. As we grew older and changed our environments and came in contact with the outside world and with other churches, we found ourselves constantly breaking the long-established rules of the Church. One of the first to break the rules was my sister, Martha, and her husband, Dr. R. H., who so far deviated from the good order of the Society of Friends as to attend the marriage of a relative, which was not solemnized in accordance with the Friends discipline.[17] My sister and her husband refused to make the required acknowledgment and were disowned. They never returned to church fellowship with the Society of Friends, although they lived and died happy Christians, members of another denomination.

---

[17] It is generally thought that many Friends were disowned for "marrying out of meeting," but the discipline extended even to *attending* a non-Quaker wedding. Indiana Yearly Meeting's Discipline in 1839 said: "Where any are present at the marriage, or marriage entertainment of a member, accomplished contrary to our order, they are to be treated with, and where they cannot be brought to a sense of their error, let them be disowned." (*Discipline of the Society of Friends of Indiana Yearly Meeting*, 1839, p. 39)

CHAPTER 5

The Work of my Father and Others in the Ministry

About the fifteenth year of my age, my father began to speak in our meetings in the line of the ministry. Abijah Jones sat at the head of our meetings, being a recorded minister. He frequently spoke, but not at length. His communications were in the way of exhortation and telling us how we should live. They were always given in a monotone, with great solemnity, and always with a number of Scripture quotations, mostly from the Psalms.

I remember well the first time my father spoke in the ministry. It made a deep impression upon my mind. About the same time, three other Friends began to speak in our little meeting: Prudence Teague; Smith Gregg, who was a shoemaker in the neighborhood; and Daniel H. Hutchins. Their gifts differed. Daniel H. Hutchins' communications were totally of a doctrinal nature, dwelling with emphasis upon the doctrine, of great importance to him, of the resurrection of the body, and, like theologians generally, he could not understand why everybody did not see the meaning of Scripture texts just as he did. This theme of his, the resurrection of the body, he dwelt upon on nearly all occasions. He died in Baltimore, in 1867, where he had gone to attend the yearly meeting, from a hemorrhage from the lungs. On his deathbed, between the flows of blood and while gasping for breath, he quoted to me Job 19:26, "And though after my skin worms destroy this body, yet in my flesh shall I see God." The language of the text in the new translation is different, but he knew only the old version. It was a comfort to him and he died in peace.

The ministry of my father was different. He was given to speak to conditions of meetings and individuals. Often his communications were so direct that meetings were impressed and individuals were led to surrender their lives to God. During the last forty years many individuals have come to me and told me when and where they were converted under my father's ministry. From this time on he was actively engaged in church work, though he was not recorded a minister until early in 1850, in his thirty-ninth year.

He was clerk of Mill Creek Monthly Meeting for six or seven years, and for several years was clerk of West Branch Quarterly Meeting. In the year 1848 he took a carriage and two horses and drove James Jones, a minister from China, Maine, and his brother, Elisha, who was his companion, through Indiana and Illinois and the State of Iowa, visiting the meetings in Iowa as far as the way opened. They also attended some meetings going and returning. They were gone six weeks. In 1849 he went, with Enos G. Pray as companion, to visit New York and New England yearly meetings and most of the meetings belonging to them.

In the autumn of 1850 we left the old home at Randolph, Ohio, and moved to Marion, Grant County, Indiana, and became members of Mississinawa Monthly Meeting and Northern Quarterly Meeting. In looking over the minutes of the monthly meeting I find that in 1851 my father took out four minutes for religious service; in 1852, five; in 1853, three; in 1854, two. One of these last was to attend Baltimore and North Carolina yearly meetings, and the other to the meetings in Iowa. In 1855 he took out four minutes; in 1856, four minutes, one to Canada and another to New York.[18] About the same ratio was kept up until the year 1873, when the number of visits was not so great.

---

[18] These "minutes for religious service" were what Friends today often call "traveling minutes." They were a minute stating that the bearer was traveling with a

In 1864 he attended Baltimore and Ohio yearly meetings. In 1865 he visited New England and New York yearly meetings, my mother going with him. In 1867 he made a general visit to North Carolina, my brother, Walter D. Jay, going with him; in 1869 a general visit to Canada; in 1870 a general visit to Iowa. In 1871 he visited Baltimore and North Carolina yearly meetings again, my mother going with him.

This little summary will serve to show his activity in religious visits. Sometimes he would return a minute and obtain another one for service the same day. In all his travels, he paid his expenses out of his own pocket, and at the same time paid his proportion of the meeting money at home, was liberal to the poor, and his home was always open to entertain Friends. He died Fifth month 15, 1880. He had visited all the yearly meetings on this continent except one, most of them more than once, traveling more or less within the limits of all of them, and during his ministry visiting all the particular meetings belonging to them, except a very few of the most isolated and remote.

He took a deep interest in those young in the ministry and bestowed on such much encouragement, wise counsel, and loving care. Having a great memory for faces, he could recognize a large number of Friends and enjoyed meeting with them. The following incident shows his power of memory. A number of years ago he attended a weekday meeting in the State of New Hampshire. After meeting, as he was passing out, he reached out his hand and spoke to a Friend, and asked him his name. Fourteen years after that, at the close of a meeting in Illinois, he went up to this Friend, spoke to him, and called him by name, and when the Friend asked him how he knew

---

religious concern, to visit Friends in a certain area, and that the issuing meeting was in unity with their concern. In a time when other forms of identification hardly existed and when communications were slow, these minutes served to identify Friends who were on a legitimate mission. Also, during the period of separation, such minutes implicitly vouched for the theological "soundness" of the bearer. When a traveling Friend visited a meeting or stayed in a home, he or she would present their minute for inspection. The clerk would write a short acknowledgment that the individual had visited their meeting, and the entire document would be returned to the issuing meeting when the traveling Friend returned home.

him, he said, "I met thee in New Hampshire fourteen years ago," and gave him the year, the month, and the date, also the day of the week.

I feel that it is due, in this connection, to speak a word in memory of my dear mother. She was a faithful wife and a loving mother, and freely and willingly bore her part in the work of the Church, never hindering my father from engaging in any work that he believed the Master called for at his hands, but bearing the burden of caring for the home during his absence and never murmuring, cheerfully giving him up and encouraging him always to be faithful to the Divine call.

I have often been impressed with the belief that the one who remains at home and looks after the family and the daily cares of the home deserves the prayers and sympathy of the Church as much or more than the one who goes out into public service. Sometimes their work may not be appreciated as much as that of those who appear more in the public eye, but the dear Master knows their peculiar trials, their worries, and their lonely days and nights, and in the end He will give the proper reward.

On several occasions my mother accompanied my father on his journeys, at one time going with him to New York and New England, at another through a portion of the West and to North Carolina. She lived fourteen years after my father's death, making her home with my sister, Mary E. Baldwin, in Marion, Indiana. She died Eleventh month 15, 1894, aged eighty-two years. When the end came, she was ready, saying at the beginning of her illness of two weeks' duration that she expected it would be her last. She often said, "I believe all will be well," and in the last day and night she would say to those around her, "Be good. I want you to do right," and then passed away saying, "Jesus, precious Jesus!"

I have dwelt a little while on the work of my parents, in order to show the young ministers of the present day something of the self-denial that the Friends minister of seventy-five years ago was called upon to make, not only in leaving his home and business, but also in bearing his own expenses. There may be a danger of the young people of the present day forgetting what the inheritance they now enjoy has cost others. I have been afraid sometimes that some have spoken too lightly of the sacrifices made by the older Friends and dwelt too much upon the smaller sacrifices which they are called upon to make. Many others were just as faithful in laboring to build up the Church that we now enjoy. May we be worthy sons of such ancestors and see that we do not lower the standard of genuine Quakerism, but labor to make it what the twentieth century demands that it shall be.

> There may be a danger of the young people of the present day forgetting what the inheritance they now enjoy has cost others.

Having thus dwelt upon my father's life, it seems but just to refer to two of his brothers, Thomas and William Jay, who were also called to the work of the ministry, both of them filling important places in the field that they occupied. Uncle Thomas was nearest my father in age, only one brother being between them, but as we labored together a few years later in North Carolina, I will leave what I have to say about him until I come to give an account of that labor, and briefly refer here to Uncle William Jay (1823–1881).

He had a birthright membership in the Friends Church and remained a member until 1857, when he and his wife, Esther Furnace Jay, united with the Sugar Grove Christian Church (sometimes called the New Light Branch of the Christian Church), of which he remained a member until his death. He was chosen pastor of that congregation and held the position for twenty-one years, when he resigned. He received into this church 230 members during his pastorate. During his ministry he preached about 1,000 funeral sermons, going long distances willingly under all circumstances.

He was for a long time prominently identified with the educational interests of Miami County, both as an educator and as a county examiner. He and his brother, Eli Jay, erected a school building in Frederick, in which they taught for years. He also had the principalship for a time of the West Milton schools. Perhaps I cannot better describe him and the love in which he was held than to give an extract from a sermon preached at his funeral by one who knew him well:

> Few men were more gentle than he. With the wisdom of the serpent was seen quite as conspicuously the gentleness of the lamb, and to his gentleness he added kindness, and this kindness was the very milk of his nature. Towards all men he extended this spirit of kindness as naturally as he breathed. One would almost think that his nature would not permit an unkind expression. Almost as well expect discord from skillful fingers as they sweep the well-tuned harp. But to gentleness and kindness he added sympathy as an equally natural expression. The tears of sympathy flowed for every suffering mortal that had need of his aid, and the word of sympathetic expression scarcely ever departed from his lips.
>
> But his nature, like the Gospel itself, was not full when stored with these graces, nor exhausted by their bestowment. These were supplemented with love. As naturally as the eyes wept, so naturally the heart loved. With love for Jesus, he loved all for whom Jesus died. As God loved the world before sending His Son, and thus before the world came to His Son, so Brother Jay's heart of love was melted into richest expressions toward those who were yet out of Christ and in rebellion against God. Never did a man more truly love the sinner. The love of the Father was the burden of his sermon, while rich, deep, yearning love was the burden of his own heart.

Gentleness, kindness, sympathy, and love were the elements of our brother's nature. I do not believe Brother Jay's heart ever compromised with evil from any fear of the foe. He fought for Jesus against every foe of righteousness and he never shrunk from the conflict. Why should the man who never feared the voice of death nor the outstretched arms of the grave have fear of mortal man? And how effectively did he fight! The record of his church shows that in the one congregation he received over 230 members. Myriads of hearts have been melted into submission to Christ by the persuasive music of his voice and logic of his argument.

But when you think of his leadership, his weapons, his possession of the Holy Ghost, and his genial spirit, why wonder at the good results of his labors? And did ever man battle more disinterestedly than he? The gain that he chiefly sought was souls for his Master and salvation for the perishing. Refusal was not possible to one whose heart was all sympathy and love. The cold wind, the hot sun, the drenching rain, the midnight darkness—none of these could deter the man whose life was duty. His nature gave promise of old age, but to-day, at fifty-seven years, he sleeps in death. Few men have more fully and generously given their lives to the people. He sleeps in death, a martyr to his devotion to humanity.

CHAPTER 6

Origin and Influence of West Branch Quarterly Meeting

In my twentieth year my parents came to the conclusion that it would be right for them to leave the old home in Ohio and move to a new one, located at Marion, in Grant County, Indiana. Although young, I had become attached to the dear old Friends, whom I had been accustomed to see sitting in the galleries of the various meetings in the quarter. So I pause a little while to dwell upon the origin of West Branch Monthly and Quarterly Meetings and the influence they have had upon the Society of Friends in the Middle West, and especially upon Indiana Yearly Meeting, religiously and educationally.

The monthly meeting was opened at West Branch Meeting-house, two miles south from West Milton, Miami County, Ohio, First month 17, 1807. The West Branch Quarterly Meeting was opened Sixth month 13, 1812, to be held alternately at West Branch, Ohio, and Richmond, Indiana. The charter members of West Branch Monthly Meeting all came from North Carolina Yearly Meeting, most of them from Bush River Quarterly Meeting, South Carolina.

It appears that the line of descent of West Branch Monthly Meeting is from and through the following meetings, established in the years given: Chester, 1681, and Concord, 1684, both in Delaware County, Pennsylvania; Newark, 1686, and New Garden, 1718, both in Chester County, Pennsylvania; Nottingham, 1730, in Cecil County, Maryland; Hopewell, 1735, in Frederick County, Virginia; Westland, 1785, Fayette County, Pennsylvania; Miami, 1803, Warren County, Ohio; West Branch, 1807, Miami County, Ohio.

From the foregoing we might conclude that West Branch Monthly Meeting was a child of Philadelphia Yearly Meeting, but we learn that in 1790, the meetings then in Western Pennsylvania and Virginia, which had belonged to Philadelphia, were transferred to the yearly meeting for Maryland, which was thereafter to be held at Baltimore, and which seems then to have taken the name of Baltimore Yearly Meeting. Since the Redstone (Pennsylvania) Meeting belonged to Baltimore Yearly Meeting in 1803, all the Friends meetings west of the Alleghenies are to be reckoned descended from Baltimore Yearly Meeting.

The minutes of Miami Monthly Meeting show that from 1803 to 1807 there were 306 certificates received from sixteen monthly meetings belonging to North Carolina Yearly Meeting, conveying the rights of membership of 1,418 members to that monthly meeting.

I have been permitted, in the providence of my Heavenly Father, to visit within the limits of all those monthly meetings, except the one in Georgia, and, so far as I have been able to see or hear, the location of Friends in this fair Southland was desirable and pleasant, so far as outward comfort and ease were concerned. Their land was fairly productive and their climate almost ideal. Their communities were prosperous, their societies were harmonious and pleasant to live in, and there was loving fellowship among them as brothers of the same household of faith.

But as the eighteenth century drew to a close, there was unrest among them and a general feeling that a change of location was desirable. Friends at first, in common with others, held slaves to some extent. There was all the time a protest against the practice as inconsistent with their Christian profession.

When they located in South Carolina and Georgia, slave-holding was still tolerated amongst the Friends, but during the years of their residence there the Society had taken a very advanced position on the subject. The change had been gradual and was the result of heartfelt conviction. It was laid upon their hearts and conscience that it was wrong to hold their fellow-men in bondage, and one by one they freed their slaves.

This conviction soon became a concern to the whole Society. By loving though persistent persuasion, pressing the truth as it was apprehended upon the consciences and judgment of the membership, the Society of Friends as a body became united in forbidding the practice of holding slaves by its members.[19] This profound stand, of course, put them in opposition to the prevailing sentiment of the country, and they soon felt the disadvantage to which their free labor would put them in competition with slave labor.

This conviction of conscience in the line of duty and judgment as to economic considerations came to them as a divine voice to go out of that country to a land that would be shown them. That land was the new Northwest Territory, then opening to settlers, with its fundamental ordinance, dedicating it forever to freedom and free institutions, and they were not disobedient to the vision opened before them, but came with great rapidity, as a vanguard of the mighty host of free citizens that soon followed to lay the enduring foundation of great States and prosperous commonwealths.

Among those who came are the names of Ballinger, Brown, Coate, Coppock, Elleman, Evans, Furnas, Haskett, Hollingsworth, Jay, Jenkins, Jones, Kelly, Macy, Mendenhall, Mote, Neal, Patty, Pearson, Pemberton, Teague, Thomas, and many others whose names are not familiar among Friends throughout the West.

---

[19] Although all of the yearly meetings in America adopted minutes forbidding their members to keep slaves or sell them to others, the situation in many of the southern states was complicated. In some states, slave-owners were forbidden by law to take slaves out of state in order to free them. Friends in these states, notably North Carolina, were caught in an impossible situation. This double bind was what caused many Friends to leave for the free states in the Midwest.

We will now advance a little while, to their method of solving the educational question and its effect on others. In the first half of the last century many Friends found difficulty in providing for their children as good opportunities for acquiring education as they would gladly have given them. The public school system in Ohio was not developed then as now, and the subscription schools on which the Friends largely depended were inadequate in equipment and were often of necessity taught by teachers poorly qualified, both as to knowledge and method.

My grandfather, Walter Denny Jay, though having but little school learning himself, was desirous that his children should have better opportunities than they had. His three youngest sons were now grown up and were beseeching him for better educational advantages. To meet this demand and to help other parents similarly situated, he hired and placed as teacher in a school-house near his home a young Friend of advanced education. This was the autumn of 1845. That winter, and also the following winter, he taught a four-months' school, ranking in grade of studies with academies and high schools of later day.

Young people desirous of better education came into the school from other neighborhoods. The school was a success, a very beehive of activity in search of knowledge and an inspiration to surrounding neighborhoods to provide more advanced education among the youth. It was quite gratifying to my grandfather, whose wise thought and liberality started the school.

One of his sons, Eli Jay, and Mahalah Pearson, who came from another neighborhood, were among those [who] greatly profited by the advantages of these schools in the knowledge of the natural sciences and mathematics. In 1847 they both began teaching near their respective homes, in Miami County, Ohio, he in a settlement school, she in the public schools of the State. They were married Tenth month 24, 1849, and soon after began teaching together in a school of their own with a set purpose to make teaching their lifework.[20]

---

[20] Eli Jay (1826-1911) and Mahalah Pearson Jay (1827-1916)

Two years of this school deepened their consciousness of their own need of better education for their intended work. They arranged to go to Oberlin College, in northern Ohio, then the only co-educational college in the country, and which then, as now, was eminently Christian in all its appointments and pervaded by a deeply religious atmosphere.

At this day we are surprised at the opposition and denunciation they met with, both in private and in public, when their plan of going to Oberlin became known. A seemingly exercised minister had the shutters opened at the close of quarterly meeting and used the occasion to dwell upon the awfulness of what they were about to do and the terrible and everlasting consequences to which it might be expected to lead. His discourse led one Friend to say, at the close of the meeting, to another who was approving what had been said, "You talk as though you thought there was no God in Oberlin." But more of the Friends present seemed dazed by the minister's exercise and avoided the customary cordial shaking of hands at the close of the meeting. To such an extent did ignorance and narrow-mindedness prevail in that day, even in supposedly high places.

The purpose of Eli and Mahalah Jay was not changed by this demonstration. It rested upon too firm a conviction of what was right for them to do to be disturbed by such an incident, and they went to Oberlin the next week as they had planned. It was a comfort to them after leaving this scene of grim-faced men and tearful women, to find that their parents on both sides and their near relatives encouraged them to go. They had scarcely left the meeting-house grounds in the carriage with Grandfather Jay when he said to them, "Children, I want you to know that I have no unity with such doings. You know I have not encouraged you in going to Oberlin, but now I want you to go."

As all college courses then required Latin and Greek, which they had not studied, it was necessary for them to give two years to preparatory work on the languages, then four years in the regular college course. The first two years they took at Oberlin, the last four years at Antioch College, Yellow Springs, Ohio, nearer their home, a new co-educational college opened in the autumn of 1853 under the presidency of Horace Mann, one of the most distinguished educators of that day.[21]

They graduated from this college in 1857, and in 1860 received their second, or Master's, degree from their alma mater. Mahalah Jay taught a large class in preparatory Latin all through their senior year, and after their graduation she continued for more than two years teaching in the preparatory department of Antioch College. Eli Jay taught in the public schools of Yellow Springs two years. In 1859 he took charge of a school near Lafayette, Indiana, which was under the care of the Friends of Greenfield Monthly Meeting, where he taught one year.[22] The next two years they both taught at Spiceland, Henry County, Indiana. They also taught at Tippicanoe City, Miami County, Ohio.

In the summer of 1864 they were asked to take places at Earlham College, and, as events turned, Richmond, Indiana, has been their home ever since. Their connection with Earlham College, which began Tenth month, 1864, closed, so far as regular work there was concerned, in Sixth month, 1884. In these twenty years they were out of the college but six years. One of these years was spent in the Indian work near Fort Sill, Indian Territory (now Lawton, State of Oklahoma), and two years in teaching at Rich Square, near Lewisville, Henry County, Indiana.

In their years as officers and teachers at Earlham College, Eli Jay was employed in various positions, first as governor, having charge

---

[21] Horace Mann (1796-1859), was one of the outstanding educators, reformers, and abolitionists of the nineteenth century. He was president of Antioch from 1853-59. He headed the first state board of education in Massachusetts, and introduced new programs such as "normal schools" for teacher training and tax-supported public schools with compulsory education till age sixteen. He strongly opposed sectarian education in public schools, which brought him under attack by some religious leaders. He is often considered the "father of education" in the United States.

[22] This school, Farmers Institute, was the same school which Allen Jay attended in 1852.

of the boys; then as teacher of mathematics, natural science, and history in the Preparatory Department. In 1874–75 he was the acting president of the college in the absence of Joseph Moore, during the latter's visit to the Hawaiian Islands.

The last five years he was Professor of Mathematics, Physics, and Astronomy in the College Department. Mahalah Jay's work was principally in the Preparatory Department of the school, teaching Latin and English the greater part of the time. She was also the principal of the Preparatory Department, which then embraced more than two-thirds of all the students attending the school.

Since 1884, they have not been engaged in much regular teaching, but have given a good deal of private instruction to students who have mostly come to their home to recite. Altogether, they have touched and aided in their preparation for life several thousands of the generation of men and women who are now on the active stage of life. These years of semi-retirement have been filled with plenty of work in various lines, preventing the rust of inactivity, and now, having both passed their fourscore years, and having lived together nearly threescore years, with thankful hearts they look back with much interest upon what they have seen and known and been a part of in the past, and forward with good hope of what the future may yet unfold to them, both here and hereafter.

CHAPTER 7

Moving to Indiana

It was in the summer of 1850 that we left West Branch. The public sale being over and the time having arrived for moving to our new home in Indiana, we, like other movers in those days, started with wagons loaded with household goods and such other things as we wished to take with us, while the younger members of the family walked and drove the cattle. At night it was customary to camp out, which was done by building a fire by the roadside, cooking the meal, and then lying down to sleep by the fire upon straw and bedding, while the older members of the company and the women or children would sleep in the wagons, which were covered.

When we remember the great emigration of Friends from the South to Ohio and Indiana, and then later from these states to the far West, it gives an added interest to the wagons used for this purpose. The wagon bed was built in such a shape that it turned up at the fore end and also at the hind end. It had wooden bows bent over the bed in such a manner that the ends of the bows ran into iron staples on each side of the bed. Over these bows was drawn a cover, made of cotton or linen canvas, which would turn the rain and in some degree keep out the storm. Then, with two horses or four horses, or sometimes six horses, hitched to the wagon, the driver would sit on the saddle horse and drive the lead horses by a single line, held in his hand.

Fifty or seventy-five years ago it was a familiar sight to see these emigrant wagons going along the main roads leading westward. Sometimes in the autumn they were very numerous, especially along the National Road, which was laid out by the Federal Government to run from Cumberland, Maryland, directly across the mountains west to St. Louis, Missouri. The act of Congress authorizing the laying out and making of this road was passed by Congress and approved by Thomas Jefferson, March 29, 1806. Upon the admission of Ohio, Indiana, Illinois, and Missouri to the Union, a certain revenue from the sale of land was to be set apart for the making of roads and canals within their limits. Although thus early provided for, the National Road was not finished through Indiana until about 1830 and 1831, and has never been finished all the way to St. Louis, but, as someone has said, "was lost in the prairies of Illinois."

This was a great thoroughfare for movers going West, and it is said that often in the autumn season such moving companies were almost always in sight. These wagons, in the West, were sometimes called "prairie schooners." In this way most of our forefathers came over the mountains and through the wilderness to Ohio and Indiana, sometimes swimming their horses and wagons through the rivers and cutting their way through the forest. At night, they would have their campfires burning to keep the wild animals away from them. When the spirit later came upon our fathers to move westward, they took the same means to remove their families, and while there was not so much forest to pass through, yet there were broad prairies, with tall grass, so that the danger of prairie fires had to be guarded against, for these fires sometimes swept over the plains with great rapidity. This danger could be overcome by burning over a piece of ground, driving into the center of it, and making the camp there, where the grass had been burned.

Our moving was more modern and not of so great length; we camped out only three nights. We reached our new home and were greeted with a pleasant reception from the Friends of Mississinawa Monthly Meeting. It was a good-sized meeting, with a great many young people. It was established in 1833 and belonged to Northern Quarterly Meeting, which was settled mostly by Friends from the "Old North State," as North Carolina was sometimes called. This quarterly meeting was set off from New Garden Quarter in Third month, 1841. At that time, Northern Quarterly Meeting was held alternately at Back Creek and Mississinawa, these two meetings receiving their names respectively from a stream called Back Creek and a river called Mississinawa.

Back Creek Monthly Meeting was established in 1838. The quarterly meeting embraced all the territory that is now included in the limits of Fairmount, Marion, Wabash, and Vandalia quarterly meetings. It was a large quarter and the meetings were largely attended. On First-day of quarterly meeting great crowds came from far and near. Sometimes there were so many that it was necessary to have an overflow meeting in the grove. It was at Back Creek, within the limits of this quarterly meeting, that one of the first "general meetings" was held, by a committee from Indiana Yearly Meeting, in 1869.[23] I shall have more to say in regard to this general meeting work later on.

In Boarding Schools and College

My life was spent on the farm, similarly to that of other young men of that day, and in taking part in the social and literary entertainments of the young people of the neighborhood until the autumn of 1851, when my father took my brother, Milton Jay, and myself to Friends Boarding School, Richmond, Indiana. About one week after reaching there I broke my leg while playing football. I was carried to the nursery and lay there for nearly four weeks, and then went around on crutches and continued my studies during the term, which closed in the spring of 1852.

---

[23] The "general meetings" were the precursor to the revivals which later became common in pastoral Friends meetings. General meetings, lasting several days, were originally for teaching and instruction, with opportunities for preaching and for discussion.

This institution has had such an important influence on the history of our Society in the Middle West, indeed, throughout the Church in the great Northwest, that it may be right to dwell a little on the struggle Friends went through to secure it. It is a long history. Friends were poor and it required great self-denial on their part to make it a success.

In reviewing its origin, I am reminded of a lecture which I heard delivered in Washington, a few years ago, by an old German who was connected with the Educational Bureau of our Government. His subject was, "Educational Laws of the World." He reviewed hastily the laws of the various civilized nations of the earth, pointing out their good and bad features. Finally, he came to the United States, and took one State after another. He had a map of each State, intending to show by the color of the map the grade of the school laws. The lighter the map was, the better the educational system.

The last map to be placed upon the wall was that of Indiana. I shall not attempt to give all of his exact words, but I think I can give a correct rendering of what he said and quote some of his own words. "According to the map of Indiana, ladies and gentlemen," he said, "There is a State that has the best educational system in the Union, yes, the best there is in the world, and the Quakers are to blame for it. Of their number, the Hon. Barnabas C. Hobbs had more to do with it than any other man."[24] He then spoke of his work as superintendent of public instruction and his connection with the State Normal School[25] and with other educational work, and closed by saying that he was not appreciated by the State nor by his own church while he lived.

After saying the above, he went on to give an account of Friends leaving the South and why they left; told how they came to Indiana,

---

[24] Barnabas C. Hobbs (1815-1892) was the first president of Earlham College, serving from 1867-68, and also Indiana Superintendent of Public Instruction, serving from 1868-71.

[25] "Normal Schools" were what we would now call teacher training schools—schools where teachers could observe classes and practice teaching techniques.

settled in the woods, cleared a little patch of ground, built a log cabin, and then selected a suitable location and built a log church. "No; excuse me, I do not mean church. They built a meeting-house." "Then, in a few years they united and built a monthly meeting school-house, and their children went to school under religious teachers; on Fourth-day or Fifth-day they went to 'mid-week meeting,' and learned to worship with their parents. The Quakers have the true idea of education. They educated the body, intellect, and heart together, which is the true system of education, for if you educate the intellect alone, you have a cold and formal Christian, or if you cultivate the heart and emotions alone, you have a fanatic, with his hobbies. Quakers solved this problem by training their children to manual labor on the farm, while their minds were trained in the school-room, and their spiritual training was promoted in their meetings, where they worshiped with their parents and were taught to listen to the voice of the Spirit and obey His commands."

This is what our parents meant when they spoke of a "guarded religious education." It was this desire to give them such a training that was at the bottom of the monthly meeting schools and, as their children grew older and wanted a more advanced education, caused the yearly meeting to think of a central boarding school at Richmond, Indiana. But more about the institution and some of the men and women connected with its history later on, when I tell of how I became connected with it in a different capacity than I was in 1852, when a student.

Upon going home in the spring, I had such a strong desire to continue my studies that my father listened to my entreaty and permitted me to go to a new school that had just been established the year before, under the control of Greenfield Monthly Meeting, located some nine miles southwest of Lafayette, Indiana.[26] Arrangements being completed, I started, with my trunk, one spring morning, with two other passengers, in the hack running from Marion to Wabash, twenty

---

[26] Farmers Institute

miles distant. The "corduroy bridges," which were made by cutting down trees and saplings, cutting off logs twelve or fourteen feet long and laying them crossways in the mud holes, were floating in some places, on account of the water, and in other places the wheels of the hack would sink in the mud up to the axles.

Our conveyance mired down nine times during the day, and we had to get out, secure rails from the fences or cut poles from the woods, get our pry under the wheels and help them up, while the driver would whip the poor horses and make them pull the hack out. Then we would get in and ride until it dropped again, when a similar scene would take place. We passengers walked about half the way in the mud, helped to get the wheels out of the mud holes for a change, and paid two dollars for the privilege of being transported to Wabash. You can now go on an interurban car for fifty cents, making the journey in fifty minutes. I went over the road a few weeks ago and tried to find the places where the mud holes were, but there is a gravel road all the way now. The young men of the present day will never know the healthy pleasure of walking and carrying a rail to help out of a mud hole. They will have to ride in fine cars and breathe the microbes that they tell us have come into our modern society.

We reached Wabash between nine and ten at night, tired, muddy, and hungry, but, after washing and eating a hearty supper, I was ready for the canal packet boat that came along about midnight on its way to Lafayette, eighty miles farther down the Wabash River. Sleep was sweet that night, and the next night I landed, a stranger, in Lafayette, where I stayed until morning. I then started out for a nine-mile walk over the Wea Plains. It was my first introduction to prairie scenes. The morning was pleasant, and when I came to the Wea stream I pulled off my shoes and stockings and waded through.

I had the name of Buddell Sleeper, at whose home I was to board and whose nephew and niece I had become acquainted with the winter before at the boarding school. Stopping to inquire the way, I found the home of Dr. Turner Welch, who knew my parents well and remembered me when I was a child. I remained there for dinner, then walked on to the place I had started for, and soon reached the home where I was to spend the next nine months, and became acquainted with the family, the eldest daughter of which was to walk with me nearly forty-five years as my wife.

On the following Second-day morning the school opened, with something like a hundred pupils. The principal teacher was Moses C. Stevens, a young man of twenty-five from Providence, Rhode Island, who had taught in the Friends boarding school of that city. He had now come West to teach. We were all strangers to him and he to us. It was a time of sizing up on both sides. After we had taken our seats, he read the ninetieth Psalm, and, after a time of silence, he rose and made a few remarks, closing his speech by laying down his first rule, which was, "I expect you all to behave yourselves." It was short, but comprehensive. We understood it.

A few words about this man who had come out to the West to engage in teaching and who was to play an important part in helping to mould the educational spirit among Friends and others in Indiana. He had taught several years at Farmers Institute and made a name for himself. After that he was at Green Mount Boarding School for some time. This institution was located near Richmond and was under the control of the Hicksite branch of the Church. After several years it went down, and is now the site of an orphans' home, under the care of the Lutheran Church, and is called the Wernle Orphans' Home.[27] After this, he was a professor of mathematics at Earlham College for a number of years, but he left his mark on that institution even more when afterwards he became one of the trustees, appointed by Western Yearly Meeting, to manage the institution.

Perhaps his greatest work was done as professor of mathematics at Purdue University, located at Lafayette, Indiana, a State institution, where he remained until age reminded him that the time had come to rest. He then retired to a comfortable home near the institution,

---

[27] Still in existence as the Wernle Children's Home, 2000 Wernle Road, Richmond, IN.

where he and his lovely wife are spending the evening time of life, except when, to avoid the cold weather, they are in their Southern home, Tallahassee, Florida. He has impressed his life upon many. It must be a comfort now, when he has passed his fourscore years, to look upon the lives of so many whom he has taught and sent out into the world to do their work.

Farmers Institute was an academy that was built by the Friends of Greenfield Monthly Meeting, in order that they might have their children educated at home. It was located in a grove between two prairies, one Wea Plain, and the other, Shawnee Prairie, not far from the meeting-house. They erected a boarding house that would accommodate about thirty boarders. There was a good literary society connected with it, in which a number of the parents took an active part. The spirit of education was felt throughout the surrounding community, and it became the center of a widespread influence for good, a number of Friends moving into that neighborhood to educate their children.

At the close of the summer term, I went home, helped through the harvest and sowing wheat in the autumn, and returned at the opening of the winter term. The following spring I returned home, helped in the sugar camp while we were making molasses and sugar, and then went on to Antioch College, in Ohio, where Uncle Eli and Mahalah Jay had offered me a home with them while I attended the college. This institution was at that time under the presidency of Horace Mann.

CHAPTER 8

Early Married Life

At the close of the three months' term at Antioch College I returned home and made arrangements for my marriage to Martha Sleeper, in the autumn, which took place at Greenfield Meeting House, Ninth month 20, 1854, before a very large concourse of people. The house could not hold them all. There had not been a Friends wedding there in ten years, and it was a great curiosity. Perhaps there was more excitement on the part of the congregation than solemnity.

There were two couples of us to be married at the same time. My wife had a double first cousin who had been brought up by her parents in the same home, and they were just like sisters. Her name was Chloe A. Sleeper. She was to marry Pleasant A. Winston. When the time came, the dear old Friend at the head of the meeting announced that the time had come for us to proceed to perform the ceremony. I spoke first. Taking Martha Sleeper by the hand, I said: "In the presence of the Lord and before this company, I take thee, Martha Ann Sleeper, to be my wife, promising, with Divine Assistance, to be unto thee a loving and faithful husband until death shall separate us." Then she followed, repeating the same, putting my name in the place of hers and "husband" in place of "wife," and "wife" in the place of "husband." Then, after the other two had said the same, we all sat down, and the marriage certificate was read, and the meeting was dismissed.

For the information of my young friends, I may say that we had to "pass meeting." That is, we had to be present at the monthly meeting before the day of the marriage, when I went into the women's meeting, the messenger going before and opening the door. There I found my intended wife, sitting on the "lower facing seat." I sat down by her, and the clerk read the minute made at the last monthly meeting regarding our intention of marriage. Then we arose, took each other by the hand, and I said: "Friends, we continue our intention of marriage with each other." She then said the same thing. Then the messenger opened the door, and we walked into the men's meeting, sat down on "the facing seat," and the minute of our intention of marriage was read there. Again we stood up and, taking each other by the hand, declared that we continued in our intention of marriage, and the clerk read the minute liberating us to proceed, and appointed a committee to attend the marriage and the marriage entertainment and see that good order was preserved and that the marriage certificate was recorded.

> I am inclined to the opinion that if more care were taken to-day, on the part of parents and children, in approaching the subject of marriage, there might be fewer unhappy homes, and our country would not be disgraced by so many divorces.

Some will say, "why so much ceremony and care?" I am inclined to the opinion that if more care were taken to-day, on the part of parents and children, in approaching the subject of marriage, there might be fewer unhappy homes, and our country would not be disgraced by so many divorces. Indeed, every lover of home and country must mourn over the unhappy homes and the frequency of divorces as we read of them in our daily papers. I would appeal to my young friends to approach marriage as a divine institution, one of the most solemn, and yet one of the happiest transactions of life if sanctioned by God. Young men and women, do not look upon courtship as a trifling matter. Approach it prayerfully. Never trifle with each other's affections. If ever honest, be so while you are seeking each other's love and affection. You cannot afford to deceive each other. When a boy, I never remember hearing of a separation where Friends had been married in a meeting.

Early Married Life

Teaching School

The following day we started in carriages to my home, some ninety miles through the country, reached there on the second day, a little after noon, spent a few days, and then went on to Indiana Yearly Meeting, which was large and interesting. We remained in my parents' home that winter, and as my wife had taught school for two years, the Friends asked us to teach the school at Mississinawa. We agreed. We had over a hundred on the roll, and an interesting and satisfactory term. It was agreed that my wife was a good teacher, and I tried not to spoil her reputation, but to learn all that I could about teaching and other things that teachers generally learn when they enter upon that profession.

As spring came on and our school closed, I felt it would be right to move down to the neighborhood of Greenfield Monthly Meeting. So I went down on horseback, found a small farm, and returning, as soon as the roads were passable, we loaded our household goods in a wagon and started for our new home, which caused one of our old friends, by the name of Eli Overman, to quote the text of Scripture, with an addition, "For this cause shall a man leave his father and mother, and cleave unto his wife and wife's people."[28]

The Home in Greenfield Monthly Meeting

The first of Fourth month, 1855, we landed on what was called "The High Gap," one mile from the meeting-house and the same distance from the school-house, where I had spent nine pleasant months at school, and two miles from my wife's old home. We were between the meeting-house and the railway station, which in fact opened the way for us to have many visitors coming and going. Here we were to live for nearly fifteen years. Here our five children were born, and

---

[28] Matthew 19:5; Mark 10:7. "With an addition" refers to the phrase "and wife's people," a joke referencing their move to be near Mahalah Jay's family home.

here the two older ones died. The second son, Charles A., died when fifteen months of age; Rhoda E., when little over six years of age.

It may be right for me to say a little in regard to Rhoda. She was going to school. One day she said to her mother, "When I die, I want you to bury me by the side of little Charlie." Her mother made the promise, and soon afterwards she went over to the home of Jeremiah A. Grinnell, who lived a few rods from our house, and told him that she was going to die and be buried by her little brother. He took her on his lap and talked with her a few minutes about dying, and after she left, he told his wife that Rhoda's father and mother might just as well give her up, as she was not going to live. She came to me one day and told me the same thing. Looking out of the window upon the snow, I asked her if she would not be afraid to die and be put down in the ground, under the snow. She looked at me with a smile, and said: "Why, no, father! Jesus will not let me lie in the grave. He will take me home to be with little Brother Charlie in heaven, and there we will wait for thee and mother to come."

Perhaps a week after this, one morning, she came out of her bedroom and said, "Father, I am sick. I do not want any breakfast." I went to the table with the rest of the family, but did not feel like eating much. I went back into the room, and when I asked her how she was, she said, "I am growing worse," and then added, with a faint smile, "I am not afraid to die." The next morning she passed away to her eternal home.

> We were now settled down to the life of farmers in the midst of a prosperous farming community, where a man's success was too much judged by the money he made and the number of acres of land he owned.

We were now settled down to the life of farmers in the midst of a prosperous farming community, where a man's success was too much judged by the money he made and the number of acres of land he owned. Greenfield Monthly Meeting, to which we belonged, was composed of two preparative meetings, Flint Creek and Pine Creek, about twelve miles apart.

Pine Creek was on the west side of the Wabash River. The monthly meeting was set off from Sugar River Monthly Meeting and Western Quarterly Meeting, now Bloomingdale Quarterly Meeting. But at the time we moved there, it belonged to Concord Quarterly Meeting, held alternately at Honey Creek and Sugar Plain, the former now New London and the latter Thorntown Quarterly Meeting.

It was about twenty miles from any other meeting, Pine Creek having been laid down. There was no minister or elder belonging to it. Neither had there been for some twelve or fifteen years. There were few who spoke in meeting except Enoch Moon. His communications were largely made of Scripture quotations. Occasionally some one else spoke. Vocal prayer was rarely, if ever, heard, unless some traveling minister came along, which was not very often. Yet, the meeting was kept up and well attended by the members and by others living in the neighborhood. The Farmers Institute Academy was a source of strength in the community, and a number moved into its limits to educate their children.

The Bible School and Religious Awakening

We appointed a committee each spring to open and keep up a First-day school during the warm weather, but when the frost came it went into winter quarters, until the next spring, and the committee would report that it had been "held to good satisfaction." In the spring, when the buds were opening, it would be resurrected again. One autumn, after we had been there three or four years, several of the young Friends came to me after the meeting. They had decided to discontinue the school, and said if I would take charge of a class, they would come all winter.

Being one of the trustees of the school, I arranged for a room in the school building, and we met every First-day afternoon. The class averaged about twenty, and has never been laid down since. On the other hand, a few years later the whole school adopted the plan of continuing the entire year. It is pleasant to look back to the work of that winter. A number of the members of that class have been useful in church work. The majority have finished their race on earth. Several years afterwards a young woman, who had been a member of that class, just before she died requested her sister to write to me that she thanked God for that class, because while a member of it she gave her heart to God.

It was while working with those young people that I first offered vocal prayer in public. I felt the need of it. Sometimes the spirit of prayer would come upon us, and several of the members of the class would engage in prayer. This revival influence was finally felt in the academy, and several of the young people at times were heard in prayer during the morning devotions at the opening of the school.

One evening after dismissing the class, while walking home I noticed one of the youngest members of the class, a girl of fourteen or fifteen years of age, weeping as we walked along. I queried of her what the matter was. After some persuasion, she said, in a broken voice, that they did not have family worship in their home, and added, "I feel like I ought to ask father to let me read the Bible to-night and pray in the family." Dear child! The burden was great. I encouraged her to be faithful, and when parting from her at the gate I told her I would pray for her that night.

The next morning the father, who was working for me, came into the barn and, with deep emotion, told how his child had come to him and asked if she might read the Bible to the family. He said: "I called all the family, mother and six children, around the table and we sat there. She took the Bible and read a few verses, but the tears so blinded her that she could not see how to read. But she could pray, and as she knelt, we all knelt and wept together." It was only a few weeks until the whole family were praying Christians. It was a lovely Christian home to visit. Three or four years after this, as the sun was setting across the Western prairie, that mother lay dying. She looked up into the face of this daughter and in a feeble voice whispered, "Thank God for a praying child," and passed away.

My own Christian life was growing during this time, and the feeling was so pronounced among the young that in several instances when a company was gathered for social visiting, a chapter would be read and a season of prayer would close the visiting. I remember several of these occasions at our house, when the students came in to eat apples, crack nuts, and have a pleasant time socially, and when we would close with a prayer meeting. Indeed, in looking back, I am impressed with the belief that often this was one of the motives that influenced those young people to come.

Thus, in a quiet way, in this little Quaker community out by itself on the prairie, during the years 1859 and 1860, began this wave of revival work that a few years later began to spread abroad over our branch of the Church in various places, of which I have more to state in the other chapters on the revival work in our Church. Other localities have claimed that the movement was born in their midst and that some special person was the instrument in bringing it about. It may have been that the sign of the "going in the tops of the mulberry trees"[29] may have been first heard by those who have never said much about it. The Master will know where to bestow the crown.

---

[29] See 2 Samuel 5:24, "And let it be, when thou hearest the sound of a going in the tops of the mulberry trees, that then thou shalt bestir thyself: for then shall the Lord go out before thee, to smite the host of the Philistines."

CHAPTER 9

Beginnings in the Ministry

During the year 1859, in our silent meeting on First-day morning, I rose and spoke a few words in the way of the ministry. It was a memorable day to me. It had an effect on the congregation. It made me a "speckled bird" from that time forward, for in those days, if any one spoke in meeting it was expected that he would become a minister, for there was no other door open whereby he might exercise his religious gifts. There was no Home Mission, no Foreign Mission, no Christian Endeavor, and but little Bible-school work. This fact may have been the reason why some who would have been good workers in these fields of religious labor were recorded ministers when they had never had the call nor had a gift in that line, and now it may happen that some who are called to the ministry may try to substitute missionary or some other religious work in the place of the ministry. Therefore they do not succeed. The gifts and callings of God are without repentance.

It was at the monthly meeting held Fourth month 16, 1859, that a removal certificate was received from Blue River Monthly Meeting held in Washington County, Indiana, conveying the right of membership of Jeremiah A. Grinnell, a minister, and that of his wife, Martha Grinnell, and their seven children. Their coming was a great blessing to our meeting. He was a man twenty-five years ahead of his time. He "understood the signs of the times," and he knew what Israel ought to do, and withal he had the wisdom of a serpent and the harmlessness of the dove.[30]

He was a reformer without being a revolutionist. Different from some of our revivalists, who walk rough-shod over the feelings of those who differ from them, or who do not change as fast as they think they should, he produced a great change in our meeting without hurting the feelings of those who differed from him. In two years all were ready to go with him as he led the way.

He knew how to get work out of others. At one time he proposed that a committee be appointed to visit the families of our monthly meeting. He met with us and helped make out the program. It was read in our First-day morning meeting so that all Friends would be at home at the proper hour. We were to meet at a certain house. When we met he sent word that he would not be there, but that we must go ahead. Every member of the committee was heard in prayer and testimony before we got through, and three of the number have since been recorded as ministers of the gospel. He knew how to encourage and also how to direct in a loving manner.

One First-day morning, as I sat under a great burden, a text came to my mind and I rose and commenced, as I believed, under the leading of the Spirit. After a little I got warmed up and spoke vigorously, condemning some severely indeed, judging and finding fault with the way they were doing. After meeting he came to me with a smile and said: "Allen, after dinner, sit down and read the account of our Savior going to a certain village where they would not receive Him, what the disciples wanted to do with them and His rebuke."[31] I read it and have not forgotten it to this day, and am often reminded of it when I hear some of our ministers opposing and condemning those who do not act as they think they should. I believe to this day my concern was right. My text was right and the meeting needed the message, but I

---

[30] Matthrew 10:16; 1 Chronicles 12:32.
[31] Luke 9:51-56.

got away from the leading of the Spirit and put a good deal of Allen Jay into it.

When I hear ministers ranting and stamping, pounding the desk and talking about people going to hell, I fear they do not know "what manner of spirit" they are of. They show there is more human nature in what they are saying than there is of the spirit of the Master. Let me ever remember the command of the Savior when he said, "Judge not that ye be not judged, for with what judgment ye judge ye shall be judged."[32]

> My text was right and the meeting needed the message, but I got away from the leading of the Spirit and put a good deal of Allen Jay into it.

Soon after Jeremiah Grinnell came to our meeting he obtained a minute to visit the families of Friends and others and to appoint meetings in the surrounding neighborhood. He asked me to go with him, which I did, and it was a help to me. At our monthly meeting, held Eighth month 20, 1859, he obtained a minute to attend Ohio Yearly Meeting, to be held at Mt. Pleasant, Ohio, and some meetings belonging to it, also some religious service in Indiana Yearly Meeting. The monthly meeting gave me a minute to go with him and it proved a great encouragement and help to my spiritual life.

On this visit I first met David B. Updegraff, at the home of his grandmother, Ann Taylor.[33] She introduced him to me by saying, "This is my grandson, David Updegraff. He is not doing what he ought to in the Lord's work." It was not long after this that he gave himself to the Lord and entered upon the work that made him such a power in the Church.

In connection with our academy we had a literary society, called the Western Literary Union, which met weekly at night. Although

---

[32] Matthew 7:1; Luke 6:37.

[33] David B. Updegraff (1830-1894) was a prominent Quaker minister and revivalist. His family was acquainted with the pioneering revivalist, Charles G. Finney. Updegraff introduced many features of revival meetings to Friends, such as the "altar of prayer" or "mourner's bench," and took a controversial role in advocating that Friends allow the use of the sacraments.

living a mile from the school-house, I made it a rule to attend. After working on the farm during the day, I would go and spend the evening, taking my part with the young people in composition writing, declaiming and debating such questions as came up for discussion. It was there that I learned to stand on my feet and think. I was naturally very bashful and avoided talking in company. It may be rather hard for my friends to realize this fact now. Nevertheless it was a genuine fact.

Let me encourage young men and women to cultivate the practice of speaking in public, that you may learn to control your thoughts while speaking. I would also suggest your doing this without notes, for if you form the habit of speaking from notes, you will become a slave to the practice and then you must have them or fail. A person may be accurate at first by having notes, make fewer mistakes and be able to say just what he wants to say with them, but while reading his notes he cannot watch the audience. The speaker who can look his audience in the eyes—can get them to look into his face—and have something to say is the one who will hold their attention.

Then there is another advantage. When he sees that his audience is sleepy, looking around and becoming restless, he can sit down, and that man is a success who sits down at such a time instead of going ahead and trying to rouse an interest by scolding, storming, and shouting the louder. Noise will not fill the place of thought. Some noisy sermons would look ridiculous if written out and printed. Now, what I have said does not mean that the sermon shall not be written out and thought over and the mind filled with it. On the other hand, it makes it more necessary. Then, from a well-filled storehouse let the Spirit draw out things new and old.[34] It may require the burning of midnight oil to prepare the sermon, but let the Spirit so permeate it that it will take all the smell of the oil out of it.[35] Thus, with a heart

---

[34] Matthew 13:52

[35] See Matthew 25:3-8. It may be important to note that the "midnight oil" in Allen Jay's day was kerosene. Allen Jay's readers would all have been familiar with the smell of kerosene, and would have laughed heartily at his comment about letting the Spirit get the smell of the midnight oil out of the sermon.

filled with love, send the message forth to the hungry souls of those who are longing for it. It will find a place.

When once you have hold of an audience, don't go on until you lose that hold. Study, if necessary, in order to preach short sermons. You can preach a long time without much thought by going over stereotyped phrases and telling anecdotes, talking about these and what you have done. Let your illustrations be appropriate, to the point, and short. Above all and over all, hide behind the cross. Remember Jesus says, "I, if I be lifted up, will draw all men unto me."[36] He is the greatest preacher who can lift up the Lord Jesus Christ, he who can sound with a bugle note, "Behold the Lamb of God."[37]

At Greenfield Monthly Meeting, held Eighth month 18, 1860, the proper authorities brought the names of my wife and myself before the monthly meeting to be appointed elders. This was very trying, especially to my wife, who had been brought up in the meeting, for there were a number of old people sitting on the front seats whom she had been accustomed to look up to as elders. The proposition being united with, we accepted the responsibilities devolving upon us in the spirit of resignation, praying that God would help us to fill the place to His glory. Our friends were kind and excused us from taking prominent seats in the meeting.

The Call to Preach the Gospel

During all these months of active labor in farming, church, and educational work, the impression was consciously growing upon me that the Lord was calling me to preach the gospel. It brought me into a deep spiritual trial. I was born with a harelip and a cleft palate, and, notwithstanding the fact that my lip was sewed up the day I was eight months old, and the operation proved successful, so that the deformity was not noticeable, the cleft palate remained and could not be fully remedied. At the age of fifteen I began to wear a false palate.

---

[36] John 12:32

[37] John 1:29, 36

Although this helped some, my voice was still very imperfect and it was difficult for strangers to understand me. Often when I began to speak the young people in the congregation would begin to laugh. But I will not dwell upon this deformity. No one will ever know what I passed through. It was my thorn in the flesh and cost me many bitter hours of sorrow. I wanted to preach and felt I could not. In a measure I believed I knew how Paul felt when he prayed that his "thorn in the flesh" might be removed, and in some degree, I have heard the message, "My grace is sufficient for thee."[38] To this day I never rise to speak, especially before strangers, without thinking about this affliction, though I have reached the experience that enables me to say, "Here I am, and if Thou canst get any glory out of my infirmities, I will rejoice and give Thee all the praise." It is said that so many who have good voices refuse to use them to speak well of His name who has crowned them with so many blessings.

One day about this time, while working in the harvest field, a messenger came, saying that David Tatum, who was paying what we called religious visits to the families of our meeting, had come to visit our family. I went to the house and on my way prayed that if the Lord was calling me to that work He would show it to his servant and that he would be led to tell me. Soon after we sat down in silence, he commenced speaking, and his subject was faithfulness in the ministry. Just as I was thinking it might be for my wife, he turned towards me and said, "I mean thee, my brother." Then he went on to tell me that the Lord had called me and I must not be disobedient, adding: "If thou art faithful, thou shalt see many souls saved by thy ministry, and thou shalt cross the ocean more than once and preach the gospel in other lands," and more that I need not mention here. The dear old man is living yet, in Chicago, over ninety years old. A few months ago, when I met him, we spoke of that day. He had a clear remembrance of the message.

---

[38] 2 Corinthians 12:7, 9

Not long after this I was called to visit a young woman who was thought to be near the close of her life. As I returned home through the woods, about one o'clock that night, I threw myself down on the ground and surrendered all to my Heavenly Father, promising to say what He wanted me to say and go where He wanted me to go.[39] From that hour I have loved to tell the story of the gospel the best I can.

I continued to live an active life on the farm and to attend to such religious work in connection with the church and school as came to me. To the satisfaction, I believe, of my friends, after the proper authorities had paid the necessary attention to the matter, they proposed my name to the monthly meeting as one called to preach the Gospel. Greenfield Monthly Meeting, held Fifth month 21, 1864, recorded me a minister of the gospel of Christ.[40] I think it right to say here that I have often thanked my Heavenly Father that He gave me a wife who encouraged and helped me in the work, always giving me up cheerfully when I felt that duty called me to leave home. It meant much to her, with the care of the home and the little children. Often when my friends encouraged me and spoke of my faithfulness, I felt she needed it more than I did. Hers was the greater sacrifice. The Master will know how to bestow the reward.

She was a real helpmate and was anxious that I should do the work well. She would tell me of my mistakes in grammar, pronunciation, and gestures, sometimes showing me how I stood in the gallery, and what I did with my hands. She taught me to keep my hands out of my pockets while I was talking. She labored hard to break me of the habit of speaking so loud and being so boisterous when preaching. She never became discouraged, but kept on and sometimes in a way that bore fruit.

---

[39] Referring to the hymn, "I'll Go Where You Want Me to Go," by Charles H. Gabriel and Carrie E. Rounsefell.

[40] Recording, at this time, was done by the monthly meeting; in most yearly meetings today, it is still initiated by the monthly meeting, but recording is usually done by the yearly meeting after a lengthy process of discernment, testing, and education.

I will always remember one morning when I was going to drive ten miles to attend the quarterly meeting. I had bade her farewell and started to drive away when I heard her calling. Looking around, I saw her coming down the steps. She came up to me with a very solemn face and said very deliberately, "My dear, I am going to be very busy to-day and will not have time to listen, so thee need not preach loud enough for me to hear." Then she turned around without a smile, leaving me sitting there, and went into the house. When I commenced speaking that day, I remembered she was ten miles away. Blessed is the preacher who has such a faithful wife, and twice blessed is he who listens to her.

Visiting Families and "Speaking to Conditions"

The first minute that I ever took out for religious service after I was recorded a minister of the Gospel was dated Tenth month 15, 1864. It read as follows: "To hold myself resigned to visit, in the love of the Gospel, the families and individuals of our old quarterly meeting (Concord), and perhaps a few who have been but are not now in membership with us."

I was accompanied on this visit by a very dear friend, William E. Morris. We were closely united in the work, felt the burden resting upon us, and endeavored to keep our minds open to the leading of the spirit, that our message might be adapted to the conditions of those we were visiting. It is a strain, both physically and mentally, upon those who labor thus day after day for a number of days.

I remember well after we had visited the last family, and we started to walk to the nearest station where I could take the train for home, we went through the woods for some distance. We felt like two boys, telling stories, jumping over logs, climbing bushes, laughing, and enjoying ourselves generally. It might have looked foolish to others, but to my mind it was a relaxation that the Heavenly Father gave to two of His children who had been trying to do His bidding. To this day, I look back with pleasure to that boyish romp in the woods that beautiful afternoon. It was a relaxation that was good for mind and body, a fit preparation for the next work the Master might give us to do. I have met with some ministers whose preaching would have been improved if they had taken a good romp with some little boys on the ground and had laughed until their lungs were thoroughly expanded.

The first ten minutes that I received from my monthly meeting for religious service were largely for family visiting, which, to my mind, requires close attention to the leading of the Spirit. It is a fruitful source of good if well done. It may be neglected too much by ministers of the present day. It is easier to speak to a mixed crowd than to go and say: "Thou art the man."[41] It is the way our Savior reached the heart of the woman of Samaria, "He told me all things that ever I did."[42] The question has often been asked of me if the gift of speaking to conditions of individuals and meetings is not dying out. Why do we not hear more of that kind of preaching at the present time? In reply I will say that every good gift of our Heavenly Father can be increased by faithful use or diminished by neglect. The pound may be made five or ten pounds, or it can be buried in a napkin.[43]

As I have said, my first religious work was mostly that of family visiting; during the first three years of my ministerial labor I visited between three and four thousand families. The gift of speaking to individuals grew upon me. I would speak modestly of my experience, but these impressions grew upon me in those days, so that when I went into a home I often found myself looking at the spiritual life of different members of the family and formed the habit of speaking to individual members rather than to the family as a whole.

Sometimes individuals have come to me afterwards and inquired, "Who told you about me?" In some instances they would accuse my companion of having told their history. As an illustration, I will give one instance, if my friend will excuse me for doing so. I was visiting

---

[41] 2 Samuel 12:7

[42] John 4:29

[43] Luke 19:20

the Friends' homes in a certain town. There were forty families that I wanted to call upon in one day and return home on the train that night at ten o'clock. The program was made out the night before, and messengers were sent ahead the next morning telling each family about what hour I would reach their home. I requested the friend who walked with me not to talk with me or claim my attention, but simply to show me the way.

Coming to one home, as I opened the gate the text found in Psalm 42:11 came up, and as I opened the door the father and mother were sitting there with their two little children. So as I walked to the chair waiting for me, I repeated this text: "Why art thou cast down, O my soul? and why art thou so disquieted within me? Hope thou in God: for I shall yet praise Him, who is the health of my countenance, and my God." I then delivered a message to the wife, then to the husband, and a few words to the children, after which I offered prayer and went out. I thought nothing more about the message. It was lost, with a hundred others.

Some five years afterwards, while living in North Carolina, a letter was received from this woman telling me I had saved her life, as she had poison in the drawer with which to take her life, which she intended doing at ten o'clock that morning, but just before the hour the messenger came and told her that I would be there at eleven o'clock. So she had concluded to wait until after the visit, during which I told her that she had been so disobedient to her Heavenly Father's call that she had brought darkness upon her soul and had been tempted to take her natural life, and then, in the words of the Psalmist, told her to hope in God for she would yet praise Him who was the health of her countenance and her God.

So after her husband and I had gone out, she said to an intimate friend who came in immediately, "I will try once more to be faithful, and see if the message is true," then rose and going to the drawer, took out the poison and threw it into the fire. The next time I met her she was a recorded minister and was engaged in religious service.

Others have come to me as I have traveled around the field where I visited thirty-five or forty years ago, and have told me that when visiting their home I had spoken to their condition so closely that they were enabled to settle the question and give their hearts to God. Let all the praise be given to Him who has said, "I will guide thee with Mine eye."[44]

At the end of four years, in 1868, I entered the field to labor in connection with the Baltimore Association work in the limits of North Carolina Yearly Meeting. There my labor was different. I was called to look after the school work, talk on education, preach to large and hungry congregations, many of whom had not heard preaching during the war. It was the multitude now that I ministered to instead of the individual. So in the exercise of my gift my work was not pointing out the conditions of families and individuals, but preaching the need of salvation to the unsaved multitude. Consequently the special gift became of a more general character.

Another reason why we do not have this special gift to point out states and conditions is that when the revival spirit came upon the church the ministry was changed. The revivalist stirred the sinner by appealing to the emotions, telling stories, giving illustrations, and warning the sinner to flee from the wrath to come, until sometimes perhaps the emotional entered into the work in undue proportion. Then, as usual, another extreme came. The doctrinal followed and we produced a generation of theologians who endeavored to present the gospel in a systematic way. Again, these have been followed by those who were trying to reach the heart through the intellect, and their sermons appeal to the reason and judgment. Finally, we have the sermons on moral and reformatory subjects, and the various issues of the day, which sometimes savor more of a lecture than a sermon.

Now, all these are good and have a tendency to advance the Redeemer's kingdom, and I am not ready to condemn those who

---

[44] Psalm 32:8

are called to labor in that way, but I have prayed that the remaining time of my ministry may be more and more like that of the blessed Master—simple, easy to be understood, and direct to the heart of the hearer. I wish we all preached more like Him who "spake as never man spake."[45]

> I have prayed that the remaining time of my ministry may be more and more like that of the blessed Master—simple, easy to be understood, and direct to the heart of the hearer.

---

[45] See John 7:46. The line that Jesus "spake as never man spake" was commonly used in evangelical sermons.

CHAPTER 10

The Draft During the Civil War

The year before the close of the war a draft was made through Indiana for soldiers. There was a sentiment among those in authority that Friends were not bearing their proportion of the expense and privation in carrying forward the war. There had been no draft made within the State, so that those who did not believe it was right for them to volunteer and enter the army had been left out.

Those in charge of conducting the war proposed that a draft be made upon those who were conscientiously opposed to fighting and that they thus be called upon either to enter the service or to pay the sum of three-hundred dollars to carry forward the war.[46]

When the draft was made, my name was one that was drawn along with those of several other young Friends, two others in our little meeting. It created a good deal of excitement among some of our Friends. The two other young Friends paid their three-hundred dollars each, but I felt it right to do nothing, feeling that I could not go myself nor give money to hire others to go.

---

[46] The practice of paying $300 to "hire a substitute" was common in other states as well as Indiana. Many states also paid $300 as a bounty to new recruits. It is worth remembering that, at this time, working men were glad to be paid a dollar a day, thus $300 represented a very substantial sum of money.

The proper military officer came out and notified me that I would be expected to report in the military camp at Lafayette, Indiana, for training, on a certain day. I told him that I could not conscientiously be there, that as I could not fight it would not do any good for me to report. Then he demanded the three-hundred dollars. To this I replied:

> "If I believed that war was right I would prefer to go myself rather than hire someone else to be shot in my place."

"If I believed that war was right I would prefer to go myself rather than hire someone else to be shot in my place." I said that I believed our Savior meant what He said when He said: "Thou shalt not kill," and "My kingdom is not of this world,"[47] and that therefore His followers could not fight, and that I took the position of the Christians during the first century, when called upon to bear arms, whose simple reply was, "I am a Christian and therefore cannot fight."[48]

After a long conversation he left. A few days later he returned and asked me to reconsider my decision and place three-hundred dollars so he could find it. He came the third time, to the orchard where I was gathering apples, and told me I would either have to come, or pay the three-hundred dollars, or he would be forced to sell my property and collect the money. As I was firm in my decision, he went into the house and tried to get my wife to tell him where he could find the money. She told him she felt as I did and that she could do nothing but suffer.

He then went out and looked over the farm, selecting the stock that he proposed to sell and then sat down and commenced writing bills for the public sale of our horses, cattle, and hogs. While he was writing, dinner was ready, and when we sat down to the table we insisted on his eating with us. We tried to keep up a pleasant conversation on various subjects, making no reference to the work he was engaged

---

[47] Matthew 5:21; John 18:36.

[48] A famous quotation from the early Christian, Maximilian. Allen Jay very possibly learned this story through reading, *The Example and Testimony of Early Christians on the Subject of War*, by Jonathan Dymond, published in 1821 by the Tract Association of Friends.

in. After dinner he turned to me and said, "If you would get mad and order me out of the house, I could do this work much easier, but here you are feeding me and my horse while I am arranging to take your property from you. I tell you it is hard work."[49]

We told him we had no unkind feelings toward him, as we supposed he was only obeying the orders of those who were superior to him. I went out again to my work and when he had prepared the sale bills he placed one on a large tree by the roadside in front of the house and then rode around and placed the others in different parts of the neighborhood.

A few days before the time had arrived for the sale, I was at Lafayette. He came to me and said, "The sale is postponed. I don't know when it will be. You can go on using your horses." I heard nothing more about it for several years. After the war closed I learned that Governor Morton,[50] who was in Washington about that time, spoke to President Lincoln about it and he ordered the sale to be stopped. My dear wife and I never worried a moment about it, for we felt that we were doing the will of Him who had condemned all war. So we were kept in peace and quietness through it all. But some of our neighbors who were not Friends were much troubled, and when the war was over we were informed that three or four of our wealthy farmer neighbors had agreed among themselves that when the sale came off they would buy up the horses for the three-hundred dollars, pay the money over to the officer, and leave the horses on the farm as mine, so that we should not be at any loss on account of our religious principles.

When we see how incompatible war is with the Gospel of Christ it is indeed strange that those who claim to be His followers so utterly ignore His teachings and substitute that of man in place of His decla-

---

[49] cf. Romans 12:20-21: "If your enemies are hungry, feed them; if they are thirsty, give them something to drink; for by doing this you will heap burning coals on their heads. Do not be overcome by evil, but overcome evil with good."

[50] Oliver Morton (1823-1877) served as governor of Indiana during the Civil War; he was later elected to the U.S. Senate and was one of the "radical Reconstructionists" who wanted to punish the South after the war.

ration that it is no longer an "eye for an eye," or a "tooth for a tooth," but "love your enemies, and pray for them that despitefully use you and persecute you."[51] It has always been pleasant to look back and to feel that in a little measure we bore our testimony to the peaceable nature of the kingdom of Christ.

---

[51] Matthew 5:38-44

CHAPTER 11

The Setting Up of Western Yearly Meeting

In 1858 Western Yearly Meeting was set up by Indiana Yearly Meeting. The opening was conducted by a committee appointed by Indiana Yearly Meeting and several other yearly meetings were represented by committees who were present and added interest to the occasion. Iowa Yearly Meeting was set up by Indiana and opened at Oskaloosa in 1863; which was followed by Kansas Yearly Meeting, opened at Lawrence, Kansas, in 1872; and Wilmington Yearly Meeting, opened at Wilmington, Ohio, in 1892.

In the setting up of Western Yearly Meeting, our quarterly meeting at Honey Creek was included in its limits, so that we were members of Western Yearly Meeting until 1868, when we moved to North Carolina. But more of that later on.

In the year 1860, Western Yearly Meeting appointed a committee to visit all of its subordinate meetings, and individuals as way might open, and labor for their help and encouragement. This committee was continued in 1861, and was composed of the following Friends, namely, Eleazar Bales, Henry Wilson, Calvin Wasson, Robert W. Hodson, Nathan Elliott, Isaac Baldwin, Matthew Stanley, Andrew D. Tomlinson, Martha Wilson, Sarah Hiatt, Drusilla Wilson, Mary Day, Hannah B. Tatum, Margaret M. Bradfield, Rachel H. Woodard, Catherine Elliott, Phoebe G. Taylor, and Allen Jay. I remained a member of this committee for four years, during which time we visited all the quarterly meetings, and many of the individual meetings and families.

All the members of this committee except myself were advanced in years and religious experience. I was a boy among them, being in my twenty-ninth year. It was a School of the Prophets to me. They had all been in the service of the Church for a number of years. They have all passed away except myself and one other, Margaret Bradfield, now Margaret Newsome, who lives in California.

As we went from one quarterly meeting to another, trying to estimate conditions, build up the Church, and laboring to draw the young into active service, I had the opportunity of studying the lives and characters of the members of this committee and becoming acquainted with their Christian spirit and spiritual discernment in matters connected with the Lord's work. I was often impressed with the gentle and loving spirit manifested by the different members of this committee towards those who through weakness and frailty had missed their way. I could not but realize the fact that they had known and experienced a definite religious experience and knew the voice of God, though their training had been such that they did not often say much about it.

Perhaps it would have been better for the Church had they been faithful in telling what the Lord had done for them. It would have strengthened others and honored their Savior. But unquestionably they were men and women of God, and knew the leading of His Spirit. Especially were dear Calvin Wasson and Drusilla Wilson led to see the spiritual struggle through which I was passing and to extend a helping hand in the right way and at the right time.

Now I come to speak of the sadness which was brought over my mind when, a few years later, after I had left the yearly meeting, I learned that several of these dear Friends felt that they must leave the yearly meeting and set up another nearby, because they felt that those who called themselves revivalists were introducing extremes and practices in the meetings for worship that they could not endorse or submit to.

I believe to this day that it was a mistake on both sides. Indeed, I think it is doubtful whether separations are ever beneficial in advancing the kingdom of God. Those who remained needed the weight, stability, and spiritual judgment of those who left, and those who left needed some of the earnestness and zeal of those who, as they felt, had driven them out by trying to force them to adopt some practices that they could not conscientiously adopt. Had they remained together, some of the extreme things that have been done would not have occurred. Neither would those who went out have seen their numbers diminishing and their young people drifting away from them. They needed each other and the Church needed them all.

> Indeed, I think it is doubtful whether separations are ever beneficial in advancing the kingdom of God.

The student of church history will not have to go far to find that, in those yearly meetings where the greatest extravagances have taken place and spiritual fanaticism has come in, the conservative element has been eliminated by separation. Sometimes when I hear some of the evangelists boasting of how they carried on the revival work in spite of the old Friends of other days, I wonder whether He, who has said that it would be better for a man to have a millstone hanged about his neck and be cast into the sea than to offend one of these little ones,[52] does not see something on the other hand that the evangelist in his zeal does not see.

It was a sad picture that day to see those old Friends, with tears rolling down their aged cheeks, walking out of the meeting-house because they felt they could not worship with their brethren. They were mistaken, but was all the mistake on their side? The Master knows.

Thinking this over, I have sometimes been reminded, when seeing the zeal of some in pressing their views and doctrines, of a little incident in my schoolboy days. In our neighborhood we had a school in the summer, called a subscription school, which was attended by children who were not old enough to work in the field during the

---

[52] Matthew 18:6; Luke 17:2.

summer. For some reason there was one grown young man among us. He had no one of his age to play with. He tried to find some way of entertaining himself. One day he stood up against a tree and said to us little fellows, "I am going to yon tree, and you cannot hinder me."

It was a dare and we took him up and prepared to resist. Two or three got hold of each leg, two or three hung on to each arm, and the remainder lined up in two rows in front. We then announced that we were ready for the fray. He started, striking those who were hanging to him and walking right over the line of opposition in front of him, stepping on some of the poor feet, knocking others down, kicking those loose who were hanging to his legs, and finally reached his goal. But when he looked back, some were lying on the ground crying, and others were going to tell the teacher and show their wounded toes and fingers. He had reached the tree, but did he have much to boast of when we count the wounds that he had inflicted?

The revivalists may walk over the feelings of those who cannot endorse their actions and still love the Master as well as they do. God holds them all alike precious in His sight.

George Fox said, "Friends, be careful where you place your feet, for you may tread upon some of the precious flowers springing up out of God's earth."[53] John Woolman said, "I waited several years until Philadelphia Yearly Meeting was ready to receive my message on the subject of human slavery, so as not to create discord in the body."[54] He lived to see the results he longed for without making bitter feelings and separation. The Master said, "I send you forth as sheep among wolves. Be ye therefore wise as serpents and harmless as doves."[55]

---

[53] Today's readers can find this quotation in *The Journal of George Fox*, John Nickalls, rev. ed. (London: Religious Society of Friends, 1975), p. 312. Allen Jay would of course have used an earlier edition.

[54] I have not been able to locate the source of this quotation. It may be a paraphrase, although it is certainly in the spirit of John Woolman.

[55] Matthew 10:16

CHAPTER 12

The Era of Separation

Anti-slavery Agitation

The first testimony that we have concerning slavery is that of George Fox, while in the Island of Barbadoes, in 1671. In this he urges humane treatment of the slaves, and, after a time of slavery, that they be set free.[56] Friends, for a time, did not regard the holding of slaves, when well treated, as wrong; but their point of view gradually changed, and in 1783 they sent their first petition to Parliament. The same year a Quaker Committee was formed, consisting of William Dillwyn, George Harrison, Samuel Hoare, Thomas Knoles, John Lloyd, and Joseph Woods. Friends never ceased their efforts until the slaves were freed. In America, the first public presentation of the subject was by some German Friends near Philadelphia, in 1688, but neither the monthly nor quarterly meetings took it up. In 1774 there was a minute disowning any member of Philadelphia Yearly Meeting who continued to hold slaves or had any part in the slave business.

The history of this change of sentiment in Philadelphia is very interesting, and even more so is the history of North Carolina Yearly Meeting, as it labored to free itself from the evil of slavery, located, as

---

[56] See *The Journal of George Fox*, Nickalls edition, pp. 602-6. Many Quaker books of *Faith and Practice* to this day quote approvingly from the doctrinal sections of Fox's letter, but ignore the searingly prophetic sections having to do with the treatment of slaves and Indians.

it was, in a slave-holding State. It is not our purpose to go into this in detail. It has been written by Friends better prepared to do so. In 1836 an epistle from London to Indiana Yearly Meeting expressed the sympathy of English Friends with those in America, and, while recognizing that the difficulties of American Friends were greater than those of Friends in England, in a similar struggle, urged Friends to be zealous in testifying against slavery. This was well received, and Friends were urged to practice and testify in favor of abolition.

From 1836 to 1840 the testimonies remained about the same. Some, more zealous than others, began forming abolition societies and opening the meeting-houses for abolition lectures. This the more conservative members opposed, believing it well to keep the testimony clear and faithful, but discouraging the more aggressive zeal. The slavery question was at this time causing great excitement all over the country, and the yearly meeting minutes to the monthly and quarterly meetings urged Friends not to join with those who did not profess to wait for divine guidance, and under the weight of this concern to watch attentively for every right opening and to move therein in a united body. All this time the yearly meeting had a standing committee, called the African Committee, who were doing all they could towards schooling colored children, holding Bible schools for the adults, circulating tracts, and seeing that they received justice in individual cases.

Separation in Indiana Yearly Meeting

The immediate causes of the separation in Indiana occurred during the yearly meeting of 1842. On Seventh-day morning, Tenth month 1, 1842, a minute from the meeting for sufferings was read, stating that four members of that meeting were disqualified for usefulness in that meeting. These members were Benjamin Stanton, Jacob Grave, William Locke, and Charles Osborne, who were leaders in the antislavery movement. The meeting accepted the report and appointed a committee to present names to fill the vacancies.

Then, on the next day, Henry Clay, who was a slaveholder and, it was understood, was seeking the Whig nomination for the Presidency, was received and taken to meeting in the carriage of the yearly meeting's clerk and given a prominent seat. This, many Friends thought, was only common courtesy to a stranger and a man of superior talents, but the antislavery element regarded it as an open insult. Accordingly, they made an effort to organize before the close of yearly meeting, but this effort was unsuccessful. However, on Second month 7, 1843, at Newport, now Fountain City, they organized a meeting of their own. The meeting-house was divided by permanent partitions, and each party had its own side of the house. The feeling was also very strong at Deer Creek, Grant County, Indiana, where there was a division. These were the strongholds of the separatists, though some members throughout the yearly meeting sympathized with them. The next autumn the antislavery Friends sent an epistle to London Yearly Meeting, which it refused to open.

A committee from England came over to labor and to restore unity among the membership, but it refused to recognize the antislavery meeting. There was no question of doctrine involved, simply their attitude towards slavery. The antislavery Friends accused the yearly meeting of thrusting them out without a hearing and silencing their testimonies against slavery for the sake of popularity. They always claimed they did not secede, but were driven out. They delighted to call the Friends who did not secede "proslavery Friends" (a name which they resented), and it was with a touch of sarcasm that they represented the body of the yearly meeting as attending elections and voting for slaveholders and proslavery committees, faring sumptuously every day on the wages of unrighteousness, the gain of oppression, namely the unpaid toil of the downtrodden slave. As they had forbidden the antislavery meetings, they designated the leaders of the yearly meeting the Scribes and the Pharisees, and themselves the followers of Christ who had been cast out.

On the other hand, the meeting at large was careful to have nothing to do with antislavery Friends, and, in the opposition to their zeal, failed to see that it was under a very real sense of duty and a feeling of the magnitude of the evil that antislavery Friends felt that they could not even modify their own testimony without compromising principle. The too rigid conservatism they would not submit to. The members of the yearly meeting, however, were in favor of abolition, but were conservative enough to want to test the new movement. In the minutes of the yearly meeting for sufferings it was plain that they advocated unconditional emancipation, but it was too much in theory and not enough in aggressive action. They were much grieved over the separation, and doubtless the decided action of the antislavery Friends did much towards awakening the yearly meeting to more aggressive action in regard to the measures they advocated.

After about fourteen years of separate meetings, there being no longer a call for separation, the antislavery Friends returned, about 1856. The coming back was gradual, in most places occupying four or five years. Perhaps some concessions were made on both sides. The yearly meeting had become more open and aggressive as the evil grew in magnitude. The other party had lost some of their overactive zeal, but none of their principle. Each side was more ready to listen to the other with a kindly feeling.

Here, again, the future historian will be able to see that there was no real cause for separation. The proper exercise of Christian patience on the part of both would have enabled them to have gone forward unitedly in the work they were both interested in. It is easy for us sometimes to imagine that we are persecuted when in our zeal we are not permitted to go ahead and denounce those who do not see things as we do. There were no differences in their views on the evil of slavery. It was a difference in their spirit and manner of fighting it. Those who remained thought it best not to open their meeting-houses for political meetings where the speakers said bitter things against the Church and all who did not join with them and use their weapons of warfare.

> The future historian will be able to see that there was no real cause for separation.

In our quarterly meeting, these meetings were held in the school-houses. I remember going to our school-house, with my father, to hear one of their strongest men speak. He pronounced bitter judgment upon the Friends who were not letting him speak in the meeting-house. While my father's house was one of the Underground Railroad stations, and for a while he bore his testimony against slavery by buying free-labor goods, thereby showing his belief in the evil of slavery, yet he, with others, felt it right to keep in harmony with the yearly meeting, and consequently in harmony with another. Bitterness was kept out and no wounds were made to be healed afterwards, and when the time came to receive the dear Friends of Deer Creek, in Grant County, Indiana, back into unity with the church, my father's voice was heard in Mississinawa Monthly Meeting, advocating receiving them back as a body and recognizing them as a monthly meeting at once, and as soon as possible, recording their ministers and appointing their elders.[57] There a monthly meeting was born in a day, in harmony with Indiana Yearly Meeting. That was a good day at old Mississinawa Monthly Meeting. The past was to be forgotten, and henceforth they were to walk together in the work of saving souls.

Those who were active on both sides of the controversy are nearly all gone. Here and there is one who remembers those days, but these would draw the curtain over the past and turn their faces toward the duties of the twentieth century. Slavery is gone. It died in a way that none of them expected. How much one may have hindered or the other hastened this end He only knows who knows the end from the beginning. May we not hope that the Church has learned a lesson that will make it harder for divisions to ever come among us again? If so, those trials will not have been in vain.

---

[57] Deer Creek Friends Meeting separated from Indiana Yearly Meeting in 1843, and was received back into the yearly meeting as a preparative meeting in 1858. They were set up as a monthly meeting ten years later, in 1868, and laid down in 1928.

The Beginnings of the Revival-Separation

I have already alluded to the Conservative or Wilburite separation in Western Yearly Meeting. Here it may be right for me to go into this subject more fully. All the later Wilburite, or "Conservative," separations were caused by the breaking out of the revival spirit.

Indeed, the "general meetings" were the fruit of this revival work. There was created a hungering for the Gospel. The membership was moved by the Spirit to seek something definite in the way of religious experience. As I have said, we felt it in our school at Farmers Institute, where a number of children were converted, and in the neighborhood prayer meetings, which were held in the homes. When we met socially, we would often read a portion of Scripture and have a time of prayer before closing. This went on quietly from 1861 to 1865. Jeremiah A. Grinnell was the human instrumentality that God used to lead it forward so quietly and wisely that but little opposition was ever raised against it.

In the winter of 1866–67, it broke out in Earlham College, when twenty young men were converted in one term, and before the end of the year almost the whole student body was swept into the movement. A young man from Canada, by the name of Seaburn Dorland, was especially active in this movement. The following year the Earlham report gave the following: "Early in the year the officers and Christian students were actively concerned for the spiritual welfare of the scholars. The meetings for worship were attended with life, and the students' prayer meetings gradually increased in numbers and interest. Souls became awakened to a sense of their need, and some were converted. The work went quietly on throughout the first two terms. Early in the third term a deeper and more general interest was awakened, and continued to grow, until there were but few who did not acknowledge the pardoning love of Christ." Some of these students carried the fire to different parts of the yearly meeting. Especially at Walnut Ridge was this manifested, where a great revival broke out and was followed by some extreme excitement, which, to some degree, marred the work at that place.⁵⁸

After having been actively connected for the last forty years with the educational work in four of the American yearly meetings, and in addition to that, having visited nearly all of the Friends colleges, boarding schools, and academies in the world, I am prepared to say that I believe that the minds and hearts of the young are better prepared while pursuing their education to receive and embrace the truths of the Gospel than at any other period of life. Good, healthy study in our colleges fits the mind so that it is susceptible to religious influences. The personal experience of those who have gone through college will demonstrate this fact—that they feel the need, while thus young, of something higher and more spiritual.

I believe, if you select two-hundred students from any of our colleges and compare them with a like number of young persons selected from any of our communities in any of our large meetings, you will find the religious experience and spiritual life lower among those taken outside the college life. We hear much said by some of the danger of education, but they forget the dangers found in ignorance. We mark one who is tinctured with skepticism who comes from the college, and pass by two or three skeptical ones who live in ignorance in our own meetings or neighborhood. Yes, I firmly believe that an occupied and trained mind is better soil to receive the good

> We hear much said by some of the danger of education, but they forget the dangers found in ignorance.

---

⁵⁸ Elbert Russell provides a graphic description of the Walnut Ridge revival: "A group of earnest members of the meeting began to meet in private homes for Scripture reading. It grew into a Sunday evening meeting held in the meeting-house to pray for a revival in that community. The interest spread to regular meetings for worship and there resulted violent manifestations of religious emotion in praying, testimony, shouting, and singing. Many of the older members and even elders and overseers professed conversion. Here for the first time among Friends a 'mourner's bench' was arranged, where 'seekers' could come for prayer." In a footnote, Russell adds: "A story current at the time says that Calvin Wasson, a minister from Western Yearly Meeting, finally got the floor in one of these meetings and exclaimed, 'Solomon says there is nothing new under the sun; but Solomon never was at Walnut Ridge.'" Elbert Russell, *The History of Quakerism*, pp. 426-7.

seed than the vacant and idle mind of the uncultured and ignorant. Fox understood this when he left some of his worldly possessions to establish a school, where the youth should be taught everything "useful in creation."[59]

This revival spirit was carried up to Plainfield in 1867, so that in nearly every house along Main Street, where Friends boarded, prayer meetings were held. Some of us who were young then remember that in seeking board for yearly meeting we sought those homes where we knew there would be no objection to such meetings. The Conservative Friends were watching us.

Until the revival era, night meetings were almost unknown among Friends. They never occurred except when a traveling minister was present and had one appointed. But the liberty and spiritual life which Friends always had in theory, and in some measure in practice, would not long submit to this rigidness. Perhaps we were too determined in declaring that we would hold meetings where and when we pleased, while the Conservatives were just as determined to prevent them. The spirit of controversy was raised and indulged in by both sides, until it culminated in a separation at Plainfield, in 1877.

---

[59] George Fox, *Journal*, 1667: "Then I came to Waltham and established a school there [for teaching of boys], and ordered a women's school to be set up at Shacklewell to instruct young lasses and maidens in whatsoever things were civil and useful in the creation." (Nickalls edition, p. 520)

CHAPTER 13

Reflections on Separation

"Separation is no cure for the evils of Church or State." These words, spoken in Western Yearly Meeting in 1861 by that Christian scholar and minister of the Gospel, John Hodgkin, of England, are weighty and full of wisdom. Had the members of Western Yearly Meeting believed in them and acted accordingly, the separation in that yearly meeting in 1877 would never have taken place.

Therefore, in the place of trying to give a history of the separations in Western and Iowa yearly meetings, thereby stirring up bitter feeling and tearing open old sores, I prefer to use my pen in healing them and hastening the day when they will be forgotten. So I will say but little about the separations, but endeavor to give my views and feelings about them in general. Although aware that I shall lay myself open to attacks from all sides, yet, upon examination into this subject, I am fully persuaded that the statement placed at the head of this section, taken from a sermon of John Hodgkin's in Western Yearly Meeting, is true, and if Western Yearly Meeting had listened to these strong words, it would be in better shape to-day. Yes, both factions would be in a better spiritual condition and many unkind words would not have been spoken, homes would not have been divided, and brothers and sisters would not have been arrayed against each other. The history of separations proves that they are destructive to the growth of the Church. Many illustrations could be given to prove this contention, but one will be sufficient to illustrate my point. I take the facts from a publication by the Nantucket Historical Association, Volume I, Bulletin No. 1, entitled, "Quakerism on Nantucket Island."

Our Society was established there about the year 1700 in a prosperous way and about 1790, with 5,600 inhabitants on the island, half of them attended Friends meeting, but in the year 1900 not a Friend was left on the island. First came the Hicksite separation, with all its bitterness, which was carried so far that some were disowned because they "sympathized with the other party." Then later came the Wilburite separation, in 1845, which again stirred up strife and bitter feeling, and, of course, each side claimed to be the original Friends. During the controversy not much was said about doctrine, but after it was over, each accused the other of holding views which were not in accordance with the teachings of George Fox. There may have been some truth on both sides.

Then came the Otis separation, which took place in Scipio, New York, when the Scipio Yearly Meeting decided to publish the journal of Joseph Hoage which contained "some remarks made by him which were construed derogatory to the temper of judgment of Job Otis."[60] The Otis family wanted to omit the criticism. This was enough for another separation. James Otis led one party and John King the other; so in 1859 they separated. The spirit of separation, which had so long lived among Friends on Nantucket, was ready to take sides, so under the leadership of Peleg Mitchel, Nantucket, that meeting was nearly all carried for the Otis party, which continued to dwindle under the fault-finding spirit until the last one had gone, and when I was there in 1900 they told me there was not one Friend left.

The old meeting-house where I preached many years before is now occupied by the Nantucket Historical Association, and there you can sit and study the history of Friends when they held control of the island and there was no other denomination there. Now the

---

[60] *Journal of the Life of Joseph Hoag, an Eminent Minister of the Gospel in the Society of Friends* (Auburn, NY: Knapp and Peck, 1861).

visitor sees fine church buildings of other denominations. As you walk through the streets, out over the commons and through the graveyard, you feel that these people died fighting each other. As you pass through the Wilburite portion of the graveyard you see no stones. The graves are unmarked. You feel as though you were walking through a pasture field. On the Orthodox and Gurneyite side you see names on the low stones that are familiar. You have seen the same names in New England, the Middle States, among the pine and red hills of the South, throughout the great Middle West, and far away beyond the Rocky Mountains.

Then you sit down and wonder if their descendants have learned wisdom from the fathers. Have they learned the great truth that, "Separation is no cure for the evils of Church or State"? Have they been able to grasp the fact that you cannot make people see the great truths of the Gospel just alike? The Saviour presented himself in His glorious saving power to one in one way and to another in another, but was precious alike to them all and they all alike precious to him. These were some of the thoughts that came over me as I visited these scenes and read of the past while sitting in the old meeting-house, but as I listened methought I could hear a voice saying: "My children have not learned the lesson. They are still finding fault. They are still judging. They are still asking if they may call down fire from heaven to burn up those who do not see me as they do."[61] And the voice of the Master bade me look the Church over from New England to California, from the Lakes to the Gulf, and along the fertile Mississippi Valley, where He had sent the rain and the sunshine, and behold the same spirit exists in those places.

But I turn away from these dark, sad pictures and come to the present. Now, as I hold my pen and look around upon my desk, I need only to reach out and turn over the pages of some of our church periodicals and see that the controversy is still going on. The fire of persecution is still burning. If some one is proclaimed a heretic, there

---

[61] Luke 9:54

are those who are ready to throw the wood on the fire, and all this in the name of the meek and lowly Jesus. Then comes the question: "How long shall these things continue?" The answer from those who judge is: "Until everybody believes as we do. We are right. God has chosen us to stand for the faith once delivered to the saints." Such are their actions, though they do not dare to put them into words.

But I have said enough to give my views on separations, and close by asking: Has a separation ever caused more people to hear the Gospel? Ever enlarged the Church? Ever shown to the world more of the gentleness and meekness of Christ? Has a separation ever caused the world to exclaim, "Behold how these Christians love one another?"[62] Has it ever caused those who held wrong views to turn and hold right ones?

> Has a separation ever caused more people to hear the Gospel? Ever enlarged the Church?

On the other hand, some of us who have been connected with families in which husbands and wives, brothers and sisters have been arrayed against each other, know something of the bitterness that it engenders which lasts to this day. Some one says: "But we must come out and be separate from sinners." "Let him that is without sin cast the first stone."[63] During that separation in Nantucket a dear Friend who passed through it said sadly: "I have seen men of natural kindness and tenderness become hard-hearted and severe. I have seen justice turned back and mercy led aside." Enough of this history.

What was true on Nantucket Island has been more or less true in other places where these sad separations have taken place. Other reasons might be given for the losses of Friends in the island, but separation is the one I am speaking about as a fruitful cause not only in one place, but in others also.

Justice to history demands that I record a separation in Iowa. This is one thing that both sides agree on. They are also clearly agreed in

---

[62] Tertullian, *Apologeticus*, 39:7.

[63] 2 Corinthians 6:17; John 8:7.

saying that the other party was the one to blame, and the yearly meeting minutes of each party show plainly that a Christian spirit was not manifested by the other side. Each side also points out its long and faithful labor to prevent the disownment of the other. They show that they were justified in the course they pursued and that they have felt great peace of mind for being faithful to the law and testimony. So I desire to give a few statements which all appear to unite with, leaving others to tear open the wound and tell who was wrong and who was right. I prefer to let the Lord settle that. It may be that some on both sides will be surprised.

It appears that the first public manifestation of difference of opinion occurred at Bear Creek Quarterly Meeting. It took place at the quarterly meeting held at Bear Creek in 1873, when the committee on general meetings made its report. Some were satisfied with the report, and others were not. Some were especially dissatisfied with the "mourner's bench" and the "testimony meetings." The differences which first became public in the quarterly meeting continued to increase until they finally culminated in a separation in 1877.

If I were to follow these troubles, it would be a history of differences continued in private and public debates. Business meetings were so hampered that it was hard to do the necessary business. When committees were to be appointed, each faction tried to get a member from their side on the committee. But I leave others who enjoy such things to write the history.

The Conservative Yearly Meeting, in 1886, revised their discipline. In the preface are these words: "To whom it may come. In consequence of innovations in doctrine and practice which have been introduced into our meetings, or, rather, forced upon us, we have deemed it our duty to withdraw from such, and we organize our meetings in order that we may hold them in accordance with the ancient usage of the Society, and have adopted the following discipline for their government."

On the other hand, as I have said, the Liberal yearly meetings show by their reports and printed minutes that they visited the separatists and labored with them under a deep concern, but were not able to show them the error of their way. Private letters from both sides have told me how deeply they mourn the separation and how they have wept over the un-Christian spirit of those who went out from them.

I turn from Iowa and simply glance for a few minutes at Western Yearly Meeting. Here the same thing was enacted. One side, in a spirit of revival, held prayer meetings at night in private homes during yearly meeting, the evangelists having altars of prayer and condemning publicly those who did not unite with them, introducing singing and forcing those who did not believe in it to hear or leave the house. On the other hand, there was just as much stubbornness and opposition manifested in the same factious spirit against this movement.

I was a member of the yearly meeting at that time, enjoyed the revival movement, and remember how determined we were to save souls, not thinking of those we might injure in the attempt or how we might cripple the Church and mar the harmony by pressing our views too fast. To-day we would all rejoice to see Western Yearly Meeting one united body, and I believe that it would be a stronger and more healthy body, better prepared to carry forward the Lord's work, if some of the conservative element that was driven out was to-day mingled with the extreme radical element that at times manifests itself in various places. I close this article by quoting: "And now abideth faith, hope, love, these three, but the greatest of these is love."[64]

---

[64] 1 Corinthians 13:13

CHAPTER 14

How Nathan Hunt Delayed Separation in North Carolina

I have given a rather detailed account of the Conservative separation in Iowa in order that the young people and those of another generation may have some idea of the course of events and the manner of proceeding when there has been a division in the Church. If I were to go into the details of the one in Western Yearly Meeting it would be similar in many respects. Some different opinions on methods and practices and in some places an honest difference on the explanation of certain scriptural passages which grew wider as they were discussed, and in some instances resulted in each party going to extremes on the point they had taken, until they got as far apart as possible and were in no condition to see good in each other.

How sad a picture thus presented by those who professed to love each other. I have purposely avoided mentioning some of the bitter expressions and un-Christian acts which occurred in some of the meetings where actual strife took place in order to get in possession of the records—holding the clerk's table and in some instances destroying it, entering into lawsuits in order to secure the property. What a commentary on the teaching of Him who said: "My kingdom is not of this world, else would My servants fight," and "A new commandment I give unto you, that ye should love one another even as I have loved you."[65]

I prefer to throw the veil of charity over these things rather than to drag them out into the light and renew the controversy. Let the wound heal, and let the world see that we are one even as Christ and the Father are one.[66]

Sometimes when reviewing the history of these separations we are made to wish that there might have been a Nathan Hunt in each of these yearly meetings who would have had the influence he had in North Carolina Yearly Meeting, when the Wilburites sent a committee to that yearly meeting. There was also a committee sent from the regular yearly meeting, Eli and Sybil Jones being members of the latter. I remember with interest the account they gave me of what happened.

At that time the Yearly Meeting of Ministers and Elders was opened at Deep River on Seventh-day, the yearly meeting proper following at New Garden, in the old meeting-house. The subject was opened up in the Meeting of Ministry and Oversight, and each side was given an opportunity to speak. The discussion was long, lasting until nearly dark, and the usual controversial spirit was manifest. When Sybil Jones arose to speak, a dear minister whose name has been a household word through the West put up her feet to keep her away from the partition so that she might not be heard.

In order to understand the situation, it is right to say that Nathan Hunt's son, Thomas, was the clerk of the yearly meeting and his daughter, Asenath Clark, and her husband, Dougan Clark, had been on a religious visit to New England and had come fully determined to throw their influence in favor of endorsing the Wilburite body. They had secured their brother, Thomas, on their side. Nathan Hunt had a room in the New Garden Boarding-School building, now Founders' Hall, Guilford College, where he made his home during yearly meeting.

---

[65] John 18:36, 13:34
[66] John 10:30, 17:11

The First-day night before the yearly meeting opened he invited both of the committees from New England to come to his room. When they had assembled and were quiet, he said: "I want to hear from both sides all about the trouble," and suggested that the Wilburite committee speak first, giving their reasons for the separation, and that the other side keep still until they were done. After they had finished and said they had nothing more to say, he called for the other side to present their case. He kept quiet until they were done. It was then about one o'clock in the morning. He sat silent a little while, then asked a few questions and said, "Now Friends, I want you all to go to bed," and dismissed them without any one getting an idea what he thought. He tells us himself that he did not go to bed that night, but spent the night in silence before the Lord, waiting to know His will as to what North Carolina Yearly Meeting should do.

Next morning he manifested his usual Christian politeness towards the different members of the committees. No one could tell what was passing through his mind. Meeting commenced just as usual. There was intense interest, for all knew that the question was to be settled whether North Carolina would remain in unity with the main body of Friends or join a faction of New England in cutting loose from correspondence with London Yearly Meeting and the great body of Friends in this country.

There were a number of ministers there from other yearly meetings. Among them were Sarah M. Hiatt and Enos G. Pray from the West. Enos G. Pray was a young man who was coming into prominence and was destined in coming years to exert an influence upon the Church in many places in our land. Well do I remember listening to his full, musical voice with deep emotion in my boyhood days, and vivid were the impressions made upon my mind by his ministry.

Little more than the usual time was given to the public worship that morning. Then the business was entered upon in the usual way by reading the opening minute, calling the representatives' names and reading the minutes of the traveling Friends. Then the clerk commenced reading the epistles. When he came to New England he said, "There are two epistles on the table purporting to be from New England Yearly Meeting. I propose to read the one signed by the clerk of the Wilburite Yearly Meeting," calling his name. Several of those who had been posted on that side united at once and the clerk commenced reading.

Nathan Hunt, who up to that time had not said a word, then spoke out in a loud voice, saying, "Hold, Friends, there is a lion in the camp." All eyes were turned towards him. Placing his hand on the banister and standing by the clerk, he said slowly, "Thomas, sit down." Then followed a scene which those who saw and heard it never forgot. Between eighty and ninety years of age, his voice was feeble when he began, but he gradually got warmed up and his eyes kindled with their old fire. His old eloquence also came back and for an hour or more he reviewed the controversy between J.J. Gurney and John Wilbur in England and the action of London and New England yearly meetings in the whole matter, and closed by warning Friends against the spirit of division.

> Nathan Hunt, who up to that time had not said a word, then spoke out in a loud voice, saying, "Hold, Friends, there is a lion in the camp."

Turning to the clerk, he said, "Read the epistle signed by Samuel Boyd Tobey, from New England." Almost the whole meeting rose in a body and endorsed the proposition. He had swept everything before him. The clerk sat silent, but the assistant clerk took up the epistle and read it slowly and solemnly. The delegation from the Wilburite Yearly Meeting rose and left the house and that evening started for home.

Thus North Carolina kept up her record of having no division, but a little of the same spirit remained in two of the quarterly meetings, namely Eastern and Contentnea, which a few years ago began to manifest more plainly by finding fault with the acts of the yearly meeting and refusing to pay their money if any of it was for evangelistic work. In 1902, at the time of the adoption of the Uniform Discipline, it was made an excuse by those indulging in this spirit to separate.[67] They were encouraged by a few persons outside the yearly meeting, but be it said to the credit of North Carolina Yearly Meeting, they have permitted them to hold their meetings in the house they occupied before. While they have no title to the property it is far better to let them alone, and if they find more pleasure in meeting separately, let them enjoy it.

In giving this account of how Nathan Hunt prevented the separation, I have repeated it mostly from memory as I have heard it related by those who were present that day. At one time I was permitted to read a copy of a letter written by Nathan Hunt himself, giving an account of the whole circumstance. I wish I had secured a copy myself, for it is an instance of the influence Nathan Hunt had in his old age upon the membership of that yearly meeting.

---

[67] The Uniform Discipline was one of the earliest goals of the new Five Years Meeting. It was intended to replace the greatly differing books of *Faith and Practice* which had evolved during the previous hundred years. Many of the yearly meetings which belong to Friends United Meeting continue to base their *Faith and Practice* on it, especially in the sections having to do with membership, business procedure, and other practical matters. For a fuller discussion of the Uniform Discipline, see Elbert Russell, *The History of Quakerism*, pp. 492–3.

CHAPTER 15

Visits to North Carolina and Baltimore Meetings

Preparations for the First Visit to North Carolina and Baltimore Yearly Meetings

I now come to the time when I obtained my sixth minute for religious service—service which brought me into the closest trial I had ever entered into, and a service which resulted in an entire change of all my life plans. I had no idea of the far-reaching effect upon my future work to result from obeying this call that seemed so clear and definite.

We were living on a small farm, heavily in debt, struggling along to meet our financial needs, and here was a call to drop all and go away to spend four or five months, hiring some one to gather my corn and take care of the stuff, and in addition borrowing the sum of $150, paying ten percent interest on it, to meet traveling expenses—and all this in the face of the fact that I belonged to a wealthy monthly meeting. But I knew that neither the monthly nor quarterly meeting would help. Some of our younger members to-day may wonder why the expenses, at least, were not provided for by the meeting. But some of us remember how fearful Friends were of encouraging anything like a paid ministry. The meeting very fully endorsed my concern; much sympathy was expressed and tears were shed as one after another united with my being liberated and encouraged to attend to the concern. Indeed, one dear Friend went so far as to suggest that he thought it might be right for the Friends to turn out and gather my corn, as I had to leave before corn gathering was over; but that was all there was in it, for when I returned next spring I had to finish gathering what my hired man failed to get in before winter set in. I have mentioned this, not because I regretted doing it, but to give the facts in the case for the benefit of those who may feel that they are bearing burdens to-day.

I had been away, visiting the meetings and families of Plainfield and White Lick quarterly meetings for two or three weeks, and on Sixth-day, by an extra effort, visited forty families between morning and ten o'clock at night, and then took the train for home, reaching the station three miles from our house about two in the morning. As I walked across the prairie, I settled the matter in my own mind, so that I went to monthly meeting that day and obtained a minute dated Eighth month 18, 1866, "to visit in the love of the Gospel, Baltimore and North Carolina yearly meetings and the families belonging to them as the way might open for it. Also such schools as might have been started within the limits of North Carolina Yearly Meeting since the war."

This minute was endorsed by the quarterly meeting the next week. A few days afterwards I learned by letter that my Uncle Thomas Jay, who lived at West Branch, Ohio,[68] had obtained a minute from his monthly and quarterly meetings in almost the same language as mine. We opened correspondence and decided that we would travel together and labor jointly in the work, which we did to our mutual satisfaction, and to this day it is a pleasure to dwell upon those days of united labor.

When we began visiting families of North Carolina Yearly Meeting, in the limits of Eastern Quarter, we went together for a couple of days. My uncle said to me one evening, "I am tired of sitting and listening to thee and then beginning and saying the same thing over,"

---

[68] Thomas Jay lived in West Milton, Ohio, and was a member of West Branch Friends Meeting.

and asked me if I was not tired of listening to him and then when he got through repeating it over after him. He thought we had better divide the field, with which I fully united, so from that time on when we went into a meeting we would ask the Friends to divide the families into two parts and then give each one of us a guide. We would then start out, one going to the right hand and the other to the left, until we came together once more on the other side of the neighborhood. I never felt uneasy but that those who fell to Uncle Thomas's portion got as good or better than they would have received if they had fallen to my portion.

Here I wish to pause and say a few words in regard to my Uncle Thomas Jay. He was next to my father in age (1813–1890). In early boyhood he evinced extraordinary will power, combined with remarkable habits of industry and perseverance. His morals were also of a strong order, as he was a member of the Society of Friends and an ardent adherent to their Christian faith. The elements of that deep piety that marked his character through life were early implanted in his mind. In middle life he was called by the Still Small Voice to preach the Gospel. In 1854 he was recorded a minister, and from that time until his last illness he continued to proclaim the message of salvation with a zeal and earnestness commensurate with the importance of his mission.

Thomas Jay was a man with a purpose. He never sought worldly distinction nor courted popularity. Controlled by the dictates of his conscience, he fearlessly performed his duty towards God and his fellow-men regardless of criticism. His gift qualified him to visit families. He was often led to speak to states and conditions in a remarkable manner. So when we learned of the similarity of our concerns, we decided to go together. In this work we became closely united. It being soon after the war, and the roads bad, we did much of our traveling on horseback or mule-back, whichever was the most convenient.

We soon got our names up as fast riders. We did not idle away much time. Each had a guide to go with him, and, although Friends were scattered and the roads bad, yet we succeeded generally in visiting from fifteen to twenty families each day. In the case of my Uncle Thomas, his communications so fitted the conditions of the families that his guide was accused of telling about the individuals beforehand.

I have said that we were closely united in Christian fellowship, and when my uncle came to the close of his life I went to visit him. The night he died he had me called to his bedside, and while struggling for breath he said, "I just want to say I am glad that thee loves to preach the Gospel. Be faithful to the end." His close was triumphant.

Visits to Baltimore

I find in an old diary I carried in my pocket the following entry, dated Tenth month 5, 1866: "This day I parted with my dear wife and children and departed on my intended journey to Baltimore and North Carolina yearly meetings, and the meetings and families belonging to them, as set forth in my minute already given." It was the year after the war, and the country was in an unsettled condition, especially in the South. No picture of the past lives more vividly in my mind than that of my wife, who, as the train pulled out that morning, was standing at the depot with our three children, the youngest in her arms and one on each side holding to her. She had eight miles to drive home alone.

I stayed that night with William B. Johnson and his wife at Indianapolis. I quote the following from my diary: "In thus leaving home my mind was brought into a close trial and fervent are my desires that the Lord will be with me and preserve me. My dear wife felt the parting keenly, yet with a Christian spirit bade me go and do my Master's will, and I believe we can acknowledge with thankfulness that we were enabled in solemn prayer to commit each other into the watchful care of Israel's unslumbering shepherd. O Lord, keep me and preserve me from marring Thy glorious cause; strengthen me to do Thy will, and if consistent therewith, grant that I may return to my family with the reward of peace. Amen."

The next day I went to Richmond and attended Indiana Yearly Meeting, where I met with my parents and many of my friends. At the close of the yearly meeting I went to Uncle Thomas Jay's, at West Milton. Tenth month 12, 1866, we left his home, going to Dayton and there taking the train for Baltimore, by way of Bellefonte that we might attend that meeting; also to Curwensville, where we visited the meeting and the families belonging to it. We also attended the Hicksite monthly meeting, having a good service and receiving a warm and cordial welcome. They insisted on reading our minutes and recording our attendance.[69] We reached Baltimore, Tenth month 20, at midnight.

Next morning the Yearly Meeting of Ministers and Elders opened. Our home was with our dear friend, Richard M. Janney. It was a pleasant home and one that in coming days was to be a resting place for me, and to the members of his household I was to become closely attached. This was my first visit to Baltimore Yearly Meeting. It was an occasion of much interest. It was my first visit to Friends east of the Allegheny Mountains. To a young man brought up in the West, in a country home, it was an education and made an impression upon my mind, having something to do with shaping my future work.

After years of close acquaintance with Baltimore Yearly Meeting, I am of the opinion that no yearly meeting of its size has done as much to mould the character of Quakerism in the Church in America as Baltimore. It was the first yearly meeting to open and establish another yearly meeting, which it did when Ohio was established by its authority in 1813. Then Ohio set up Indiana in 1821. All the yearly meetings in the United States since that date have descended from Indiana Yearly Meeting.

> I am of the opinion that no yearly meeting of its size has done as much to mould the character of Quakerism in the Church in America as Baltimore.

The yearly meeting proper opened on Tenth month 2, and the following Friends were in attendance from other yearly meetings: Eli

---

[69] The rift between Orthodox and Hicksite Friends may not have been so deep, or so spitefully maintained, as some histories assert. As in many other parts of his *Autobiography*, Allen Jay's actions here show that he was eager for the division to be healed.

and Sybil Jones, William Beard, James E. Bailey, Daniel Hill, Thomas Jay, John B. Elliott, Daniel H. Hutchins, John Bean, Seneca Hazard, Samuel Heaton, Jesse Green, and myself. The yearly meeting was a time of great favor.

Visit to North Carolina Yearly Meeting

At the close we started to North Carolina Yearly Meeting, going by way of Richmond, Virginia, where we stopped at the home of John B. Crenshaw. As we drove through the city and out to his home, we saw the dire effects of the war. We were impressed by what we saw on every hand. Our dear friend and family were remarkably preserved during the conflict. Although their home stood within sight of the outside batteries erected for the defense of Richmond, yet no injuries came to them except the loss of some property.

Our dear friend was engaged in relieving those in distress. He was often called upon to intercede in behalf of those who were conscripted and forced into the army, but who were entitled to be exempt on account of their religious belief. Friends who were consistent members of the Society, members of the Dunkard Church, and Mennonites were all exempt. He told me that he never failed where he felt sure that the parties were consistent members of the church to which they belonged. In some instances he was fearful that the parties had joined in order to keep out of the army. That put him in a close place, for the authorities threw the responsibility upon him to decide whether the applicants were really entitled to their freedom.

There were so many of these cases that they required much of his time, and in some cases there was much danger connected with securing their release. In one instance, about which he told me, he had, after great effort, secured the release of two young Friends who lived in North Carolina. It was late in the day and the battle was going on, these young men being in the trenches with their regiment around Petersburg. He secured a carriage and drove out to where the conflict was raging. It became very dark, but he pressed on until he had gone as far as he could with the carriage. He stopped with the prospect of waiting until morning.

Then the thought arose, "Suppose these young men should be killed during the night. Would I be clear?" After weighing the matter, he felt it right to go ahead, so leaving the horses and carriage with the driver, he started afoot through the trenches, inquiring for the regiment. After walking several miles through a heavy storm, with the roar of artillery all around him and shot and shell flying about him, about one o'clock in the morning he found them, and, presenting his orders for their release to the officer in charge, they were turned over to him. He started back with them and reached the carriage about the time that the Federal troops made a charge upon the breastworks which their regiment was defending and carried it with great slaughter, capturing those who were not killed. He drove home, arriving safely.

He told me of other similar instances. It was always interesting to hear him tell his experiences with the Confederate Government, including President Jefferson Davis and the various members of the Cabinet, and with the generals and officers in the army. He often joined with the committees appointed by North Carolina Yearly Meeting in going before Congress and the proper legislative authorities to secure proper laws upon freedom of conscience and other subjects that Friends were interested in. He was at one time a member of the Legislature of Virginia and endeavored to carry out the views of Friends on all occasions.

It was a rule which he adopted to always rise and go out to attend a little Friends meeting when the hour arrived. One day, while sitting in one of these meetings, the room above the Legislative Hall (which I believe was a courtroom) was crowded so that the floor gave way and came down upon the members of the Legislature, so that several were killed and many wounded. His seat and desk were crushed to pieces by a heavy beam which fell across them. He felt this escape was a cause of great thankfulness.

He also edited a little paper called *The Southern Friend*, during the war, to keep up an interest among the members and to encourage faithfulness among those who were shut off from association and communication with their Northern friends. It no doubt did good. I have a part of one of the copies published while Sherman was marching through Georgia. While it would be interesting to dwell upon the services of John B. Crenshaw and many other Friends who labored so faithfully during the war to uphold the cause of truth—and there were many of these silent heroes who let their light shine—yet I must hasten on.

On First-day we attended meeting in the city, held at the home of Jane Whitlock, and in the afternoon and evening visited the work among the freedmen, under the care of Sarah F. Smiley and her faithful assistants. Then we went on to North Carolina Yearly Meeting by way of Black Creek and Somerton. The former place was where the Virginia Half-Yearly Meeting was formerly located, but it is now held here and at Richmond alternately. From there we went on to Jamestown, North Carolina, which we reached Eleventh month 2, about midnight, and spent the remainder of the night at Dr. Coffin's.

The next morning, Eleventh month 3, 1866, we went to Deep River Meeting-house, where the Yearly Meeting of Ministers and Elders opened. It was a time of deep religious feeling. Much sympathy was felt and expressed with our dear Friends in their present situation, and they were encouraged to be faithful in the discharge of their duties. It was believed by those who spoke that there never was a time when the fields were more fully open for our beloved Society to labor in North Carolina. We went home that night with Jonathan Harris, and in the evening walked over to Daniel Barker's and had a religious opportunity with his interesting family.

"Eleventh month 4. This was First-day, and we went to the old New Garden Meeting-house, where the yearly meeting has been held for many years. The meetings were large, both in the morning and in the afternoon. The visitors boarded in the school building, and at night we had a chapter read in one of the schoolrooms and another good meeting was held, there being many young people present at these meetings."

"Eleventh month 5, 1866. The yearly meeting proper opened this morning with Nereus Mendenhall as clerk. The following Friends were in attendance from other yearly meetings: Eli and Sybil Jones, William Beard, Pharaba Toms, Miriam Huff, James E. Bailey, Seneca Hazard, John B. Elliot, Daniel D. Barton, Alson R. Walls, Peter Osborn, Thomas Jay, and myself," all of whom have passed to the Beyond except the author. The yearly meeting continued until Sixth-day afternoon.

"In reviewing this yearly meeting, I think it may be truly said that it was a time of real favor and that the business was conducted in unity and much love, some of the sessions being especially blessed. The one on the State of the Society was a time of searching of hearts; the one when the Meeting for Sufferings reported the sufferings of Friends during the war and their faithfulness brought feelings of praise to God for the evidence of His protecting care. Many instances of his loving care were brought to remembrance. Through it all, Friends who have been faithful have been kept and their lives have been spared. The evening meetings in the schoolroom were seasons of real spiritual awakening to many of the dear young people, several of whom have given their lives to God for His use, and I believe, if they are faithful, will be useful members of the Church."

These words, written at the close of the yearly meeting forty-two years ago, I have lived to see more than realized. The years of my connection with North Carolina Yearly Meeting have been among the best of my life, and my prayer that day has been answered far beyond my fondest hope. My heart was knit to that people at the closing session as to no people before. Little did I know how closely we were to labor together for nine years in building up the waste places and making North Carolina Yearly Meeting—then having about 2,200 members—a light in that Southland and a bright example among the sisterhood of yearly meetings with nearly 7,000 members, and that New Garden Boarding-School was to become Guilford College and take its place among the colleges of the South and stand in the foremost ranks of the Quaker colleges of our land.

As I pen these lines, I thank my Heavenly Father that he has permitted me to have a little part in helping to answer these prayers of forty-two years ago, uttered in old New Garden Meeting-house, and for the fact that my life is richer and fuller because I have worked and labored in harmony with those men and women who composed North Carolina Yearly Meeting that day, also for the brightness and happiness that have come into my Christian life, as I have known and mingled with their children who are now leading North Carolina Yearly Meeting into new and wider fields of usefulness. "What hath God wrought!"[70] It is marvelous in our eyes. Praise be unto His name.

The Peace Conference in Baltimore

At the close of the yearly meeting my uncle, Thomas Jay, went to Rich Square, in the limits of Eastern Quarter, to continue the work which we had begun, while I turned aside for a little time to attend a conference held in Baltimore on the subject of Peace. This conference was composed of delegates from the different yearly meetings and began Eleventh month 14, 1866, at the invitation of Baltimore Yearly Meeting. It resulted in the organization afterwards of the Peace Association of Friends of America, which has been kept up ever since and is now located in Richmond, Indiana.[71]

My memory is that the subject was first mentioned in Ohio Yearly Meeting by Jesse Green, one of its members, which resulted in that yearly meeting calling the attention of other yearly meetings to the matter. In their epistles to the American yearly meetings, Baltimore went so far as to propose that each yearly meeting appoint delegates to such a conference, to meet in that city on Fourth-day following North Carolina Yearly Meeting.

---

[70] Numbers 23:23

[71] The Peace Association of Friends of America was organized in 1867, and was incorporated in Richmond, Indiana, in 1894. It became one of the many boards of Five Years Meeting (now Friends United Meeting) in 1940, until all of the boards were combined during the restructuring of the 1980s. The Peace Association published numerous tracts on peace, and published *The Messenger of Peace* for many years.

Having been appointed by Western Yearly Meeting, I returned to Baltimore from New Garden, in company with Dr. William Nicholson, and attended the meeting in Baltimore and one at Deer Creek in Maryland, and in the old Friends meetinghouse. The following delegates were present: from New England, Samuel Boyce, John Page, William C. Tabor, Joseph Cartland; from New York, Jonathan DeVol, William H. Case, Benjamin Tatham, Robert Lindley Murray, Samuel Heaton, and Jesse P. Haines; from Baltimore, Francis T. King, James Carey, Dr. James C. Thomas, John Scott, John B. Crenshaw, Richard M. Janney, and Jesse Tyson; Ohio, John Butler, Jesse Green, William H. Ladd, Ezra Catell; from Indiana, Charles F. Coffin, Levi Jessup, Francis W. Thomas, Isaac P. Evans, Daniel Hill, and Murray Shipley; Western, Nathan Elliot, Dr. James Kersey, Barnabas C. Hobbs, Dr. Dougan Clark, and Allen Jay; North Carolina, Isham Cox, John Parker, Seth Barker, Allen U. Tomlinson, and Dr. William Nicholson; Iowa, Joseph D. Hoage, Jeremiah A. Grinnell, and James Owen. In addition to these, there were from Philadelphia, John M. Whitall, George W. Taylor, and Samuel Rhodes. All of these were present, except five, and all of the forty-three have passed away except Charles F. Coffin and myself.[72]

After a season of worship, during which vocal prayer was offered, the conference was organized by appointing Francis T. King clerk, and Dr. Dougan Clark, assistant. The first subject under consideration was our duty towards our own members, which occupied the first sitting. We then adjourned until 3:30 o'clock. At this session a committee was appointed to draft an address to our own membership for the purpose of stirring them up to more faithfulness in maintaining our well-known views on this important doctrine.[73]

---

[72] The list of delegates to this conference is a "Who's Who" of influential American Quaker leaders of the mid-nineteenth century. Many of them are mentioned elsewhere in Allen Jay's *Autobiography*.

[73] This first discussion, and the epistle which came out of it, suggests that Quakers were ruefully acknowledging the fact that many Friends had borne arms during the Civil War, and that Friends' discipline in the area of peace needed to be re-instilled before we could speak clearly to the rest of the world.

We met again at nine o'clock next morning, and after a long and full discussion, a large committee was appointed to draft an address to the professors of religion of all denominations. Another session was held at 3:30 that afternoon, at which a discussion took place on the question of how far we could seek the co-operation of other religious denominations. It was finally decided to ask them to labor in their own appropriate channels for the advancement of the cause.

At the meeting the next day the address to our membership was adopted, and the address to the other religious denominations was left in the hands of a judicious committee to be prepared and presented at a future meeting to be held some time the following year. The conference also recommended to the different yearly meetings to appoint standing committees on the subject of Peace, who should labor in subordinate meetings and among individuals, and hold meetings and give lectures among Friends and others.[74]

After some minor matters were attended to, the first peace conference adjourned, to meet at the call of a special committee the next year. Dr. Nicholson and I took the boat that night for Norfolk and were met at Suffolk the next morning and driven to Belvidere, which we reached the following evening, where I again met with my dear uncle.

---

[74] This pattern of plenary sessions, committees, position statements, and recommendations is so familiar to Friends today that it is easy to forget what an innovation it was at the time. True, there was a long Quaker tradition of gatherings of elders and ministers, as well as the yearly meetings themselves, but this was the first time Friends had been sent as delegates by their yearly meetings to a national conference on a particular subject. It was clearly made possible only by the development of railroad transportation, as well as by reliable postal and telegraph service for planning and coordination. Very significantly, this conference took place in 1866, twenty-one years before the Richmond conference of 1887 which focused more on doctrine and led eventually to the organization of Five Years Meeting/Friends United Meeting. The conference of 1866 came as a response to the Civil War, but it looked forward to the larger issue of peace in general. Allen Jay was a central participant in both of these events, which changed the landscape of Quakerism forever.

CHAPTER 16

Visiting Friends in North Carolina and Tennessee

Again we began the work of visiting meetings, families, and schools as we came to them. Our course was towards western North Carolina, and from there across the mountains into Tennessee, the work to be finished in that State. In taking this course we were following in the tracks of Johnston's and Sherman's armies, from Goldsboro to Greensboro, the former retreating, the latter pursuing him. We had a good opportunity to see the devastating effect of war.

It was in a Friends neighborhood that the last battle between Johnston and Sherman was fought, near Bentonsville, North Carolina. Our dear friend William Cox's house was situated in the midst of the conflict. The effect of the bullets upon the house was plainly to be seen. None of the family was hurt, as they quietly remained inside.

But it is not my purpose to dwell upon the subject of the war or the sufferings of Friends, for that has been told by others. Mine is to tell of what we found and what we tried to do. I could fill volumes in relating the stories told us as we went into the homes. Many nights after a hard day's work we would listen until a late hour to these facts which at that time were fresh in the minds of all, and the evidence of their truth was to be seen on every hand.

One dear Friend, near Goldsboro, told how Johnston's men first, and then Sherman's following, took their horses and cattle, cleared up their chickens, indeed did not leave anything alive on the farm, besides the members of the family, except a setting hen which was hidden under the barn. The soldiers would take the sheets and the linen bedclothes; would rip open one end of a bedtick, take hold of the other and run down stairs into the yard, scattering the feathers everywhere in a spirit of wanton destruction. Everything that could be eaten was destroyed or carried away.

Several years after this, sitting by the bedside of a dying soldier in Indiana, he brought up this circumstance and what happened in this home, and the part that he took in it. He spoke of the Christian spirit manifested by those dear Friends, of the father, the mother, the three children, and then added, "Oh, I wish I could see them and ask their forgiveness for the part I took in destroying their home!" When I told him I knew them well and had often partaken of their hospitality, that they were prospering, and that the children had grown up lovely Christians, he begged that I would bear his dying request that they would forgive him, and his prayer that they might meet in Heaven.

All of this I have carefully done. But, as I have said, I leave these unpleasant things and pass on to our mission. It was ours to go from house to house and bear the message of love and encouragement to those noble men and women who had silently and faithfully borne their testimony to the cause of peace. One thing impressed me day after day, in going from one home to another and from one meeting to another—that I was in the midst of a people who, without noise or any great flourish of trumpets, had fought and won a silent yet glorious victory, for "they endured as seeing Him who is

> I was in the midst of a people who, without noise or any great flourish of trumpets, had fought and won a silent yet glorious victory . . .

invisible,"[75] and as we listened to the pitiful stories of their trials, privations, and persecutions, we felt that we were among a people who believed in God, a people who had walked through the fiery furnace unconscious that, "One like unto the Son of Man was with them." They had come out "without the smell of fire upon their garments."[76]

We listened to the mothers and sisters telling of plowing and carrying on the work of the farm, while the husbands, fathers, and sons were hidden in the woods and caves that they might keep out of the army, or had passed through the lines to the North in order that they might not be forced to fight. I remember young men telling how hard it was for them, from their hiding-places on the mountains, to see their mothers toiling in the fields for their support. In one instance, one of these young men went home, dressed in his mother's clothes, and took her place in the field for three days while she rested. Women would suffer severe punishment rather than tell where their loved ones were hiding.

Day after day we would listen to these simple narratives, often told because we drew them out by questions, not because they thought they had done any great thing. They appeared little to realize that they had been making history that would place them in the list of God's heroes; that they were sowing the seed that would build up his kingdom on earth again.

While others had closed their places of worship in the country, they had kept up their meetings for worship on First-day and in the middle of the week—meetings held often in silence, yet always a bright example of their devotion to their profession and duty to God. They had heard the voice of God and were faithful to His will; men and women who knew more of God than some whom I have since met who make a much louder profession, talk more about doctrine, and dwell much upon orthodoxy and religious belief. Here were those who

---

[75] Hebrews 11:27
[76] Daniel 3:25, 27

heard His voice and followed as He led the way, and were "kept in perfect peace" because their minds were "stayed upon Him."[77]

So we continued our work, making use of the time. When we reached the Springfield Meeting, located near what was called Bush Hill, now Archdale, North Carolina, we found Joseph Moore, who was at that time superintendent of the Baltimore Association work. This was an organization formed in Baltimore at the close of the war called "The Baltimore Association of Friends, to Advise and Assist Friends in the Southern States." Richard M. Janney, John Scott, and Sarah F. Smiley were sent down at first by this association to help relieve the immediate need, but the work was afterwards put in under the entire control of Joseph Moore. We were glad to meet him and strengthen his hands in the good work, but it is my purpose to speak more of this in a short time, when, in the providence of God, I came to take the place he then occupied.

We passed on westward, visiting the meetings up among the mountains in western North Carolina, then crossed over into eastern Tennessee, going to New Hope Meeting first, then down to Lost Creek, across the Holston River to Maryville and so on to Friendsville, where William Forster, of England, who was buried in the graveyard here in 1854, laid down his life while engaged as a member of a delegation appointed by London Yearly Meeting to present a communication on the subject of slavery, addressed by that yearly meeting to the President of the United States and to the Governor of each State.

After reaching Friendsville I learned of a settlement some four or five miles distant where there had once been a Friends meeting, but which had gone down. The last meeting held in the old meeting-house, the roof of which had fallen in, had been held by William Forster some thirteen years before. There were some ten or twelve members scattered among the hills, often only one in a family. So, First month 15, 1867, on horseback, with a Friend on another horse for a guide,

---

[77] Isaiah 26:3

we started soon after daylight, rode over twenty miles during the day, and visited ten homes.

Soon after beginning, the word got circulated in the woods that a preacher was holding meetings in the homes where there was a Friend. After that we had a company in each house when we reached there. While eating dinner at John B. Jones's, I felt it right to appoint a meeting that night for the people in that community. He freely offered his house, a two-roomed one, with a door between. His wife, though a Presbyterian, very cordially joined with him in granting the home.

When we reached there at meeting time, both rooms were full, people standing and sitting on the floor. I took my position in the door between the two rooms and for an hour or more was engaged in exposition and prayer. Soon after this a new meeting-house was built and a meeting established, and in a short time a monthly meeting was opened, called Hickory Valley. I believe that day's work was owned and blessed by the Lord.

After the meeting, I rode two miles to Joseph Bales's, a Friend who had long been confined to the house, and did what I could to encourage him and his family before leaving them. The next day I visited families and reached Francis Hackney's in the evening, where I found my uncle and our dear Friends, Joseph Moore and Isham Cox. We all went to meeting First-day and had a large and favored meeting.

I visited families that afternoon, and on First month 17, awoke very early and felt clearly the command to return home, which was a joyful message. When Uncle awoke, in a few minutes he said, "Allen, I am ready to go home." We started that day, and I was favored to reach my home on the afternoon of the nineteenth, when the wisdom of returning was made plain. I found our little boy, fifteen months old, very sick. We were united in returning thanks to our Heavenly Father for His watchful care over us and our loved ones during our separation of one hundred and seven days. Thus ended my first visit to North Carolina Yearly Meeting, which was soon to become the field of several years' work.

CHAPTER 17

The Call to the Work of the Baltimore Association

I now settled down to farm life, which was mingled with a few visits of a religious character of more or less importance. The next winter I obtained a minute to visit families of those within the limits of our meeting and surrounding neighborhood who were not Friends, and held some meetings among them. Early in 1868, in company with my dear wife, I visited the meetings of Indiana Yearly Meeting, located within the States of Ohio and Indiana.

Returning from this service, the summer was occupied in raising a crop. One day, after harvest, while finishing "laying by" some late corn, my wife came to the field, saying, "Here is a letter from Baltimore." I asked her to read it while I sat on the plow to rest. It was from Francis T. King and began by saying, "We have just had a meeting of the Baltimore Association of Friends to Assist and Advise Friends of the Southern States, and at the earnest request of many Friends in North Carolina, we are united in appointing thee our superintendent, to take the place of Joseph Moore, who has resigned in order to return to his place as president of Earlham College." He then went on to tell how much they would pay and what they would provide for myself and family if we would come for one year, and closed by saying, "We want an answer by return mail."

The proposition was entirely unexpected. We sat in silence a few minutes. I then rose and, turning my horses round, proceeded to finish my plowing, then went to the barn and occupied the rest of the day in putting away my farming utensils where they belonged. That evening we did not mention the subject, neither the next day. It being First-day, we went to school and meeting, spent the afternoon with my wife's parents, and upon returning home that evening the same silence was maintained on that subject, each waiting for the other to work it out.

On Second-day morning, after breakfast, I remarked, "I must now answer F. T. King's letter. What shall I say?" My wife simply replied, "I expect we will go," and went out to wash the dishes. I went to the desk and wrote an answer, saying we would accept if they should furnish a cow in addition to what they had already promised. In a few days I had an answer saying, "We accept thy proposition. Thou art our man. Go to Iowa Yearly Meeting and secure all the funds thou canst for the work. I have written to the Friends there to give thee an opportunity during the yearly meeting."

In two days I reached there, a stranger and very much depressed with the thought of making a public appeal, which was not made lighter by the fact that I could see that they did not want the appeal to be made. The yearly meeting was new, it being the third one that they had held. The country was new and they had not yet paid for their house. They told me plainly that they felt they had their hands full, but as Francis T. King had helped them financially in their educational work, perhaps it would be best to grant me a little time.

> It doesn't take much thought to talk an hour, but to say something in fifteen minutes requires much preparation.

So one evening I was informed that I might have fifteen minutes the next morning. I was frightened and laid awake most of the night to prepare a fifteen-minute talk. It doesn't take much thought to talk an hour, but to say something in fifteen minutes requires much preparation. The hour came. The house was full. There sat before me men who had fathers and mothers, brothers and sisters and dear relatives in the Old North State and in Tennessee, who had gone through the horrors of war, whom they did not hear from for four long years, and I had been in their homes and heard of their sufferings. I was full of these tales of sorrow.

Joel Bean, who was clerk, like a Christian gentleman as he has always been,[78] politely introduced the subject and said that they were very busy, but thought best to give me fifteen minutes. I rose trembling all over and so frightened that I did not remember anything that I had made up to say, but plunged into the subject and did not stop for nearly an hour. When I sat down there was weeping all over the house. James Owen rose at once and proposed that I should go upstairs and lay the matter before the women's meeting. A messenger came back soon, saying that they would give me a few minutes; so with an escort I went up, was introduced by the clerk, Hannah Bean, with the reminder that time was precious. When the few minutes were out many were wiping their eyes; so I spoke forty-five minutes, and then they entered into a collection, and when I went downstairs I had four-hundred dollars in my hat. They reported that they had raised one-thousand dollars among the men while I was upstairs. I slept well that night. That was the beginning of my public solicitations in raising money, but it has not been my last.

At the close of the yearly meeting I returned home and in three weeks we were on our way, moving to North Carolina. We had left our farm and everything on it under the care of a man and his wife, expecting to return in one year, but we have never done so. God has led, I believe, in another way. After we had been in the South two years my parents came down to see us and to attend the yearly meeting. My father went with me for a few weeks, seeing the work. He then said, "We would be glad to have you back in Indiana, but thee is engaged in a work here that thee must not leave. Better let me go home and make a sale and close up thy affairs in Indiana." Next morning we had

---

[78] Joel and Hannah Bean were deposed as ministers by Iowa Yearly Meeting in 1893 for alleged "unsoundness," an action which shocked many Friends like Allen Jay who knew them well. Their membership was "accidentally" dropped in 1898 and was restored in 1899.

an offer for the farm which was better than we expected. We made the deed and father wound up the affairs at the old home.

When we reached North Carolina, the house we were going to move into was being repaired. It was located on a lot adjoining old Springfield Meeting-house. There was a good sized school-house on the meeting-house grounds, and we had taken a teacher with us from Indiana, Deborah Steere, who was a graduate of Earlham College and one of the best teachers I ever knew. She remained with us for three years, living in our home, and then, after a year's rest, I arranged for her to take charge of the school at Friendsville, Tennessee, which was a school of some note. It had been assisted by English Friends in building and getting started. Deborah Steere is now the wife of Samuel Howell, located at Selma, Ohio. She was assisted at Friendsville by William Clark, the present editor of *St. Nicholas,* in New York.[79]

We went to the home of Allen U. Tomlinson, where we remained until our house was ready. This man deserves more than a passing notice. He sat at the head of Springfield Meeting, lived at Bush Hill, now called Archdale, had a tanyard, a shoe shop, a harness shop, and a store. He was an enterprising man in business, educational work, and church work. Two of his sons have graduated at Haverford College and were teachers of ability, being employed by our association. Another was a practicing physician. Allen U. Tomlinson had been superintendent of the First-day school for forty years. In connection with Nathan Hunt, Mahlon Hockett, and other worthy Friends, he had made Springfield Meeting one of the leading meetings in the yearly meeting. He was interested in the success of New Garden Boarding-School[80] and educational work generally, and was a member of the

---

[79] *St. Nicholas: The Magazine for Young Folks* was published from 1873-1941. It was a major magazine in its day, with a large national circulation and many famous contributors, including Charles Dana Gibson, James Whitcomb Riley, Laura Ingalls Wilder, Mark Twain, Jack London, Ernest Thompson Seton, and illustrators such as Arthur Rackham and Norman Rockwell.

[80] Later Guilford College

committee appointed by North Carolina Yearly Meeting to counsel and advise the Baltimore Association in their work.

Just before the surrender of Johnston at Greensboro, one corps of his army was located at Bush Hill. The leading generals had their headquarters in his home. At night they placed a guard around the house and bolted all the doors. He objected to the guard and unbolted the doors. It appeared later that the wives of the generals were afraid of their own soldiers, as they were poorly fed and had received but little pay and felt that their cause was lost. But the Friends were preserved and went on with their duties. They held their quarterly meeting as usual, while the army lay around the meeting-house not knowing how soon they might hear the roar of the cannon opening another bloody battle.

But the next day they learned that Johnston and Sherman had tried to negotiate the terms of a surrender, which was soon accomplished, and the poor, weary Confederate soldiers received their small pay, laid down their arms, and returned to their sad and, in many cases, destitute homes. It was a happy day for our Friends in the South.

Now, having told of our call and location in the South, I purpose to give some account of the organization of "The Baltimore Association of Friends to Assist and Advise the Friends in the Southern States." But before doing so, I wish to introduce a chapter written by my dear friend, Mary Mendenhall Hobbs, at my request, as an introduction, showing the need for such work and the wisdom required in carrying it forward. This chapter has been written by one who went through these dark days, a daughter of Dr. Nereus Mendenhall, a leading Friend in North Carolina Yearly Meeting, one who remained in the yearly meeting from a sense of duty and whose labor was abundantly blessed to individuals and to the Church. She has told the story as few could. Many will be glad to read it.

CHAPTER 18

Conditions in Carolina at the Close of the Civil War

by Mary Mendenhall Hobbs

As a background for the work of the Baltimore Association, Allen Jay has asked me to give Friends a glimpse of the condition which existed here at the close of the Civil War.

I was a little girl in those days, and much which would now be of deep interest was either unknown to me or but dimly comprehended. So far as I know there are no records of these things, aside from the allusions in histories and books of fiction. Our minutes are very chary [cautious] in their references to actual conditions, and being unconscious of the fact that they were making history in their daily lives, the Friends moved on in the even tenor of their way, doing the things nearest them, facing circumstances as best they could, with no thought of preserving records of events.

I well remember the anxiety and distress which was everywhere in our part of the land, and how we had become so accustomed to lives of privation and care that it seemed impossible to imagine ourselves released from apprehension and dread. Our community perhaps suffered less than many others, owing to the fact that we were not in the line of march of either army, and being, in the main, a settlement of Friends, not many of the men in our neighborhood served in the ranks. Many had fled from home and had either escaped through the lines to prevent being conscripted and forced into the Southern army or had "bushwhacked" through the period, which meant that they dwelt in caves and hollow trees and slept in barns and outhouses or crept secretly into their own or the houses of kindly disposed neighbors, never daring to be seen about their premises or attending to any business. Even if the conscript hunters, who were always roaming about, did not see them, some unfriendly person might report them and they be trapped.

At the close of the war such as had been able to survive returned to find everything impoverished—houses gone; cattle, if any, poor; the merest pretense at farming going on; tools worn out and antiquated; harness mostly ropes; vehicles in the last stages of "the one-horse shay."[81] The buildings were dilapidated, roofs leaking, windows pasted up with paper or cloth, hinges broken, fences gone—burned up in many cases for wood, in many instances houses and property destroyed by fire. Eastern Carolina suffered more than we, because the Southern army destroyed as it went, and the Northern army, even after the country had surrendered, in pure wantonness burned buildings for spite.

Those left at home had battled along as best they could. Many women were left with families of small children and almost no resources for their support. Such had been assisted by their neighbors and relatives as far as possible. We learned to do with little and to live on corn bread, which was more easily provided than wheat. We could no more get coffee, sugar, or tea than we could get papers from "beyond the lines," and those who had these articles on hand saved them for sick people. We drank hot water tea sweetened with sorghum, and made coffee of parched wheat and dried sweet potatoes, which was a great deal better than many modern substitutes for coffee. We

---

[81] *The Deacon's Masterpiece: Or, the Wonderful One-Hoss Shay*, poem by Oliver Wendell Holmes, first published in 1858.

were almost all upon the same level and were in what we should now consider *very straitened circumstances*, but, so far as I remember, were always ready to give each other such aid as was in our power.

Little boys with the assistance of their mothers and sisters had been obliged to do what farm work was done. There were no stores, and nothing to buy goods with if there had been. We were all clothed in homespun cloth, which had the redeeming quality of lasting a long time. Our shoes were of the coarsest leather, made from the skins of animals butchered on the farms and the hides carried to some near or far tanyard and there tanned for a toll of one-half. The shoes, which were not "Queen Quality,"[82] were made by a neighborhood cobbler, and we were as delighted with a new pair of these as children nowadays are with the finest. Stockings were made from yarn spun and knit at home, from the wool of the few sheep which almost every family kept.

I remember that lights were quite an item, and sometimes we could not get tallow to make candles, which we did in "moulds" which were borrowed by the whole community. As father was a great reader, he always made a special effort to procure tallow and wax for his candles, but sometimes he failed and we had to resort to a queer little grease lamp with a wick which hung out of a little spout. This was beyond his ability to manage, and he gave up his books for the time being. Generally, people sat by the firelight. I recall that the first purchase father made "after the surrender" was a good lamp, and with what delight and enthusiasm we children welcomed it into our home. Previous to the war we used what was called a "fluid lamp," but during the war we could not secure the "fluid," whatever it may have been.[83]

Our roads are none of the best now, but at the close of the war they were well-nigh impassable. We have many streams and the bridges had almost all gone to wreck or been washed away by "the big freshet" which preceded the close of the war. In this Piedmont section the

---

[82] Queen Quality Shoes were a famous brand of women's shoes in the early 1900s, made in Boston, Massachusetts.

[83] Probably camphene, a mixture of turpentine and alcohol. Camphene lamps often had two wicks to increase the light output. News accounts of the time were filled with reports of injuries and fires started by lamp explosions.

streams rise suddenly, owing to heavy rains near the sources, and since all had to be forded this often caused great inconvenience. I recall the fact that at the time of the surrender a near relative of my mother was dying at the home of Aunt Delphina E. Mendenhall and she could not get to the place, although it was not very far away.

The household furnishings were in as dilapidated a condition as the farm tools. There had been a constant wear and tear, with no opportunity to replace or repair. "It will do" had come to be the verdict, and anything which would do was made to do, had to be; and this attitude was a mental factor which had to be dealt with. During the war if any of our cooking utensils or table-ware were broken, we had to do without these necessaries. Blacksmiths did make knives and forks sometimes, and for plates, if worse came to worst, we could use tin pans or earthen dishes; for there were some rude potteries which made many useful articles, amongst others a little stew kettle which we could set on the coals on the hearth and cook our apples or dried fruit. The women dried all the fruit they could, and dried cherries cooked in sorghum tasted as good then as Heinz's dainties do now. Sorghum was raised generally and made into molasses. Chickens, turkeys, and guineas were raised, and gardens were planted and worked by the women and children, who were obliged also to make, as well as weave, the clothes for the family.

It may be remarked that since the war only lasted four years it would seem possible that people might have had on hand materials to satisfy their needs for so short a period. No Joseph had arisen to warn of the coming danger;[84] and while there had been an apprehension of the evil days, no one knew exactly when or how they would come. The Friends were a simple, rural people, depending largely upon their own labor on the farms for their sustenance. Such money as had been saved was lost, and stored provisions were more likely to feed the

> The Friends were a simple, rural people, depending largely upon their own labor on the farms for their sustenance.

---

[84] Genesis 41

army than those for whom it was provided, as there were foragers all the time seeking for food and provender who unhesitatingly carried off what they could find.

Our "Sunday clothes" were made and remade out of the old dresses of our mothers and aunts, but their old shoes were not so pliable; so we would appear in a pretty old faded muslin dress and shoes as coarse as brogans. Some young ladies in the community acquired great skill in plaiting straw, which they made into neat little hats, and old bonnets and hats were made over and worn and worn. I know we looked like composites of all styles and ages to those dear Friends who came first after the close of the war, but they looked marvelous to us, too. I never shall forget how their finery impressed me far more than their messages. I could not remember how people dressed before the war and no silk dresses were on parade anywhere during that period. There must have been many packed away, but they did not come forth; and to suddenly behold people, actually folks, sailing around in silks and satins and wonderful soft shawls and *kid gloves* and silk hats and all was as much of a spectacle to my eyes as I could have been to them. When you have no opportunity to buy anything, your wits become active and you invent fashions adapted to the quantity of material.

The only new thing which I remember as being bought for me was a new toothbrush—father bought us each one and paid four dollars apiece for them in "Confederate paper," as he called it; he never would call it money. As soon as the war was over the Yankees flocked in and put up stores, but we had nothing but "paper" to buy with. Debts had been paid either in Confederate money or State bank notes, and both were alike useless.

Some schools had been kept up a part of the time in different places and New Garden Boarding-School had never been closed. I have seen it stated that the trustees kept this school from closing. They were trying to close it, as I understand, but decided to allow Jonathan E. Cox to run it upon his own responsibility. For a time he did this and employed the teachers himself; and if I mistake not, it was under this arrangement that my father came for the third time to the school. John R. Hubbard had resigned and gone West and father was sent for to take charge.

There were so many changes constantly going on, and there is such an imperfect record to draw upon, that it is difficult for one who but faintly comprehended matters to say why things happened as they did; but after teaching in the boarding-school for a while some new arrangement left father at liberty, and he went over to Jamestown, and there, at Flint Hill Academy, conducted a fine school, to which several pupils from a distance came. The family remained at New Garden, living in the farm house whither they had been removed from the charming little home in Florence, North Carolina, situated within the limits of Deep River Meeting, to which the Mendenhalls had belonged for more than a century.

Another change, I cannot say what, returned father to the boarding school. This time, if I remember correctly, he and Jonathan E. Cox took the school jointly. Father was to teach for the tuition of the boys and such girls as studied any of the languages, and Jonathan E. Cox was to operate the boarding department.

About this time, or perhaps previous to it, father's brother-in-law, Dr. Nathan B. Hill, determined to move to the West, and he persuaded father that it would be best for us to go also. The school was very full and there were several young men here rather in hiding to keep out of the army. If father left, the school would have to be closed, and he was in a very great strait as to what was his duty. Every instinct for the safety of his family urged him to go, but the responsibility for the meeting and the school called him to stay. Our trunks and boxes had already been sent to the station and we were ready to follow, when, with tears streaming down his face, he told mother he could not feel clear to go, and she told him to send for the things and remain.

Our property had been sold and was gone, but mother gathered articles as she could and soon had a comfortable abiding place arranged; and father went to the old school-room and remained through all the distress and perplexity of the time, true to his convictions.

The boys' school was full, and as they nearly all paid their bills in provisions, we had stores of flour and meat and corn and molasses—more than we had places to keep or knew where to hide; for it had to be hidden. I remember that one boy paid his tuition in gold dust which he had washed out of the sand in a creek near his home, but that was all the gold I saw during the war.

The task of keeping the school was difficult and unremunerative from a money standpoint, as the charge for tuition was small, and in a way it was unappreciated self-sacrifice; but he did the thing he determined to do and without doubt was instrumental in saving the school.

This is somewhat of a retrogression, but it explains a situation which is not always understood.

Our meetings had been kept up better than one would think possible. All of the yearly meetings had been held. John B. Crenshaw, of Richmond, Virginia, had visited us and gave us great encouragement and cheer. He, too, edited a paper called *The Southern Friend,* which was very refreshing in those troublous times when nothing in the shape of the magazines and papers to which we had been accustomed could be obtained. I heard some Friends from the West call it "a rebel sheet" and rejoice that it had been discontinued. But it was not a rebel sheet. It was a good, clean, wholesome little paper, started and kept going to help to hold the breath of life in us while we were being battered about. Joseph Neave threaded his way through the lines and was one of the most welcome visitors who ever crossed a Quaker threshold.

There is much of interest, to one who can fill in between the lines, contained in the yearly meeting minutes of those four years, but the reading between the lines is necessary, because they did not record historical fact so much as spiritual needs and conditions. In 1860, just previous to the outbreak of war, occurs this bit of warning in the Minute of Advice, which shows that Friends were feeling the effect of the general exodus: "It is to be feared that some have their minds so much set on moving away from this part of the land that they are neglecting their proper duties. Whatever may be right for us in this respect may we not forget that there is an emigration for us all, and endeavor so to walk that when the period for it arrives it may indeed be to a better country—that is, to a heavenly; and though a voice be heard in Ramah, lamentation and bitter weeping, Rachel weeping for her children,[85] the encouraging language still remains: 'Be thou faithful unto death and I will give thee a crown of life.'[86] Let us wait upon the Lord and we shall experience that renewal of strength which is so much needed, not for ourselves only, but that we may be instrumental in encouraging others both by example and precept and so far as may be building up the waste places. And even if we do not succeed there is no condemnation to the faithful, the language to him being, 'Let alone, he hath done what he could.'"[87]

When I remember how they stood their ground and braved everything and never once thought of themselves as heroes, I cannot restrain the tears; and, when I recall how they divided their stores and fed the hungry and clothed the naked and took the wayfarer in out of the cold and gave of what they had, I know that they were of the faithful to whom God has said, "Well done."[88]

At two homes within a mile of Guilford College, poor, distressed Yankee soldiers who had escaped from prison were tenderly cared for, and the physician secretly conveyed to them, from whom they received every care; but nothing could save them, and they rest in our burying ground where British soldiers of the Revolution sleep, together with hundreds of our own people who were enlisted under the banner of the Prince of Peace.

The meetings and family worship, which we were more faithful to keep up then than we are now in more prosperous times, kept us together; and, although at the close of the war our property was gone and we ourselves in rather a forlorn condition, we did not entirely give up to discouragement, but went to work to gather up the pieces that remained. Our work of recuperation would have been slow, and

---

[85] Matthew 2:18, quoting Jeremiah 31:15
[86] Revelation 2:10
[87] Mark 14:8
[88] Matthew 25:23

most likely we should have been beaten in the fight, had it not been for Francis T. King and the Baltimore Association.

The tide of emigration which had been started before the war now rose to an appalling magnitude. The following quotation from the first annual report of the Baltimore Association will give an idea of what was going on: "During the spring and summer of 1865, directly after Sherman's march, two of our number twice visited North Carolina to distribute provisions, clothing and money, and during that year we forwarded to the West about 400 members, adults and children, fifty of whom arrived here destitute at one time. Though we discouraged this emigration, we could not wonder at it, as they fled to escape the ravages of war to join relatives who had prospered in the West, and who gave them cordial welcomes." Our people left by car loads, and we were in danger of being depopulated so far as Quakerism was concerned.

Francis T. King came here and investigated the whole situation and decided in his own mind that it was better for the people to remain here upon farms which they still owned and begin anew to build for themselves rather than seek homes in the West, to obtain which they would necessarily have to encumber themselves with debt. He was a seer in the broad sense of the term. I distinctly remember hearing him in our own home arguing this point with Addison Coffin, who was at that time running emigrant trains to the West. Francis wanted the people to stay here and Addison believed they would be better off on the more fertile land of the West. To stay this tide of emigration, the Baltimore Association was formed, and to its beneficent work the yearly meeting is indebted to-day for its existence.

It is difficult to ascertain how many Friends there were in North Carolina at the opening of the war. In one of their memorials they say, "The entire number in the whole South does not exceed 5,000." Whether this included Baltimore I cannot say, but I presume it did. There were not many in Virginia. They seem to have kept no statistical records except as connected with the use of intoxicants. A yearly report of this matter is made under the heads of "Clear Members,"

"Who Use It," "Not Inquired Of." These we infer to have been adult members. In 1860 there were 1,361 clear. Use it, 81. Not inquired of, 71. Total, 1,513. In 1864, clear, 1,573. Use it, 18. Not inquired of, 81. Total, 1,672. In 1865, clear, 1,659. Use it, 60. Not inquired of, 77. Total, 1,796.

Hence it would appear that in spite of the fact that we know hundreds left the State during the war, we had more members than at the beginning. In 1866 we began counting children, and our spirituous liquor report is as follows: Clear, 1,957. Use it, 53. Not inquired of, 75. Children between 5 and 18, 840; and next year the number of children is given as 998.

While this is not, as we know, an accurate account, it is the best I have been able so far to find and will serve as a kind of working basis for what the Baltimore Association began with.

These were situated in seven quarters—

> *Eastern*, in the extreme east, on the Atlantic coast.
>
> *Contentnea*, embracing meetings situated in Wayne County, in the middle of the State, below the fall line.
>
> *Western*, in central Carolina, toward the South.
>
> *Southern*, still further to the west and south.
>
> *New Garden* and *Deep River*, in the Piedmont section of the State, embracing the northern counties, and the latter extending into the Blue Ridge.
>
> *Lost Creek*, in Tennessee, since transferred to Wilmington Yearly Meeting.

Thus it will be seen that Friends dwelt in almost every part of the State. They had always been influential citizens of the commonwealth. Archdale, the Quaker Governor,[89] had favorably introduced them, and

---

[89] John Archdale (1642-1717) served as governor of the colonies of North and South Carolina from 1683-86 and from 1695-96. He was a Quaker, and had been elected a member of Parliament in 1698 but did not serve because he could not take the oath. He was the first to introduce the cultivation of rice to the Carolinas.

while during slavery times they had excluded themselves from office, they were well known and held in high regard by men prominent in public life. One of the most stirring speeches ever delivered by Governor Graham[90] was on the subject, "Test Oaths and Sedition," and was spoken in the State convention at Raleigh, December 7, 1861. As an evidence of the position held by Friends, I quote a part of this speech:

> Now, sir, the requirement of this affirmation to be taken by the denomination called Quakers is as effectual an act of banishment of that sect as if it had been plainly denounced in the ordinance. And the same may be said, I presume, in relation to Mennonists and Dunkers, though I have less knowledge of them. There were some of the last named class in the County of Lincoln during my boyhood; whether they remain and keep up their peculiar tenets, I am not informed.
>
> But the Quakers are a well-known sect, numbering not less than 10,000 persons in the State—and it is equally well known that they will not engage in war, and are conscientiously scrupulous against bearing arms. Our laws, from the Revolution downward to this day, have respected their scruples, and extended to them the charity and toleration due to the sincerity and humility of their profession.
>
> This ordinance wholly disregards their peculiar belief, and converts every man of them into a warrior or an exile. True, they are allowed to affirm, but the affirmation is equivalent to the oath of the feudal vassal to his lord, to "defend him with life and limb

---

[90] William Alexander Graham (1804-1875), was U.S. Senator from 1840-53, governor of North Carolina from 1845-49, Secretary of the Navy from 1850-52, and ran for Vice President in 1852 on the Whig ticket. He was a senator in the Confederate Congress during the Civil War, and after the war was a trustee of the Peabody Fund, which helped educational institutions in the South.

and terrene honor." It is, that they "will, to the utmost of their power, support, maintain, and defend the independent government of the Confederate States of America against the United States or any other power that by open force or otherwise may attempt to subvert the same," etc.

If this does not include military defense, it is difficult to find language that would. It is so well known that the ordinary oath to the State implied defense with arms that the Quakers have ever refused to affirm its terms, but have had a special affirmation provided for them, as may be seen in the present Revised Code, and in all former editions of our laws.

This ordinance, therefore, is nothing less than a decree of banishment to them. Sir, this humble denomination, who in the meekness and charity which so distinguished their Divine Master, yield precedence to none, were the first white men who made permanent settlements within our borders. Scourged and buffeted by Puritanism in New England, and Prelacy in Virginia, they found no rest or religious freedom until they had put the great Dismal Swamp between themselves and the nearest of their persecutors. In the dark forests of its southern border, they obtained a toleration from the savage red men which had been denied them by their Anglo-American brethren.

There they opened the wilderness, reared their modest dwellings, and filled the land with the monuments of civilization. There, and upon the upper waters of the Cape Fear, which they subsequently colonized, their posterity has remained to this day—a quiet, moral, industrious, thrifty people, differing from us in opinion on the subject of slavery, but attempting no subversion of the institution—producing abundantly by their labor, paying punctually and certainly their dues to the government and supporting their own poor. Sir, upon the expulsion from among us of such people the civilized world would cry "shame!"

Up to the time of the war the Friends had generally carried on schools in their communities, and their children had been educated at the boarding-school. During the war most of these schools perished, and at its close there were many just entering young manhood and womanhood who had had little opportunity to secure any education. Previous to the Civil War there had been an educational committee, composed of two men and two women Friends from each of the nineteen monthly meetings. This committee was appointed in 1848, and in the Summary Report for 1851 there were 804 children between five and sixteen years of age, and 334 between sixteen and twenty-one. Of these, 1,104 were reported as receiving some education.

As times grew more strenuous and doubt and discouragement were abroad in the land, this committee relaxed its efforts and was finally discontinued, and nothing of the kind was attempted during the war. In 1865 another education committee was appointed to act in conjunction with the Baltimore Association, which reported regularly thereafter. This committee was Joseph R. Parker, Isham Cox, Thomas J. Benbow, Thomas Pearson, Allen U. Tomlinson, and Nathan F. Spencer.

First-day schools had not been general, although there had been a few scattered through the yearly meeting. In 1864 this minute is recorded: "The importance of the establishment of First-day schools within our limits claiming our attention, it is advised that subordinate meetings adopt measures for that purpose," and thereafter there was a yearly report of this work.

The peculiar views and testimonies of Friends were much dwelt upon by our ministers and overseers during the war, and we were exhorted to be faithful in all these peculiarities. The following from a Minute of Advice will illustrate the general attitude: "We verily believe that the great distress in which our country is now plunged is in a large degree traceable to the hireling ministers of the present day. We fear that some of them, feeling that their places and living may depend upon the doctrines which were preached, have failed to enforce the truths of the Gospel in its fullness; while others from the same cause have advocated doctrines directly at variance with the teachings of Christ. Let us then be careful, while treating all men with kindness and love, that we do not lower this important principle—that a pure Gospel ministry must be free."[91]

We had been a little band of believers in peace in the midst of war, of antislavery abolitionists in the heart of slave territory, of hearts almost to a unit loyal to the Union in the midst of secession. The way had not been strewn with flowers. Espionage and a degree of persecution had drawn us closer together and intensified both our principles and our prejudices. We had had almost no intercourse with the outside world. Almost everything was gone except the bare hills, the abundant forests, and ourselves. I flatter myself that even thus we had a goodly heritage, and under the kindly nurture of some of the noblest men who ever blessed God's earth, we were enabled to rise from the dust and discouragement of the past and set our faces toward the rising sun.

The association first sent us Joseph Moore, whose presence was that of light-bringer. Then Allen Jay, who somehow anointed us with the oil of gladness and kept us from faltering. But these matters are not for me, but will be told by one who knows both sides of the situation.

---

[91] In this minute, North Carolina Friends are not criticizing pastoral ministry in their own meetings, since it did not exist at this time; they are warning about what they saw happening in other denominations, where pastors felt compelled to support slavery and war because speaking out against them would lead to their being fired.

CHAPTER 19

Work and Leaders of the Baltimore Association

The Field Opened for the Baltimore Association

The foregoing account by Mary Mendenhall Hobbs, telling in her own pleasant way the privations and trials of Friends in the South during the war and the condition they were left in at its close, is a fit introduction to the organization in the city of Baltimore having for its name and object, "The Baltimore Association of Friends to Assist and Advise with the Friends in the Southern States." The need of this can never be fully known except by those who passed through it. We of the North will never be able to appreciate the condition that our dear Friends of the South were in at the close of the war. We will give here a clipping from the *Baltimore American*, dated Eighth month 6, 1883, in which a short *résumé* of the work is made:

> One First-day morning, towards the close of the war, two men appeared in front of the Friends meeting-house, on Courtland Street, and quietly waited until the services were over. As the members were coming out of the building, the two strangers informed several of the congregation that there were some North Carolina Friends at one of the city wharves in destitute circumstances.

A committee at once repaired to the locality and found there fifty persons, of all ages and conditions, whose homes had been ruined by the passage of Johnston's and Sherman's armies through the section in which they lived. They had obtained permission to go to their friends in the Northwest. Their suffering excited a warm sympathy, and steps were at once taken for their comfort. But the charity did not stop there. Permission was obtained from President Lincoln to send a vessel load of provisions and agricultural implements to the other Friends in North Carolina, and 450 more soon passed through the city, and they, too, received assistance.

The temporary aid thus extended became an established permanency, and the Baltimore Association of Friends in the South was formed. This society, in a quiet way, has been accomplishing a great deal of good in North Carolina. It has expended over $122,500 since the close of the war in educational and agricultural work. The magnitude and efficiency of the results have recently been brought to light through extended notices in the North Carolina papers and the dedication of large school buildings and meeting-houses.

In 1750, New Garden, in the western part of the State, was settled by a colony of Friends. This settlement formed a nucleus of a still larger settlement and the Friends increased both in numbers and influence. Over half a century ago a school was established. It has continued prosperously ever since.

The Baltimore Association has organized a system of schools in thirteen counties of the State; took great interest in the institution at New Garden, and has just expended $22,000 in the enlargement of the buildings and the extension and addition of new halls and general improvements, making it one of the most prominent institutions in the State. The opening exercises took place last week in the presence of a thousand people, among them being Governor Jarvis; General Scales, member of Congress; Dr. Worth, treasurer of the State; and a large number of the leading editors of the State. The Baltimore Association was represented by Francis T. King and Dr. James C. Thomas. All the gentlemen made very interesting and able addresses. Dr. Mendenhall read a full historical account of the Yearly Meeting of Friends compiled from the original records as far back as the year 1704, when George Fox landed in Carolina and gathered a church near the waters of the Albemarle.

The Friends first landed in this country in Massachusetts in 1656. They made their way down to North Carolina and at one time formed over one-half of the colonists of the State.

The labors of the Baltimore Society have been fraught with gratifying results. Its system of schools has given education not only to all the children of the Friends, but to 1,300 children of other denominations. The establishment of the institution has stopped all emigration of Friends from the States to the West, and increased their membership from 2,200 to 5,641, and the number of meeting-houses from 28 to 52. A similar work has been carried on in Eastern Tennessee, where there are 700 Friends. The Society has also conducted a model farm at a central location, and has established agricultural clubs in various parts of the State. Some years it has sent as much as two tons of clover seed from Baltimore to North Carolina.

The officers of the Baltimore Association are: President, Francis T. King; treasurer, Jesse Tyson; secretary, John C. Thomas; directors, Dr. James C. Thomas, Francis White, Dr. Caleb Winslow, James Carey, and Joseph P. Elliott.

Mr. King was seen by an American reporter yesterday and asked what improvements he had noted in the South. "I notice," he replied, "that a great stimulus is being given to education in the South. New schools are springing up, many of them being of high grades. In one town of 5,000 inhabitants, two large post-grade schools are being established, each of which will have a brick building and would be an ornament to the city of Baltimore. The money was contributed by the people."

In 1874, the *Friends Review* had the following to say:

The Friends of the yearly meetings on this continent, with those of London and Dublin, rendered Friends of North Carolina, through the agency of the Baltimore Educational Association, the assistance they so much stood in need of after four years of trial and suffering, and have been greatly blessed in promoting their religious and material interests, and we believe it has always been a blessing to their neighborhoods generally, commending to many hearts the Gospel message of "Peace on Earth, Good Will to Men."

North Carolina Yearly Meeting abolished slavery within its limits at the beginning of the eighteenth century, from which period to the breaking out of the rebellion there was a steady and large emigration of their members to the West, composed mainly of families escaping from the power and influence of slavery, that they might bring up their children under free institutions. The character and extension of this emigration seriously diminished their numbers, and had their members been able to sell their farms in 1861, there would have been a general movement to the free States. But we believe it was providentially overruled, and they were left isolated for four long years from their brethren and their government, the history and suffering of which period have already been given.

When the war closed in 1865, the same desire to move away again seized upon them, and, but for prompt aid and counsel through the Baltimore Association, serious consequences would have resulted to the organization of the yearly meeting, and great pecuniary and personal sacrifice to Friends individually.

In 1861 there were seven quarterly meetings, 31 meetings for worship, 12 Friends schools and 2,200 members. In 1873 there were eight quarterly meetings, 44 meetings for worship, 42 Friends schools and over 5,000 members.

The educational and agricultural work in the South, undertaken in brotherly love by the United Yearly Meetings, had been so rich and varied in its character, so speedy and permanent in its results, so economical in its management, and so evidently blessed of the Lord, that we desire to encourage our Friends of North Carolina to continue the work.

The Master Hand at the Helm

Having given the cause and origin of the Baltimore Association, it will be appropriate to pause for a little time and speak of the man who, more than any other, saw the necessity of such an association, and who, during its years of existence, did more than any other one to make its work a real success. Others labored faithfully and efficiently, but I think we all recognize the fact that he was the master hand at the helm. It would be pleasant to give a word picture of this man, who was a leader and who led wisely and efficiently.

Francis Thompson King was born in Baltimore, Second month 25, 1819. He was carefully trained and educated in the Society of Friends, and early became convinced of the sin of slavery and war.

About this time Joseph John Gurney, while on a visit to this country, stopped at Joseph King's house, and his son, F.T. King, became an avowed Christian in 1838. He fully accepted the doctrine of the Gospel as held by Friends and ever remained loyal to the interests of Baltimore Yearly Meeting, with which he was actively connected through the remainder of his life. He served as clerk of the yearly meeting for many years, was an elder worthy of double honor,[92] and a member of various committees. For sixteen years he engaged in business, but in 1856, having obtained the amount he had previously fixed upon as needful for his support, he retired from active business that he might give himself more directly to the Lord's work.

John C. Thomas knew him well, and in a recent letter to the writer, gives this brief word picture of our mutual friend: "He was a remarkable combination of widely differing and valuable qualities, a sanguine temperament with a conservative disposition, enthusiastic, but cautious; quick to devise plans, yet holding all in subjection to religious principles and to his understanding of God's will for him; an elder with spiritual discernment and earnest concern for the growth of the Church and for the development of gifts; though a zealous Friend, yet with a wide outlook, broad and sympathizing; a genuine fellowship with all believers in the Lord Jesus Christ."

Being faithful with his early covenant to retire from active business as soon as he became possessed of a moderate competency, and devote himself to benevolent work, it was not long before appeals for

---

[92] 1 Timothy 5:17

his services and help pressed upon him and met a hearty response. Many institutions and associations and individuals were guided to success by his advice and assistance. I remember him telling me at one time that he was connected with over one dozen benevolent institutions and Christian associations, as president, vice-president, trustee, or director. For many years he took active interest in the Maryland Bible Society, and was one of its active managers. He took great interest in the work of the Y.M.C.A. of his native city. Also in the orphan asylums and hospitals and similar institutions. He was president of the Board of Trustees of the Johns Hopkins University and the Johns Hopkins Hospital.[93] He gave much time and labor in getting those institutions started and in proper working order. He was also one of the trustees of Bryn Mawr College, and was actively engaged in the promotion and building up of that institution.

So when the Baltimore Association was formed, as described in a previous chapter, those who knew him would naturally expect to see him taking a leading part in the organization and one of its active spirits in carrying it forward. He felt that North Carolina Yearly Meeting should continue to be the center of religious influence in the South, and that Guilford College should be made a center of Quaker education in the Old North State, where early Quakerism found a foothold in the days of Fox and Edmundson and others of the early pioneers, but which bid fair to be routed out.[94] He saw the danger, and

---

[93] Francis T. King was a personal friend and close associate of Johns Hopkins (1795-1873). Johns Hopkins' Quaker parents were tobacco farmers, who freed their slaves in 1804, without asking any payment, providing lifetime financial support for their older and less able-bodied slaves. The cost of freeing their slaves ended Johns Hopkins' education, and he went to work for an uncle in Baltimore who owned a wholesale grocery business. He and his first cousin Elizabeth fell in love but could not marry; they remained single for the rest of their lives. Johns Hopkins made an enormous fortune as a wholesaler, banker, ship owner, and developer, and especially from his interest in the Baltimore and Ohio Railroad. Francis T. King was one of the trustees hand-picked by Hopkins to head the university and hospital, and along with fellow Baltimore Association director, Francis White, was one of the executors of Hopkins' estate.

[94] William Edmundson visited North Carolina in 1671 and again in 1676. George Fox visited Friends in North Carolina in 1672.

with others threw himself into the breach and turned back the tide of emigration to the West. He visited every yearly meeting in this land, also London and Dublin yearly meetings on the other side, endeavoring in this effort to build up the waste places in North Carolina Yearly Meeting and restore it to its proper rank among the yearly meetings of this continent. He labored both with men and boys, in public and in private. His correspondence was extensive, laying the work before Friends everywhere.

During the time of the association work he made about forty visits to the field in North Carolina and Tennessee. He wanted to see the work himself. No privation was too great. With my horse and open spring wagon, we would leave our home at Bush Hill and drive around through Randolph, Guilford, Alamance, and the adjoining counties for ten days or two weeks, visiting schools and meetings, holding religious and educational meetings in different neighborhoods. Sometimes our journey would be up towards the mountains, but wherever we went we always had a word of encouragement for those we met.

It would be interesting to dwell upon some of our conversations as he would review the field, talk over the different schools and meetings, and dwell upon what the future would be in North Carolina religiously, educationally, and agriculturally. He saw the beginning and the growth of his vision. It is the privilege of some of the rest of us to see more of it, but none of us have yet seen the full fruition of those years of patience and toil.

He died peacefully, after a few days' illness, on the eighteenth of Twelfth month, 1891.

John Scott, of Baltimore Yearly Meeting

There are one or two other persons who should claim our thoughts as we pass on. Our dear friend, John Scott, a minister of Baltimore Yearly Meeting, was among the first to go to North Carolina to spy out the condition that Friends were left in and the best way to supply their needs. Although advanced in years, he was active and energetic in the work, his mission being to look after the temporal needs of our dear Friends, and to help them get started again in a financial way. Thus he spent most of a year.

He reached Greensboro, North Carolina, Twelfth month 23, 1865, and attended monthly meeting at New Garden on the twenty-seventh. The meeting appointed Joshua Lindley, Uriah Macy, and John Carter to assist him and Joseph Moore in their work. Dover Monthly Meeting, on the twenty-eighth, appointed Thomas J. Benbow and Lewis Starbuck for a similar purpose.

It is interesting to read his diary, in which he noted all the particulars of each days' doings: "Went to Allen U. Tomlinson's on the twenty-ninth. On First-day attended a meeting at Springfield, and on the first day of the year, 1866, started two schools in the limits of Springfield Monthly Meeting, one at Oak Forest, under the care of Franklin S. Blair, whose salary was $25 per month; the other at Springfield, under the care of Alpheus L. Mendenhall, at $35 per month."

Then he goes on to tell about looking after the work at Marlboro, Centre, Cane Creek, Spring, Forbush, Hunting Creek, and Piney Woods, where he distributed calicoes, flannels, shawls, cloth of all sorts, pins, needles, etc. On the fourteenth he went to New Garden and bought John Carter's gray mare, Fannie, for Joseph Moore to use, also a bridle and saddle, paying fifteen dollars for the saddle and bridle and $125 for the mare. In this way he passed over the length and breadth of the yearly meeting, giving a detailed account of his travels, also the condition of families, schools, and meetings. But most of those homes are now changed and the individuals named have passed away.

Richard M. Janney, who went down with John Scott, did not remain very long. Sarah M. Smiley, who was a pioneer in the field, soon turned her attention to the work among the freedmen, in which line she labored faithfully for several years, and her work was much blessed.

Joseph Moore and His Work

At this point it is fitting to speak at length about Joseph Moore, who was a leader in organizing day schools and Bible schools and in lecturing along educational lines.

He was born in Washington County, Indiana, Second month 29, 1832, and was the son of John Parker Moore and Martha Cadwalader Moore. Until he was twenty years old, he spent most of his time upon the farm, helping to clear the ground for cultivation and doing all kinds of farm work. From four to six months per year were spent in school. Barnabas C. Hobbs and Myra Lindley were his first teachers. He early loved nature in her various aspects. He knew no one who had made a study of plants, but, finding a book on botany, he borrowed it and soon had a botanical garden of wild flowers, which he tried with no little pains to classify.

He said of himself, "I had strong religious convictions in my early years and a tender conscience, often suffering from doing violence to my sense of right."

He taught his first school in Jackson County in the winter of 1850 and 1851, the second at Blue River Seminary in the summer of 1852. At the age of twenty-one he sold his colt and went to Friends Boarding-School, now Earlham College. He joined with William B. Morgan, teacher of mathematics, and Zaccheus Test, teacher of classics, in purchasing $200 worth of apparatus from E.S. Richey & Son, Boston, Mass. He spent two years at Harvard, under Agassiz, Gray, and Wyman.[95]

In 1861, having received the degree of B.S., he returned to Earlham College and took the position of Professor of Science. He opened a laboratory in the fall of 1861 and taught qualitative analysis, which Professor Wylie says was in advance of the work done in any other

---

[95] Louis Agassiz (1807-1873), professor of zoology and geology at Harvard, first suggested that glaciers had profoundly changed the face of the earth. Asa Gray (1810-1886), professor of botany at Harvard, was a correspondent and close friend of Darwin. Jeffries Wyman (1814-1874), professor of anatomy at Harvard, was also the curator of the Peabody Museum and a pioneering naturalist.

college in Indiana. He was married Eighth month, 1862, to Deborah A. Stanton, who died in the autumn of 1864, leaving one son, J.E. Moore. In the autumn of 1865, soon after the opening of the college term, his health suddenly failed. He had hemorrhage of the lungs, and for several weeks recovery was thought to be doubtful. As he grew better he was asked by the Baltimore Association to go to North Carolina and take charge of the educational and religious work that they were carrying on in that State and in Tennessee. This work, as we have already seen, was to restore in part what had been lost in the war, to make a more efficient and influential body of working Christians and to stay the tide of emigration to the West and North. With the change of climate and the outdoor life afforded in traveling from mountain to sea and from sea to mountain and over into Tennessee, his health gradually returned, so that for three years he hardly missed as many days. He had three precious years, "with a people scattered and peeled by war."

With the help of the Baltimore Association and the Friends in North Carolina, schools were started, normal schools organized, and school supplies were shipped from the North. He instituted Bible schools and schools for training Bible teachers, and went from one neighborhood to another lecturing and talking on various subjects to the hungry multitude. "I never had any fear," he says, "that I was in the wrong place, with access to so many parents, so many children, so many people generally, of all grades and classes." So, what seemed in the autumn of 1865 a great personal calamity, was but the continuation of personal blessing.

After three years in North Carolina, he was called to the presidency of Earlham College, which post he held for fourteen years, from 1869 to 1883.[96] He was married again in the spring of 1872 to Mary Thorne. I will close my account of Joseph Moore by adding a description from one who was intimately acquainted with him:

---

[96] Moore actually served for fifteen years, from 1868-83. Thanks to Thomas Hamm for this correction to Allen Jay's chronology.

Joseph Moore was a singularly winning personality, though it is difficult to analyze the sources of his power over those with whom he came in contact. Certain traits, however, were conspicuous in all his relations. He had a large capacity for friendship. There was a receptive welcome in his attitude, a gracious geniality in his bearing, a kindliness in his smile and in the cordial and frank light of his eye that drew to him alike child and adult, man and woman. Loyal himself, he inspired loyalty in others, and a host of loving friends in all the places where his work was done attest to his power of giving and gaining friendship.

He loved men as individuals and mankind at large. He believed in the best in man and called out the best in response. His was a broad but practical optimism which had faith in God's good purpose for the uplifting, purifying, and ennobling of the common men and women who make up this world. His faith in the best in men and his frank and sincere appeal to it, both directly and by implication, was one of the causes of his strong hold on the young men and women with whom his teaching brought him in touch. They caught the inspiration of his ideals. He made his own spiritual vision vital realities to them, and many a one responded with the fine zeal of youth, and, striving after these same ideals, grew into new beauty of character. For though he loved beauty and truth in nature and in art, pre-eminently he loved the truth and beauty expressed in human life—the creation of noble character.

His love of service amounted to a passion; no child, no halting pupil, was too insignificant to share his gracious helpfulness, if he saw the need. Whether it was an individual, personal need or a broad and general one, if the need were there and the cause right, it met a ready response. He spent generously of his time, his strength, and his money for education, both for Earlham and for the work in North Carolina. He was most self-forgetful in his service for education wherever he had opportunity.

A further source of his power lay in his wholesome and sane simplicity, a simplicity which he saw with sure insight, the essential good, the untrammeled truth. And such essentials he loved with a sure and steadfast devotion.

Gentle to a degree, yet the strength of his character showed itself in unflinching fidelity to his conviction and unswerving loyalty to the truth. There was never any public vacillation with him. He was fearless and firm, yet tactful and considerate in questions of college administration or in the still broader problems of the Church or of politics.

To be true to the truth and faithful,
Though the world be arrayed for a lie.[97]

And we often heard him say, "Truth is the highest thing a man may keep." Along with his love of truth was a profound reverence for it. He reverenced the smallest fact of science as well as the greatest and most comprehensive laws, because either is a revelation of God. All poetry or other literature in which the truth of man's experience found expression appealed to him. His religion was a firm faith in the spirit of God, unhampered by narrow creed or difficult dogma, a truth which was livable in any human life.

---

[97] From "Wendell Phillips," a poem by John Boyle O'Reilly (1844-1890), originally published in his collection, *In Bohemia* (Boston: Pilot Publishing, 1886), pp. 17-21. Wendell Phillips (1811-1884) was a prominent Abolitionist and close associate of William Lloyd Garrison.

Withal he met his life and its opportunities and responsibilities with a glad courage and an absolute sincerity. He loved his work as teacher and minister, and felt the call to both as equally strong and equally divine. He had the same high purpose in both. It was the sincere living of the message which his lips uttered, that sent it home to men's hearts with conviction and power. Whether as teacher or preacher, he transmitted his own vital knowledge of truth to others and lived as an incarnation of the truth he taught.

One of his old students says of him, "To inspire a passionate love for truth in the hearts of young men and women is the greatest thing man or woman can do....Somehow his one tender love for truth communicated itself to us." And a lifelong friend says, "There was something in him that always seemed to make God and goodness a deeper reality to you, to confirm you in the Christian life, and to give a higher impulse to your whole being."

CHAPTER 20

Duties as Superintendent for the Baltimore Association

Having now given some idea of the condition of Friends in North Carolina at the close of the war, and an account of the formation of the Baltimore Association, also a brief sketch of some of the leading characters connected with the work, we can now proceed to speak of the work in general and some of the results that were accomplished. It would be difficult to dwell upon the particulars and give the details, because of my intimate connection with the various departments, without speaking of myself more than is pleasant or becoming, but I will try to keep myself hidden as much as possible.

I wish I could tell of Friends and their heroic sacrifice. Many whose names have not been seen in public did much to bring about the great results. When we reached there Joseph Moore and his co-laborers had started a number of schools, organized a normal training school for teachers, had held some Bible-school conferences, and had opened up the channel for securing supplies of books and stationery from William Wood & Co., New York. It was my duty to press the good work forward and into new fields; seek out places where there were no schools; assist in building new school-houses; employ more teachers; visit the meetings and schools, stir up and keep alive the interest through the length and breadth of the yearly meeting, and try to enlarge the work in all directions.

The Baltimore Association, at a meeting held in Baltimore, Twelfth month 21, 1865, adopted the following set of rules to govern the superintendent in his labors:

1. He must keep a clear cash account.
2. He must keep a journal.
3. He must report weekly to the board.
4. He must have a central office, a room that can be hired and fitted up for storage of books, clothes, stationery, etc., and to which letters can be addressed.
5. There is an Educational Committee appointed by North Carolina Yearly Meeting with which our superintendent is to confer when necessary. The committee and the Baltimore Association control the schools jointly.
6. The boarding-school is to remain under the care of its trustees. We have nothing to do with the management, but we have agreed to spend upon the repairs of the building this year $1,500, including roofing, etc., and $100 on apparatus this year, and to educate free one year in the institution twenty children of Friends who have suffered from the war, selecting the most suitable ones.
7. The Baltimore Association [is] to pay the salaries of teachers in the schools and furnish books and stationery. North Carolina Friends will furnish school-houses, board the teachers, and provide the fuel.
8. Friends who are able are to pay the tuition of their children and provide the books.

9. Those who profess with us are to enjoy the same privileges as members.
10. Those not Friends are to pay for the books and tuition of their children.
11. To employ teachers by the month. Our views are $5 to $50 per month, according to the size and grade of the school.

The above were the rules under which the association began its work. They were modified as time went on and circumstances changed. The amount of money given to the boarding-school varied each year as the situation demanded.

The first post-office near which we located was Greensboro. We changed afterward to Bush Hill (now Archdale). We fixed up one of the downstairs bed-rooms in our home for an office, where all the books and stationery were kept. Our home was located some twenty-five rods from the old Springfield Meeting-house, about a mile from the post-office. By correspondence I generally learned what books and stationery to take with me when starting out to visit the schools located in the adjoining counties of Randolph, Guilford, Alamance, Davison, Chatham, etc., and would load them in my spring wagon. For those schools located in a distant part of the State or in Tennessee, I would ship the books and stationery by railroad and then go myself by public conveyance.

In that way I would visit schools and meetings in the eastern and western parts of the State and cross the mountains into Tennessee once or twice each year during the nine years I was in North Carolina.

These visits were very interesting occasions. With my buggy loaded down, I would start out over the rough roads and through the woods. During the war but little attention was given to repairing the roads. If a tree fell down across the track it was easier to drive around it than it was to cut it off and roll it out of the way. If a gully was washing across the road, people would drive around it through the fields or through the woods and brush. In time, however, I became familiar with the roads in the territory where our schools were located. I learned to love the old ways and old places, and the localities of Friends meetings in North Carolina and Tennessee were dear, familiar spots, but more near to my heart were many of the homes. I always found a warm welcome and shared with them the best they had.

The memory of those fathers and mothers with their children is a bright spot in my life. Many of those humble homes were oases in my life's journey. They are changed now. Those children are the active members of the Church to-day. Three years ago, as we sat on the platform in the yearly meeting I said to my wife, "I think I have had nearly half of this yearly meeting on my knee when they were children." The memory of those days is pleasant.

> "I think I have had nearly half of this yearly meeting on my knee when they were children."

Those visits were frequent and were after the fashion of the Methodist circuit riders. I would send an appointment on before me to the effect that there would be an educational meeting in the school-house and a religious meeting in the meeting-house while in the neighborhood. All were invited to attend both and the company was generally large.

Some of my educational lectures would be amusing if they were compared with the lectures of the present day. The variety was sufficient to do away with all monotony. Sometimes my talks included such profound subjects as telling the young men that they should do the milking rather than their mothers and sisters, and should carry in the wood; that they should let mother sit down at the table when there was not room for all; also how hurtful was the use of tobacco. They included telling the girls to sweep up the ashes in the corners of the fireplaces and stand the broom up on the handle, rather than let it lie on the floor. I tried to tell them how they spoiled their looks by dipping snuff. Those lectures were not in vain. Soon the time came when, as I went into a schoolroom, all the snuff brushes would disappear and the boys' tobacco was pushed out of sight.

To-day North Carolina is among the leaders in its rules forbidding those who use tobacco in any form being acknowledged ministers of the Gospel or appointed elders or overseers in the Church, and the yearly meeting is in the foremost ranks in the great temperance movement that has swept over North Carolina.

Joseph Moore, who preceded me, was a college man and this reputation went before him, but upon one occasion it was called in question by a dear old woman Friend who heard him lecture. She said, "I don't believe he has college larnin', for I could understand all he said." My educational talks never raised a suspicion that I had "college larnin'." Yet these talks were times when we got close together and endeavored to strengthen and build up the schools, the neighborhood, and the home; to create in the minds of the young an ambition to aspire to higher positions in the educational and religious world.

Schools of the Baltimore Association

Reference has already been made to the normal schools that were held each summer for the purpose of training teachers in methods of instruction. The plan was to bring all the teachers from the schools under the care of the Baltimore Association together in a suitable locality and train them for the work of teaching. This work resulted in a great good to the cause of education in the State.

Other teachers connected with schools not under our care were permitted to attend, thereby introducing the normal training in the State. The result was that when the time came for our Society to give up this normal training, the State had seen its good effects upon the schools; so that it established a normal school, which has elevated the standard of teaching in North Carolina and other places in the South that have come under its influence. I believe it is not claiming too much to say that the work done by these normal schools was the beginning of an awakening on the subject of education that has been far reaching and of untold advantage in placing the educational system of the State among the best.

The first one of these normal schools was held at Springfield in 1866. Joseph Moore had charge of it. It was the practice to give practical lessons in teaching, having classes in the various studies and selecting one of the best teachers to conduct the recitations, at the close having the rest criticise the method and show how it might have been improved. In this way all the branches taught were brought in review. For six weeks this was carried on, the different teachers being called upon to show how they would conduct classes upon various subjects. In this practical way they were prepared to take charge of the schools under their care.

Much attention was given to composition, writing, reading, and spelling. The moral and religious training was not overlooked. The devotional exercises at the opening in the morning were conducted in a way to be an example to the teachers in their schools, and were led by different ones of the teachers. Then in the middle of the week all attended meeting for worship—another example for the various schools throughout the yearly meeting; and it is pleasant to record that in our morning devotions, as well as in our midweek meetings for worship, vocal exercises were frequently heard from the various teachers, giving assurance that such would be the case in their schools and in the meetings where their scholars attended. This proved to be the result, manifesting itself in a great increase in permanent membership in the yearly meeting.

As I have said, the first of these schools was held for six weeks at Springfield. It was largely attended and was a great success. The second was held at Deep River in 1867, the third at Springfield in 1868. The fourth, in 1869, and the fifth, in 1870, were also held at Springfield. The sixth, in 1871, was held at Cane Creek and was large, numbering over one-hundred, and the seventh, in 1872, at Springfield. In 1873 and 1874, the eighth and ninth were held at Greensboro, in Benbow Hall, the one in 1874 being the last one held under the supervision of the Baltimore Association. The work was then turned over to the control of North Carolina Yearly Meeting, the association retiring from the field except for a little financial assistance to the boarding-school and a few other special institutions.

It was the practice to invite well known persons and those who would be a good influence, to deliver lectures before these normals, at which times the public was generally invited. Among those whom I remember as addressing us were Judge Robert P. Dick, Dr. Nereus Mendenhall, Governor Jonathan Worth, Dr. Braxton Craven, Marcus L. Wood, Francis T. King, Samuel Collins, Calvin H. Wiley, Professor Palmer, Harry Hardee, New York; Judge Turgee, author of "Fool's Errand," and others whom I fail to call to mind at present. Some of these spoke to us several times. In this way the work was kept before the public.

Some of these occasions were special times of pleasant remembrance. During the Normal School at Springfield, in 1869, occurred the remarkable eclipse of the sun, which was nearly total. Joseph Moore had come down from Earlham to be with us, and we also had Eli and Mahalah Jay with us. The word had been given out that we would have a picnic dinner in the grove and that at the proper time Joseph Moore would give a lecture on astronomy and explain the cause of the eclipse. It was believed that there were 1,500 people present. When we had finished our dinner and the time was drawing near for the eclipse to begin we adjourned to an open field on the model farm near by, and there, standing on a wagon with the crowd around him, for some time he explained the natural phenomenon we were about to witness.

When the time approached, he pulled out his watch, which he had taken pains to have correct, and said, "Now in the next five minutes we will see the shadow begin," and told us where it would begin. As they looked through their smoked glasses and saw the shadow, there was a solemn hush, as something like awe came over the crowd. It went on until there was a complete annular eclipse, there being only a small, bright rim visible. He continued to explain the subject of eclipses until it was all over and the sun assumed its normal appearance. At the greatest obscurity there was a damp and chilly feeling in the air and some of the chickens in the neighborhood began hunting for their roosting places.

Another incident connected with the Normal School session in 1870 was the presentation to me by the teachers and scholars of the Normal School of a very large Bible. It took place at the close of the term, after I had made my closing remarks and was about to dismiss the company. Hearing a little noise, I looked around and saw a committee coming from an adjoining room bringing this Bible, with the inscription on it, "Presented to Allen Jay by the Normal School held at Springfield, North Carolina, 1870." One of the teachers had been selected to make the presentation speech, which he did very nicely and then left me to make reply, which I endeavored to do. The presentation being a surprise, my reply was rather awkwardly worded and poorly delivered, but I hope I succeeded in making it plain that I thoroughly appreciated the motive and accepted the gift in the spirit in which it was given. I have just been looking at it and living in memory the scenes of that afternoon at old Springfield. There have been great changes since then in that company.

The Bible-School Work

While giving attention to the schools for advancing secular education, the association was equally concerned to promote the moral and religious education of the teachers and scholars. It was the aim to have a Bible school in each meeting, and in order that there might be a sufficient number of teachers for these and those who could carry them on and make a success, there were established what we called Bible or First-day School Associations, which were held for several days in convenient centers.

To these were invited all who could attend, and classes were taught from the Bible. Lessons were selected from the Scriptures that would give practical illustrations of how to teach. Proper persons were obtained to lecture on the Bible and Bible teaching, the geography of the Bible, the history of the Bible and various subjects connected with religious teaching, such as "Bible Lands" and the customs and manners of the times of our Saviour, lectures on Bible schools and the methods of teaching.

Sometimes two or three were held during the year. Some of the places thus visited were New Garden, Deep River, Springfield, Centre, Providence, Cane Creek, Spring, Back Creek, Marlboro, Goldboro, Rich Square, and other places. Indeed, it was the wish to hold them all through the yearly meeting. Some of those who were invited to be with us and to help in conducting them, outside of our own workers, were F. T. King, from Baltimore; Robert Lindley Murray, Ruth Murray, Sarah Tabor, Ellen Congdon, Anna Tatum, and Thomas W. Ladd of New York, and many others. These were present and were a help, adding a pleasing interest to those occasions. Indeed, the coming of these dear Friends was looked forward to with much pleasure by a large number who had learned to love them for their devoted labor and the sunshine and gladness which they scattered in their pathway.

Some of those experiences are pleasant to remember to this day. One morning we left our home at Springfield for Cane Creek. There were three men and four women of us in an old army ambulance that General Sherman had left at the time of the surrender at Greensboro. We had three horses hitched to it and William A. Sampson, the model farmer, was our driver. That afternoon we had a meeting at Providence, stayed all night at John White's, and next morning went on our journey. Towards noon we came to a beautiful spring by the roadside, with plenty of green grass and good shade under the spreading boughs of the oak trees. We spread our wraps out on the ground, built a fire, hung on the tea-kettle, got out our meat, vegetables, bread, cake, pickles, pies, lemons, oranges, sugar, etc., which had been provided by the good women before leaving home. When we had gathered round this lovely dinner and vocal blessing was invoked amid the singing of birds, I believe every heart was thankful. We lingered long in that spot and left with reluctant looks when time reminded us that we must proceed. In my rounds I frequently passed the place afterwards, never without thinking of that company, all of whom have passed beyond except myself. But now I leave these Normal Schools, both in the secular and Bible schools, and turn to the teachers and the work resulting from this intellectual, moral, and religious training.

CHAPTER 21

Some of the Teachers and Ministers

The Teachers of the Baltimore Association

Our teachers were selected from the members of North Carolina Yearly Meeting who had been to New Garden Boarding-School and who had some experience in teaching the country schools before the war. We had others who were brought from the North and West. When the schools had reached their largest number, there were some sixty teachers under the care of the Association.

It was the duty of the superintendent to look after them, assigning them to their various schools, find boarding places for them, and see that books and stationery were supplied. It was also his duty to see that everything was running smoothly between the teachers and the patrons of the schools. It required care always to get the right one in the right place. These assignments were generally made at the close of the Normal School, so that when the teachers returned home they knew where their next year's work was to be done. No Methodist bishop ever had a more loyal set of workers to assign to their fields of service. They were willing to leave the matter to the superintendent and many times did not even inquire what the salary would be. Indeed, in looking back to the loyalty and devotion of those dear teachers I do not wonder that the work was greatly blessed.

It could not be otherwise. It is hard to resist the desire to mention their names, for I feel that North Carolina Yearly Meeting owes more to those devoted and self-sacrificing teachers than it is aware of. Only the fear of omitting some who should be mentioned keeps me from giving a detailed list of the Blairs, the Henleys, the Farlows, the Dixons, the Englishes, Tomlinsons, Davises, Worths, Fraziers, Whites, Pettys, Hodginses, Benbows, Starbucks, Mendenhalls, Wilsons, and others of the South; and from the North, the Meaders, Steeres, Hollingsworths, and Clarks—all dear names to those of us who were in the field.

Here I want to say, what I have long felt in regard to the growth of North Carolina Yearly Meeting, that this growth was due to the faithfulness of those teachers as much as the ministers, for at the close of the war there were few active members of the yearly meeting who were acknowledged ministers.

The Ministers of North Carolina Yearly Meeting at the Close of the War

Isham Cox, with gray hairs and old-fashioned saddle-bags, was a familiar picture riding around over the State, visiting the meetings, doing a good work, and preaching a gospel of good cheer. He was faithful in exercising his gift. His labors were a blessing to the Church. In the eastern portion was Dr. William Nicholson, with his strong and clear ministry, leading his hearers to a deeper and fuller understanding of the Gospel message. In the same locality was Ellen Nicholson, with her feeble body, but filled with the Spirit of her Master and fully consecrated to His service. Her ministry was on the prophetic order and was blessed to many.

In addition to these there were few who were actively engaged in the field. Daniel and Seth Barker were growing old and could not engage in much active service. Albert Peele was a rising young minister who has given a good account of himself and is still active in proclaiming the Gospel message. Many have been blessed by his ministry. Besides these, there were a few others who were old and feeble and rarely went from home. Yet their prayers held up the hands of those actively engaged.[98]

How few were these compared with the multitudes that they had to meet. Here were about 2,200 members scattered over North Carolina from the eastern coast to the western end among the mountains and across them into eastern Tennessee and down into the region of Knoxville, Maryville, and Friendsville. Surely they were separated far from each other upon the walls.[99] The line of battle was long drawn out. In addition to all this they had just passed through a four years' war, had been stripped of their property, and left destitute. Their meetings had been small during that time and many of them held under trying circumstances.

I will here insert a description of a meeting held in Virginia during the war. It was written by Susan Walker, a member of the meeting, and read before a literary society at Earlham College during the winter of 1862–63, she being a student at Earlham at that time. Perhaps many similar experiences were passed through by meetings in North Carolina Yearly Meeting.

A Quaker Meeting in Dixie

> It was a bright morning in the winter of 1861 when the Friends of Fairfax Meeting began to assemble at the usual hour around the old stone meetinghouse. Great was their surprise upon arriving there to find that it was occupied by two companies of Confederate cavalry that had encamped there during the previous night.

---

[98] Exodus 17:12
[99] Nehemiah 4:19-20

Some of the oldest and most influential men Friends immediately sought out the captains and told them of their situation, that the house was their place of worship and that there had not been a meeting missed there for over a hundred years, and if the arrangements could possibly be made they would be obliged for the use of the house for at least two hours. At first the officer thought it would be impossible, but after some consultation concluded that the building was large enough for them all and said if the Friends would wait a while they would make some room for them.

So the women sat in the carriages while the men entered the house and assisted the soldiers to place their bedding and baggage to one side. The partition was soon closed and those of the soldiers who did not wish to attend were sent into the other side of the house. However, almost all had a curiosity to be present, having heard of Quaker meetings. When the members entered the scenes presented there were strange ones for the interior of a Friends meetinghouse, and had it not been for the solemnity of the occasion it would have been truly amusing. The old ladies ascended the steps into the gallery and took their seats, though rather daintily, as arms were stacked behind them and muskets and swords stored away beneath the benches.

In one corner of the room the "stars and bars" were unfurled. In an opposite one was a large fireplace with a blazing fire, over which was roasting a large turkey, and some hominy cooking. Overcoats were hanging all about. Knapsacks and saddles were strewn around, while a suppressed titter or an amused whisper of some of the more mischievous soldiers regarding the peculiar shape of the plain bonnets could be distinctly heard.

But when all were seated it was perfectly quiet, and when an aged and feeble lady rose every countenance wore a thoughtful aspect and each attentively listened to her words of truth and love. When she rose to invoke a blessing on the little band there assembled, she also prayed that the wings of peace might be spread over our once prosperous and happy land, and for the strangers that were that day gathered in their midst, until loud sobs broke from strong men and great tears forced themselves down their sun-burned cheeks.

After the meeting many of them expressed their gratification at having been allowed to assemble with the members and said they hoped to have another opportunity. Of course, the Friends were not desirous that they should remain in the house, but invited them to attend their meetings whenever they felt inclined. Since that day there have been many assemblings for worship in the same room and amidst the same military surroundings. They have been mostly solemn and impressive, but very different from our nice, quiet little ones here at Earlham. Those who have not been surrounded by war and its attendant horrors know but poorly how to appreciate the almost perfect peace and tranquility that reigns here. I hope never again to hear the familiar sound of the booming of cannon or the noise of musketry, and that ere I return to the Blue Ridge Hills of my native state they will have passed forever from our land.

The Fruits and Lessons of the Work

Our dear Friends in the limits of North Carolina Yearly Meeting had their full share of these difficulties, as they were located in that part of the State where Johnston's and Sherman's armies passed in the closing years of the war. Their meetings were mostly held in silence, as there were but few ministers belonging to the yearly meeting. Their numbers were very few and scattered over a long distance, and yet we saw this little number, without much noise or any great show, grow in a few years from 2,200 in 1866 to 5,500 in 1876, and it has continued to grow until now the figures have nearly reached 7,000, and that notwithstanding the fact that they have set off the Friends in Tennessee to join Wilmington Yearly Meeting in Ohio. It should also be borne in mind that this increase has not been helped by Friends moving from other yearly meetings into its limits, but, on the other hand, some of our Western yearly meetings have been strengthened by members of North Carolina moving to them.

There is another fact that I wish to impress upon my readers. There has not been the backsliding in that yearly meeting that there has been in some others. If we look over the church papers for the last forty years and sum up the number who have been recorded as converted in the revivals and who have joined the Church, we should expect in the place of five or six thousand they would have ten or twenty thousand. In others, instead of ten or fifteen thousand, they should have, according to revival figures, thirty or forty thousand; and then when we hear some one of our revivalists state how many thousands have been converted under their ministry, we pause and exclaim, "Where are they to-day?"

I am not condemning revival work, but rejoice that I have had a little hand in it myself and can call to mind some who claim that they found the Saviour under my ministry during some revival work. But in view of these figures, which are stubborn things and cannot be denied, is there not room to fear that there has been a fault in our revival methods or in the shepherding care of the Church? Perhaps a future historian may see a weakness in both the evangelist and the Church.

In the building up of North Carolina Yearly Meeting, which I regard as one of the greatest works of the Society of Friends in the last hundred years, there is a lesson that I wish to impress upon the workers in other yearly meetings. Here were some sixty or more teachers, all Christians, sent out into the various meetings, requested to open their schools with devotional exercises every morning, encouraged to organize Bible schools and take the superintendency of the same unless a more suitable person could be found; they were impressed with the importance of being faithful in their meeting for worship in vocal prayer and testimony, and, above all, to visit the sick, hunt up the poor children and get them into school and under their religious instruction. This was a work that was done with no flourish of trumpets. Often have I heard of some heroic deeds done by these young teachers, deeds that were done only for the Master's eye to see. Some of these have passed on and perhaps they were surprised to hear Him say, "I was sick and in prison and ye visited me, enter ye into the joy of your Lord."[100]

With the blessing of the Lord upon the labor of these dear teachers, the monthly meetings began to receive members, a family at a time, sometimes two or three families. Sometimes the children in the school led their parents into the church. Other families were impressed by the silent and patient suffering of the Friends during the war. In some cases the women and children of those who were not Friends would come and sit with Friends in their silent meetings while their husbands, fathers, and sons were in the army. They found something in those meetings which strengthened them in the time of sorrow, and when the war was over they joined the Church where they had found help in those dark hours.

Another feature of this work was that it went on harmoniously and they

---

[100] Matthew 25:34-36

did not have the religious controversies on doctrinal points that have occurred in some other yearly meetings. Where these things have been introduced it has been done by those coming from outside.

Theological hair-splitting and fanatical extremes were never created by the kind of work that has been described above. Where the mind is trained along with the emotions, where brain and heart are educated in unison, such things do not take place. The sad result comes where one is developed to the neglect of the other. The narrow and untrained mind runs off upon hobbies and extremes. Our fathers were right when they labored for a religious and guarded education. They built well when they placed the monthly meeting school-house along by the side of the meeting-house.

I have dwelt thus upon this revival work of the Baltimore Association in building up North Carolina Yearly Meeting because there is a lesson in it that some of the other yearly meetings will do well to study, and I also feel a desire to honor the memory of those silent workers, who patiently labored day after day, walking through the cold and wet, some of them building the fires in the school-house, sweeping out the room, visiting the children in their homes, and speaking a word of comfort to the parents. Another generation has arisen and I fear if I did not say these words they never would be said.

CHAPTER 22

Revival Work in North Carolina

Let it not be inferred from the foregoing that there was no evangelistic work done in the shape of the old-fashioned revival meetings. There was more or less of that kind of work done by different ones. As has been said, I took part in some of that kind of labor which was blessed, but always with the feeling that it should never be carried further than the leaders of the meeting could go with me. I have always felt that a separation in a meeting on that account in the end was more fruitful of evil than good.

Upon returning home one morning from New York, where I had been soliciting funds for our work, my wife met me at the station, and as we rode home she told me that the Methodists were holding a revival meeting at Trinity College, some three miles from Springfield, and that some of our young Friends had gone to the mourners bench and professed conversion, and that some of the parents had forbidden their children to go, but that the young people and some who were older had gone in spite of the counsels of the older people. She feared we would have trouble in the meeting. I tried to learn what was right to do. In the evening I hitched up the horse, and when my wife asked me where I was going, I told her to the revival. She expressed fears for the result, but told me if I went she would go with me. My object was to save our young people to our own church. When we went in and took our seats in the back part of the room, the leader of the meeting came back to us there and insisted that I should come and sit by him on the platform, which I did. Looking over the congregation I perceived whispering and looking at me. Our young people were much pleased. At the close we endeavored to shake hands with all of our young Friends and told them we wanted them to remain with us. I attended the meetings for two weeks and took such part as I felt was right, and had the promise of each one of our young Friends who had been converted that they would remain members with us.

A similar revival service was held about the same time in Caraway school-house near by. The closing meeting was held in the forenoon, and one of our young Friends came to me weeping and saying, "I dread to go home, for my parents are much displeased because I have attended these meetings." She had been staying with a friend who lived near by where the meetings were held. I told her to go and get her things and we would take her home, as we passed by there. When we approached the house the father was standing in the door. I took her by the arm and said, "Thy child left home unsaved. She now returns a child of Christ, and in His name I ask thee to receive her." At this she threw her arms around his neck and weeping, said, "I love Jesus." All opposition fled, and when all had sat down, I led in prayer and then spoke. She then told what the Lord had done for her, and before closing an older sister accepted the Saviour. Before leaving the State we saw the whole family converted, and one is now a recorded minister.

The next day was our preparative meeting. At the close I told Friends what I had been doing, and that a number of their children were so under deep conviction that I believed it would be right for us to hold some meetings in our meeting-house, if they were willing. Several leaders gave their consent, and a meeting was announced for that night. It was largely attended, and a deep feeling came over all. The next night, at the close of the speaking, a young man came up and knelt down by me, and in deep contrition asked me to pray for him. The next night three came forward without any invitation, thus establishing an altar of prayer without any action on my part. But the climax was reached on the third or fourth night, when some one broke out singing. My wife came to me and asked me to stop it. My reply was, "I did not start it and I shall not stop it."

I remembered how a few years before, in Illinois, a Christian young woman stood up to sing a hymn, and as she sang with tears running down her face, an elder sitting by my side rose and harshly ordered her to stop, saying, "It is a Friends meeting and we won't have singing." At the close he spoke to me about it. I simply said, "I have nothing to say about the singing, but it was very evident that thee was out of humor when thee spoke to that dear child, and I leave thee to settle it with Him who knoweth all things, as she is undoubtedly one of His children." Two days afterwards, when I sat down after speaking, he rose and stood, weeping so he could be heard all over the house, and then in broken sentences said, "You saw and heard what I did the other day and I cannot rest day or night. The only way to find peace is to try and sing a hymn myself, and I do not know how." Poor man, he made the effort. It was poorly done. The whole congregation was weeping with him. At the close of the service the young woman whom he had sat down came to him and said, "I forgive you." From that day to this it has been a serious matter for me to ask any one to sit down. I do not say but that it may be right sometimes, but let it be done with care and in the right spirit.[101]

Our meeting went on for ten days, growing larger and a number professed to be saved. One day, at the close of our weekday meeting,

---

[101] Quaker elders had the authority to ask people not to speak in meeting, but this authority was not always exercised gently. Indiana Yearly Meeting's discipline said, "If any, in the course of their ministry, shall misapply, or draw unsound inferences, or wrong conclusions from the text, or shall misbehave themselves in point of conduct or conversation, let them be admonished in love and tenderness, by the elders or overseers where they live; and if they prove refractory, and refuse to acknowledge their faults, they must be further treated with, in the wisdom of the truth, as the case may require." (*The Discipline of the Society of Friends of Indiana Yearly Meeting*, 1839, p. 54; identical language appears in the 1892 edition). The Quaker world was changing, and many elders did their best to stop it. Allen Jay was one of the gentlest and strongest advocates for change, in this as in many other instances.

the elders gathered together in the meeting-house yard, and I could hear them talking, for the dear friend who sat at the head of our meeting, A. U. Tomlinson, was hard of hearing, and in telling him what had happened they had to speak loud. They told him of the singing and of the altar of prayer and that there had been some excitement, etc. He listened until they were done. Then he said, "Friends, my youngest son came home last night from the meeting here, came to his mother and myself and told us he had given his heart to God and that he wanted us to forgive him for the way he had lived and that he was determined to live a different life. Now, if any of you want to lay your hands on these meetings, you can do so, but I am going home." And he started down the path.

Soon they were all gone, much to the relief of my mind, for I had decided if they requested me to close the meetings I would do so without any complaint, for I had that early in my religious work decided to work in harmony with the Church, and after fifty years' active work in the ministry have never seen cause to change my mind. I do not believe the cause of Christ is advanced by pushing in innovations or change of practice faster than the weight and religious sentiment of the meeting is able to go. For if this is done separations are sometimes brought about and bitter feelings are engendered and things said and done that are contrary to the spirit of the Master. Our meetings closed a few days afterwards, and we kept all of our members and added some thirty new ones to our meeting.

The Revival at High Point

The morning we closed, some five or six ministers of other churches from High Point came in. We invited them to our house to dinner. While eating, one of them wished to know why they could not have a revival in their town. I knew their condition. There was a prejudice towards each other, and while they each had small congregations, they would not unite in religious work. I told them plainly that they never could while they were fighting each other and would not go into each other's meetings. Finally the pastor of the Southern Methodist Church said, "Brother Jay, if you will come and hold a meeting, we will all join in and help." After some conversation it was agreed that we would begin on the next First-day night, and we selected the house that would hold the most people, which was the Southern Methodist Church, to hold the meeting in. They insisted that I should do the preaching of nights, saying there would be no prejudice against me as we had no church in the place, and they would hold a prayer-meeting during the day, visit the homes, and try to get the people out. They also agreed to look after the singing, etc., all of which I am glad to say they carried out in the right spirit.

The result was that I preached for thirty-one nights. The house was soon full to overflowing, and some one-hundred and fifty professed to have found their Saviour in the pardon of their sins. The whole town was shaken and many prayer-meetings were held in the homes during the day. At the close the converts joined the churches according to their own personal wishes. Notwithstanding the fact that we had no meeting in the town, about fifty wished to join us and their names were placed on the roll at Springfield, which was fully two miles away. To-day one of the strongest meetings of the yearly meeting is located at High Point, in a fine stone building.

A circumstance happened during this series of meetings, and I tell it, trusting it may do no harm. From day to day, as my mind was on the meetings at night, more than usual I was favored to get hold of a text and see something of the line of discourse that it would be right for me to follow at the meeting that night. But one day, near the close, my mind was a blank. Look over the Bible as I would, nothing took hold of my mind. Indeed, I felt as thought I had never preached and never would again. Never had I felt such spiritual poverty. There was no life in any subject. I told my wife I could not preach that night. "But they will expect thee to do so." "Well, I can't, and that's all there is of it."

We arrived, and the house was packed, the doors and windows full as usual. By hard work I managed to get to my chair on the platform while the congregation was singing. Turning to the half dozen ministers sitting around me, I said, "Brethren, one of you will have to preach. I can't." They insisted that I must, saying that the congregation expected it and adding that they had made no preparation for it. It was a great trial to me, sitting there and hearing each one declare that he could not preach.

Finally one brother said, "We need to pray," and knelt down and led the congregation in prayer. Then another said, "While you are deciding who will preach, I will give out another hymn." So he rose and said, "Brother Jay says he cannot preach to-night, and while the brethren are deciding who will, we will sing another hymn." It was a trying time. All eyes were on me, wondering what was the matter. Before the hymn was finished some one touched me on the arm and handed me a piece of paper with my name on the back. Inside were these words, "I think you ought to preach to-night from Matthew, xxii, 11th and 12th verses." I threw it on the floor disgusted, saying, "Who is giving me a text?" Immediately the impression came, "Do I not use thee to tell others what to do? May I not use one of My children to tell thee what thy duty is?" I opened the paper, turned to the reference, and in a moment the light shone upon the text and it took hold of me. Turning to the brethren, I said, "The Lord has settled it. I will preach."

As soon as the singing stopped I rose, and for more than half an hour had wonderful liberty in giving the message. As I sat down, a lawyer by the name of J.R. Bulla, who sat in front of me, a man of the world, rose, and looking me in the face said, "You have knocked the last prop from under me; I surrender to the Lord Jesus Christ." And fell on his knees. Others followed.

This dear man was saved, joined our meeting, lived a Christian life, and died several years later in the triumph of faith. He had a wife and two daughters who were Christians. The eldest daughter was specially concerned for the spiritual welfare of her father and had spoken to me about him several times during the meetings. Some three months after this, as I was walking by their home, we met. She came up to me and said, "Brother Jay, do you know who gave you the text you preached from the night my father was converted?" Replying I said, "No, but I expect thee did." I had not thought of her before, though I had often wished that I did know.

She became serious and replied, "Come into the house and I will tell you all about it." She said, "I was so burdened for the salvation of my father that I could scarcely eat or sleep. I knew he was under conviction and that he was going away the next day to be gone a month. I felt if he got under the influence of his old companions he would settle back into his old habits. With these thoughts I departed for the afternoon prayer-meeting, but the burden was so great that I turned back, went to my room, locked the door, and on my knees for a long time asked God to save my father. He told me if Allen Jay would preach from Matthew, xxii, 11 and 12, that night my father would be saved. I rose, went to my desk and wrote a letter to you asking you to do so. When the bell rang for the night's service I started to the church, but on the way I began to reason that you were a Quaker preacher and did not believe in having a text given to you and that here I was, a young girl going to tell you what to preach about. I felt afraid that it would insult you, and listening to my fears, I tore the letter up and went on, praying that the Lord would make you preach that text. So when that minister rose and said that you could not preach that night, I secretly exclaimed, 'O Lord, what shall I do?' The answer was, 'I told thee what to do and thee refused. Thy father's blood will be on thee.' In my desperation I wrote on the fly-leaf of my hymn book the words I sent you, tore it out, doubled it up, wrote your name on the outside, and sent it through the crowd to you. I was so excited I forgot to sign my name. My heart leaped for joy when you rose with the text. It was a glorious night to me and to our household." The dear girl died a few years later. After her death I told her father about it and he said, "I knew she was praying for me."

Not long after this Mary Moon (now Mary M. Meredith) came into North Carolina and labored as an evangelist, and being a woman she opened the way for other women and did a good work. Her work is remembered by many. Later there were others who came who had the evangelistic gift, such as John Y. Hoover, of Iowa, who did good service in gathering into the church. Still later, Fernando G. Cartland and his wife, Abby Cartland, labored efficiently, and later yet James Jones has labored to enlarge the borders of North Carolina Yearly Meeting. Of their own membership, Albert Peele, Mary Woody, Mary Cartland, and others have done royal service. These have come to the front since the days of the Baltimore Association, and it is cause for rejoicing that others are coming forward in the ministry, missionary, and other fields of religious labor in the various branches of church work. The Master of the vineyard knows who have been instrumental in laying the foundation of this work. He will divide the sheaves with a loving and impartial hand.

Enthusiasm of Parents and Children for Education

Having spoken of the teachers and their work, it is but just to mention the part taken by the parents and their children in this building-up process. Many of the parents had labored hard and struggled under many privations to care for their children during the war. When the war closed and they began to get started in their new life, their minds turned to their children, who had not had any opportunity for education during those long years of trial and darkness. But few schools were kept up in the South. The boarding-school at New Garden continued through the war, and the Friends Academy at Belvidere was in operation most of the time. With these exceptions but few schools were in operation among Friends or others. At the close of the war what public school funds there were had been lost,[102]

---

[102] It is easy to forget that at the close of the Civil War, the economy of the South collapsed. All public dealings had been in Confederate money, which became nearly worthless. Local governments literally had no money for anything for years, and Southern education suffered for generations.

so that parents turned to the association and said, "We can work our way and care for our families if the association will assist us to educate our children. They are our hope for the future."

Many of them made heroic efforts to keep their children in school. Many bright examples of trust and faith came under my observation. One day after a meeting in the school, a mother invited me to go home with her to dinner. When the time came to sit down to eat we gathered around the table and there were three pieces of back-bone of a pig, some corn bread, and cold water. After the children had all bowed their heads and folded their hands, she requested me to ask the blessing upon the meal. While we were eating she talked of the blessings of her Heavenly Father—how He had preserved her and the children. She pointed out where General Sherman had pitched his tent over night, and the road in front of her house still showed the marks where the heavy artillery had been hauled along, but she had been preserved through it all and now her children were actually going to school and learning to read.

Another poor widow told how during the summer, when her vegetables and little patch of corn were all drying up for want of rain, she could not sleep one night, and getting out of bed, began to pray for rain. She then remembered that sometimes she had done wrong and was fearful that God would not hear her on account of her transgressions. She then woke up her three little children, who she felt were innocent, thinking that perhaps God would hear their prayers. When they had knelt with her she told them to ask God to send rain, and she believed the Heavenly Father would hear their childish prayers. While they were praying the rain began to fall upon the clapboard roof of the cabin. To her childlike faith it was a direct answer to prayer, and she could not speak of it without shedding tears of joy.

One more instance, among others, was that of a poor widow with six children, who was struggling to educate them. She had about half an acre of ground from which she and her children cleared off the trash and then with a hoe and shovels they loosened up the soil. She then sowed it with wheat, and with a rake and hoe covered it up.

Then with the children she asked God to bless it and cause it to bring forth a good crop, and she covenanted with Him that He should have one-tenth of the income. It was a beautiful little patch of wheat, so much so that the neighbors talked about it. When the harvest came they cut it the best they could, and with a flail beat it out on the old barn floor. When they had cleaned it all there were ten half-bushels of good wheat. The last half-bushel was heaping full, and she proposed to the children that they give that one to the Lord.

Not knowing how to use it to the best advantage, she brought it to our house saying that I would know how to use it to do the most good. My wife, knowing her condition, suggested that perhaps it would be right to keep it to help clothe and feed her children during the coming winter, but she insisted that it was not hers, that it belonged to the Lord and that she must leave it with me to dispose of in a way that would honor Him. Just then I came in, and after listening to her story, told her I would do with it as she requested, and then I had the pleasure of saying to her, "Here is a twenty-dollar bill that the Lord has sent thee, for yesterday morning, as I was leaving the home of a Christian woman in New York, she handed me this twenty-dollar bill for thee, as she had been in thy home and knew thy need." Her reply was, "I knew the Lord would do his part, and now he has given me twentyfold."

While giving a few instances illustrating the faith of a few parents, there were a far greater number who manifested this life of quiet confidence in God in their homes, never murmuring or complaining as they saw their property destroyed by the ravages of war. They bore with sweet resignation the odium that was heaped upon them and their families by the enemies of their peace principles, and as I sat and talked with them and listened to their tales of true heroism, I was often impressed with their simple narratives. They never spoke of their acts in a way that would lead me to think they had done anything much, but simply had done their duty, which is a sign of true greatness.

Sham heroism is always watching to see if it is going to be praised for what it is doing. Self is to the forefront, always desirous of coming out on top in the eyes of its friends. Not so were these leading Friends of North Carolina. They were simply faithful unto their Master. They caught the spirit of endurance and of self-denying lives. They were ready to do their duty when the opportunity was offered. When the opportunity came for them to go to school they carried this spirit into the schoolroom. So when the association opened the schools in different neighborhoods, the children were ready to fill them up. There was no need of a truant officer in such neighborhoods. It has been my privilege to be connected with institutions of learning for more than fifty years, first at Farmers Institute, then in the association work in North Carolina, then at Providence, Rhode Island, and now for the last thirty years with Earlham College. I have no hesitation in saying that I have never seen scholars, old or young, who were more keen to learn or who made better progress in their studies than these in North Carolina. They caught the spirit of education and had a determination to make up for lost time.

Many of these were young men and young women who had missed four or five years that they should have had in school. Speaking one day to a little boy of about twelve and his sister, perhaps ten, who had to walk four miles to school through the woods, I asked them what time they left home in the morning. The reply was, "We do not know; we have no clock, but the stars were still shining when we started." The teacher said they were nearly always on time. Those children have grown up and are making their mark in the Church to-day. Many walked two and three miles. Is it to be wondered at that with such teachers and such earnest scholars, backed up by the parents who were encouraging the work, and with the united prayers of the Church, that the work of the Baltimore Association was a success? It could not have been otherwise.

CHAPTER 23
Final Work of the Baltimore Association

The Model Farm

Soon after the educational work was under way the association conceived the idea of trying to improve and develop the agricultural resources of the State. On this subject it made the following record: "The low and unremunerative state of agriculture in North Carolina exercises a very depressing influence upon every effort to ameliorate the physical and educational condition of her people. Every other interest, being essentially dependent upon this, languishes under the inadequate reward of the tiller of the soil. Under this influence the disposition to leave the State after the close of the war had scarcely any limit except the inability to do so. To educate and enlighten her people without at the same time demonstrating the possibility of greater returns for labor would still further tend to her depopulation. A work so general in its character could not fail to stimulate Friends to desire improved agriculture. There had been a continual pressure upon us to establish a model farm and to place among them a practical farmer who should, by improved farming implements, artificial manures, introduction of grasses, selected seed, and stock demonstrate to their eyes the great neglected wealth of the soil, awaiting only the call of improved cultivation; and who, by the establishment of agricultural clubs within the limits of each quarterly meeting, should stimulate a spirit of inquiry and enterprise which would be rewarded by the best practical results. We have accordingly purchased a farm formerly owned by that honored and devoted servant of Christ, the late Nathan Hunt, at Springfield, on the dividing line between Guilford and Randolph Counties."

This farm was bought in 1867, after much care and investigation, Francis T. King examining it two or three times himself, with several farmers from Maryland and Pennsylvania. It contained about two hundred acres and cost $4,400. The Friends at Springfield were so anxious to have it located there that they paid $700 towards it. There was a small stream of water running through this farm upon which they erected a bone mill, believed to be the first bone mill erected in the South. By this means they secured bone dust to use as fertilizer. They selected as the superintendent of the agricultural work William A. Sampson, of Maine, who took charge of the farm, erected a model dwelling upon it, and a barn built after the most approved plan.

Fourth month 12, 1869, F. T. King wrote to his friend Samuel Bewley, in Ireland, saying that "After three years' duration it has made wonderful progress, revolutionizing the whole neighborhood. I often rejoice in tears at this true manifestation of true Christian citizenship on the part of men who were despised for a century past and who suffered patiently for conscience's sake, now returning good for evil. There are now seventeen agricultural clubs with a membership of over fifteen-hundred. They meet monthly. We make this department nearly self-sustaining. It embraces a model farm, agricultural implements and seed department, four-hundred and fifty subscribers to agricultural papers, all under the care of our superintendent, who is a farmer and a lecturer. He has solved the grass question, for in 1867 he imported and sold at cost 500 pounds of clover seed; in 1868, 5,000 pounds, and in 1869, 19,880 pounds."

The superintendent, in his fourth annual report, in 1871, writes to the association: "From a careful estimate, I am satisfied that over 10,000 acres have been successfully sown with clover in consequence of the establishment of your farm. I have hulled and cleaned several lots of clover seed for various persons this fall and now have one which was brought ten or twelve miles to be cleaned. By the sale of improved implements, several reapers, mowers, wheelrakes, ploughs, both iron and cast steel, cultivators, clover seed gatherers, etc., have been supplied by me to the farmers, greatly to their satisfaction. There is music in the click of a mowing machine which to the ear of a progressive man is more potent than the words of an orator, and which is proved in every neighborhood where one is carried. It instantly suggests the propriety of removing all stumps, stones, sprouts; underdraining the wet places so the horses can travel better; better ploughing to insure a smooth surface; all these improvements speedily followed. Hardly a day passes without some stranger visiting the farm, and in spring time they come in great numbers, so that during the second and third months it takes nearly all my time to attend to them. During the last year it was estimated that something over one-thousand persons visited the farm. Of the improved stock we now have five head of thoroughbred Alderneys, the gift of Charles L. Sharpless, of Philadelphia; James Taylor and Joseph B. Cooper, of New Jersey, and James Carey and James W. Tyson, of Baltimore."

This farm was named by the association Swarthmore Farm, but it became known far and wide as the Model Farm. In 1872, Francis T. King writes: "The effect of our operation on the community has been gratifying and can be seen for fifty miles around. About 15,000 acres have been sown with clover, in the surrounding counties, since our operations commenced. Many improved implements have been introduced. Instead of the scythe and cradle are frequently seen the mower and the reaper. A large number of people from all parts of the State continue to visit the farm to see for themselves the new way, and they very generally express themselves as satisfied that it is an improvement on the old exhaustive system. The effect of our educational and agricultural efforts in staying the tide of emigration to the West is very apparent and has already saved to North Carolina hundreds of her best citizens."

Close of the Work of the Baltimore Association

When the time came that the association felt it had done its duty in the agricultural department, the farm was sold and the proceeds used to advance the educational interests of what is now known as Guilford College. At the same time they arranged to close their care of the educational work and to turn it over to the supervision of North Carolina Yearly Meeting. In my final report I find the following closing paragraph: "In bringing this, my last, report to a close, I desire to record my high appreciation of the services of our teachers. To their devoted and earnest labors in a great measure is due the success of this noble work, a work of seven years, which I believe will stand out prominently in the history of our society in the South. Permit me to suggest the propriety of publishing a brief history of it, which I believe would be deeply interesting and useful. In conclusion, it is with deep regret that I take leave of the work in the prosecution of which I have become so closely united with the dear teachers and Friends with whom I have labored. I desire also to express my gratitude to you for your confidence and support. I feel thankful that I have had even a small part in this good cause. May the Divine blessing continue to rest upon you and the State that has been the scene of this work is the prayer of your friend."

We find upon the records of the association this closing minute: "At a called meeting of the Baltimore Association of Friends to Advise and Assist Friends of the Southern States, held at Friends Meeting House, corner of Eutaw and Monument Streets, Baltimore, Second month 12, 1891, present Francis T. King, Secretary John C. Thomas, Treasurer Jesse Tyson, and thirteen members, it was resolved that as the objects of the association have been accomplished and no further reason exists for its continuance, the said association is hereby dissolved. The books and papers of the association are to be placed with the records of Baltimore Yearly Meeting of Friends. The secretary was directed to send a copy of these minutes to the Provident Life and Trust Company of Philadelphia. Then adjourned. John C. Thomas, Secretary."

The question has often been asked, how much money did the association expend in its work and where did it come from? It has been hard to find a definite answer to this question, but after considerable research I believe the following figures approximately yield the facts in the case:

> For physical relief, including cost of the
> Model Farm $36,000.00
> Friends schools $72,000.00
> Guilford College $23,000.00
> Building and repairing meeting-house ... $7,300.00
> A total of $138,300.00

As nearly as I can ascertain, this amount was divided among the members of the different yearly meetings as follows:

> London Yearly Meeting $38,750.00
> Dublin $16,250.00
> New England $9,000.00
> New York $10,200.00
> Philadelphia $30,150.00
> Baltimore $14,700.00
> Ohio $1,600.00
> Indiana $9,750.00
> Iowa $2,400.00
> Western $5,500.00
> Total .... $138,300.00[103]

---

[103] It is very difficult to estimate the present-day financial value of the contribution of Friends in the 1870s. There was much less cash in the U.S. economy in the 1800s. Wages for teachers were much lower then, and many of the teachers

Superintendent of Education for North Carolina Yearly Meeting

Now, as the Baltimore Association had turned over the educational work to the yearly meeting, it was necessary that some one should have the superintendence of the work. The yearly meeting requested that I should hold that position for one year longer, so I continued to look after the work. It gave me an opportunity to visit all the meetings and schools, both the day schools and the First-day schools, as there was a school in each meeting in the yearly meeting, and all the Friends children were in these schools. Each monthly meeting appointed a committee to have the care of the schools within its limits.

This to me was a pleasant service, laying down the burdens on the shoulders of those prepared to receive them, feeling that the work would be continued until the public school system would be fully organized and take the education of the children throughout the State under its care. Our schools did much to stimulate the State in building up its first public school system, and our normal schools laid the foundation for the splendid normal school they now have.

In the midst of our work the Superintendent of Education of the State died, and the governor, who had to appoint some one to fill out the term of his office, sent for me, but I told him plainly that I could do the State more good to keep out of politics in those reconstruction days. I now feel that it was a wise conclusion. It was at a time when carpet-bag politics were at their height, and it would have thrown a suspicion over my work had I taken a public office. As it was, I was doing this farewell work with the satisfaction that what had been done was from a sense of duty, with only one thing in view—the good of the cause.

---

worked for the Baltimore Association on a subsistence or near-voluntary basis, so that the contributions of Friends probably went much farther than they would today. The lowest estimate, using the Consumer Price Index, is approximately $2.4 million. A more complicated estimate, comparing the average output per person correlated with income over time, shows that the contribution of Friends would be worth about thirty million in today's dollars. Whatever method is used, Quakers from the U.K. and the North gave generously and sacrificially for the work of the Baltimore Association.

CHAPTER 24

Preparations for a Visit to Great Britain

During the summer of 1874, having held the Bible conference and closed the normal school, my wife and I took our family and went West to our old home for a visit to our parents and many relatives. It was a pleasant visit. I had a minute to attend Western and Indiana yearly meetings. It was on this visit that I attended the second general meeting held by Indiana Yearly Meeting at Back Creek, in the limits of northern quarter. It proved a blessing to many and opened the door to continue the work along that line.

For a number of years the feeling had rested with me that at some future time it would be right for me to visit, in the love of the Gospel, Friends across the ocean. One day, while sitting in Indiana Yearly Meeting, I believed it was right to ask the privilege of paying a visit to the women's meeting, which was freely granted. When I returned and took my seat it came upon me with an overwhelming force that the time had now come for me to make preparations for that religious service on the other side of the ocean.

The next thirty minutes was a time of great spiritual conflict. My infirmities, leaving my family in North Carolina, away from all relatives, going among those whom I had never seen, and many other things came before me, but in thirty minutes the matter was settled;

the conflict was over; I had said "yes." Immediately there was a calm, and I began to plan how to make the arrangements. At the close of the session I told my father that I wished to walk with him to town, and told him what I had decided to do. We walked in silence until we reached the post-office, when he said: "I do not feel like discouraging thee. On the other hand, if I had known it in time, I do not know but what I would have gotten ready and gone with thee."

That night I wrote and mailed a letter to our monthly meeting at Springfield, North Carolina, requesting a minute liberating me to visit London and Dublin yearly meetings and the yearly meetings in Norway, and the meetings and Friends belonging to them as the way might open, and to such other service as might appear right. When we returned to North Carolina, I found that the monthly meeting had endorsed my concern, and the following week the quarterly meeting did the same. A few days later I laid the matter before the select yearly meeting, and then, in accordance with the discipline at that time, I brought it before a joint session of the yearly meeting at large, which proved to be a time of great spiritual blessing, and I wish to mention one thing especially which was a great comfort to me: A large number of the young people with much feeling expressed their unity and sympathy with me and my concern.

This was in the Eleventh month. The next few weeks were devoted to completing my arrangements. My passage was engaged on the steamer *Ohio*, that sailed from Philadelphia the first of Third month, 1875. My dear friends, Francis T. King, of Baltimore, and James M. Whitall, of Philadelphia, were particularly helpful in making the necessary arrangements.

Many expressions of sympathy and love were given by our dear friends both to me and to my dear wife, but perhaps none of them made a more lasting impression on my mind than that of a dear old colored woman who went by the name of Aunt Jenny. No one knew how old she was. She could not read or write, and had been a slave, but all who knew her had confidence in her Christianity. Her old master, when he came to die, turned from the minister and said: "I want Aunt Jenny to come and pray for me." She lived in a little cabin by the roadside, and had a little garden back of it which she tended, and what she raised on that patch and the provisions given to her by her friends kept her.

The white young people were very fond of her and loved to hear her talk, especially of her religious experience. They would go in to take something for her and then listen while she told of her experience. All who knew her believed that she "walked with God." I was to start on my journey one night. That afternoon my wife and I went to call upon some of our friends, as I wished to bid them farewell before leaving. As we passed along by Aunt Jenny's cabin, my wife suggested that I go in and bid her farewell. Feeling tired, and perhaps a little depressed, I was inclined to omit it, but my wife stopped the horse, got out of the buggy, and went in and told her that I was going away across the ocean to preach the Gospel, and asked her to come out and bid me good-bye.

She came out in her cheerful way, and coming up to me, said, "Well, honey, is you going away to preach the Gospel across the ocean?" And then: "I don't know where that is, but I expect it's a long ways off. Well, honey, tell the sinners if they don't repent they'll be lost. Tell the Christians to hold on and they'll get to heaven." When I took hold of her hand to bid her farewell, she saw that my wife was affected by the prospect of our separation, and she put her arms around her, saying, "Don't cry, honey, the Lord will take care of you and the children. You will all be well while he is gone, and the Lord will bring him home safely and you will live together many years."

> "Well, honey, is you going away to preach the Gospel across the ocean?"

Then, putting her other arm around me, she said: "But, honey, I won't be here when you come back. The Lord will send for me before then." After I had been gone about three months I received a letter from my wife saying that Aunt Jenny had died. Some of our young friends had gone in one morning to take her something to eat. She was very busy cleaning up the cabin, and was very glad to see them, and entertained them with her pleasant conversation. Finally one of them suggested that the time had come when they must go. She said: "No, honeys; I am not ready for you to go yet. Wait a little while." They sat quiet for a few minutes, wondering what she wanted, when she looked up and said: "I hear the chariot wheels coming. The Lord has sent after me." She went and lay down on her bed, and in five minutes she "was not, for God had taken her."[104]

---

[104] See Ezekiel, chapters 1-3; also the story of Enoch, Genesis 5:24.

CHAPTER 25

Among Friends in Ireland

Having completed my arrangements, I left home on Third month 1, 1875, for Philadelphia, and stopped with James M. Whitall until Third month 4, when I went on board the steamship *Ohio*, of the American Line, at 8:00 A.M., bound for Liverpool. We had a pleasant sail down the Delaware, and at 3:00 P.M. our pilot left us and we continued our long journey across the ocean. It was new to me, and I was soon seasick and suffered much for seventy-two hours, after which I began to eat a little and was soon well and enjoyed the remainder of the voyage, which was rather rough and stormy.

However, we reached Queenstown[105] on the morning of the thirteenth. Standing on the deck of the tender as we approached the wharf, I saw an old Friend with his broad-brimmed hat. I turned to a fellow-passenger and remarked, "There is the man I am going home with." As I stepped on the dock, he reached out his hand and said, "Welcome, Allen Jay, to Ireland." This Friend was Benjamin Haughton, the father of the present Benjamin Haughton, with whom my wife and I made our home during our last visit to Ireland eight years ago. We had never met before. He turned to the officer and said, "I'll stand good that there is nothing that requires duty in this baggage." The officer put his mark upon it, and in a few minutes we were on our way to Cork, some twelve or fourteen miles distant.

---

[105] Now Cobh/Cork, Republic of Ireland.

Upon reaching his home, he took me to my room and said, "This is thy home while in Cork," adding, "Dinner will be ready in thirty minutes," and left me. As the door closed, dropping into a chair, a real homesickness came over me. Here I was in Ireland, and had never met anyone on this side except William Green, who lived in the north of Ireland and whom I had seen while in attendance at Western Yearly Meeting several years before.

But there was no time to dwell on discouragement. Dinner would be ready soon. Making such preparations as I could, I went down to the dining-room, where I met several Cork Friends who had come in to bid me welcome. Among the number was the late George Grubb, who afterwards attended the Richmond Conference in 1887, when I had the pleasure of welcoming him to our home. He had good conversational powers and, to a large degree, the gift almost universal among Irish Friends to make visitors feel at home. This is a quality that should be cultivated in every family. Those who have never traveled among strangers do not realize the help it is to get into a home and feel that you are welcome. It will be a beautiful recollection in my life as I look back to my first landing in Ireland an entire stranger. The cordial greeting that followed caused me to feel that I was welcome and did much to strengthen me for the work I had in view.

The next morning Lydia Pike, wife of Ebenezer Pike, who had sent me a note of welcome which was handed me before I left the ship, sent her carriage after me to take me out to lunch at their beautiful home. It was an introduction to a wealthy home which was pervaded with a Christian spirit. They had several lovely sons and daughters. The father and sons were not at home, but the two hours spent with the mother and her daughters among the flowers and on the garden walks was cheering. The two younger daughters each had a large St. Bernard dog that walked with them to the dining-room and were fed while we partook of our lunch. I found myself busy answering all the questions that were put to me about the United States and the Friends in our land. Lunch over, I returned to the city and took the afternoon train to Dublin, spending the night there, and next morning went to Ulster Quarterly Meeting, which was held at Lisburn.

I was met at the station by a Friend and hurried at once to the meeting-house, where I gave my simple message, this being the first time I had undertaken to preach in Ireland. After several others had spoken came a recess of thirty minutes for lunch, after which the meeting sat down again and transacted the business. I was taken home by Joseph Richardson and family, where I found a lovely home and a nice resting-place during my stay in that part of Ireland. My wife and I visited the same home eight years ago, but it was different then. The parents had grown old, and the large family of children had nearly all gone to homes of their own.

Having visited the principal meetings in the north of Ireland, I returned to the south and visited most of the important meetings in Munster Quarterly Meeting, such as Cork, Waterford, and others. I then went to Mountmellick to attend Leinster Quarterly Meeting and some of the meetings composing it before the yearly meeting. When the yearly meeting came on in Dublin it was my privilege to be assigned to the home of our dear friend, Adam Woods, at Dundrum, in the suburbs of Dublin. It was a quiet resting-place, a real home, one that I greatly appreciated. It was a pleasure to keep up a correspondence with the members of the family long afterwards. The dear parents have long since passed beyond, but the memory of those days lives bright in my recollection. Perhaps the different members of the household never knew the strength and comfort they were to a weary laborer during the strenuous work of Dublin Yearly Meeting in 1875.

> While they spoke their minds freely, yet through it all ran the spirit of brotherly love and Christian kindness.

The business was interesting and enjoyed. The contrast was great between their manner of doing business and that of some of our large American yearly meetings, especially those in the West, but it was refreshing to listen to their frank, cheerful, and outspoken discussions. While they spoke their minds freely, yet through it all ran the spirit of brotherly love and Christian kindness. The business was transacted in harmony.

While sitting in the meeting one day I was impressed with the belief that it would be right for me to appoint a meeting for the young people. I rose at a suitable time and informed the meeting of my concern. It was soon evident that it was something unusual and that there was a little fear that there might be some young Americanism in it. But after a time of silence, dear Samuel Bewley rose and said that while it was something out of the usual line, yet he did not feel like discouraging it, and he proposed that a judicious committee be appointed to take it into consideration and report to a future sitting. It was united with, and a committee appointed which reported to the next meeting in favor of the proposition. When the question of time was brought up, several wished it postponed so that they could send home for their children. The evening of the next day was selected.

It was evident that there was much interest in the subject, and on the part of some of the older Friends a little uneasiness. As for myself, there was earnest prayer that I might simply do the will of my Heavenly Father. When the hour came, the meeting-room was packed with a company of noble young people. But few old people were present. When I arrived, Samuel Bewley was at the door waiting for me. Taking me by the arm, he led me up to the front of the meeting and sat down by me. A solemn feeling settled down over the company, and a living silence held all under its precious influence. After a time I rose and spoke some thirty minutes, then, after a pause, knelt in vocal prayer. After closing, all was still except the sounds of weeping. Soon a young person spoke, and then another, until it was said that some thirty or forty who had never spoken before had given vocal expression either in testimony or prayer.

The feeling became so deep and general that I became fearful lest it might prove hurtful to the cause among the conservative members, so I made a motion to close the service, when Samuel Bewley rose and in a tender voice said, "This is marvelous in my eyes," and added that he hoped all would be faithful. His words opened the way for others to come out and place themselves on the Lord's side. This meeting closed about ten.

The effect was to be seen and felt the next day in the meeting. Many came to me with words of appreciation for the blessing that had resulted to them or their families. Two days later several of the young people came and wanted me to appoint another meeting. I felt it would be best to encourage them to send up a request to the meeting themselves, which they did. When some one in the meeting asked if I had felt any concern, my reply was, "If the meeting is held, I hope to be there."

It was held the following night, and there was a greater number present than before, many of them being from among the dear old people. It proved to be a wonderful meeting, for the Lord was manifest. Before I had said a word, a number of the young people spoke. It was easy to deliver the message, and when I was through the testimonies and prayers continued until I had to close the meeting in order to catch the last train for Dundrum. My heart was brought near to the dear young Friends of Dublin Yearly Meeting, and I left them with the prayer that the good work might go on and that many of them might be used of the Lord in building up His kingdom.

Eight years ago, when visiting all the meetings of Ireland, I met some who are now active in church work who look back to those meetings as a starting point in their Christian life. My interest in the young people preceded me to England and resulted in my receiving invitations to hold young people's meetings in the limits of London Yearly Meeting, and in my being invited to tea-meetings and young people's associations wherever I went.

It was during the yearly meeting following this, in London, that I took an active part in founding and organizing the Young Friends Christian Fellowship Union, which has continued until the present time, and when in London eight years ago I was invited to address the annual meeting held during the yearly meeting. This organization was brought to this country and adopted in several yearly meetings, but has now mostly given place to the Christian Endeavor organization in most of our American yearly meetings.

CHAPTER 26

At London Yearly Meeting

At the close of the yearly meeting I remained in Ireland until the Second-day following, being at Monktown on First-day morning, and at a meeting near Dundrum in the evening. I had now attended all the larger meetings in the yearly meeting, and the Brookfield School for boys and girls, and the Lisburn School, also for boys and girls, in the north of Ireland. I had also been at Mountmellick Boarding-school for Girls, and Newtown Boarding-school for Boys, at Waterford, and I will add that I specially enjoyed visiting those schools.

So on Second-day morning I took the train to the boat, crossed over to Holyhead, and went by the first train to London, where I arrived in the evening and was met at the station by my dear friend, Joseph Bevan Braithwaite,[106] who took me to his home at 312 Camden Road, N., where I found a warm welcome, and not only then but several times since, until I have felt almost like calling it my London home. Many of our American Friends who have visited London at various times during the last thirty or forty years can bear testimony to the same experience. The father and mother, with their nine children, all of whom were at home, soon made me feel that I was one of the circle.

---

[106] Joseph Bevan Braithwaite, Sr. (1818-1905), was the editor of the memoirs of Joseph John Gurney, and also the primary author of the Richmond Declaration of Faith.

I enjoyed the social and religious atmosphere of the home life very much. Joseph Bevan Braithwaite was a remarkable man, a great student, having an extensive library, and his mind stored with a fund of useful knowledge upon all subjects, so that his conversation was always elevating and instructive. Sitting down on a First-day afternoon while there to read the Bible for an hour, which was customary when there was nothing to hinder, I heard it read in six or seven different languages, no one reading in English but myself.

He had visited America in 1865, just after the close of the war, having for his companion Joseph Crosfield. They were in North Carolina, and gave some aid and advice to Friends, F.T. King consulting especially with Joseph Crosfield about how he found things down there. J.B. Braithwaite visited the United States and Canada several times so that he became well posted about the condition and welfare of our Church in this country, and did much valuable labor in several of the yearly meetings on this continent. I shall have occasion to allude more fully to his work in connection with the Richmond Conference of 1887, as a delegate from London Yearly Meeting, which I will speak of when I come to tell of the organization of the Five Years Conference which resulted in the establishment of the Five Years Meeting.

The next morning after my arrival was the Meeting of Ministry and Oversight, held at Devonshire House. It was a large and solid body. It was a good time for me to sit and learn. My earnest prayer was that I might be kept in my proper place throughout the various sessions of the yearly meeting. I had often looked forward to being in this yearly meeting, and now I was there in the midst of those whom I had heard about but never seen.

This was historic ground, and there were men around me who had helped to make history in our Church; such men as Isaac Brown, Isaac Sharp, Joseph Storrs Fry, Edward Backhouse, Charles Tyler, Charles Brady, Thomas Harvey, Caleb Kemp, Henry Wilson, John Bright, Arthur Pease, Stafford Allen, Arthur Albright, and George Gillett, and among the women, Hanna Stafford Allen, Christine Alsop, Sarah S. B. Clark, Martha Braithwaite, and many others whose names are familiar to those who attended London Yearly Meeting. It was said at that time that there were some eighteen members of the Society of Friends who were members of Parliament. I do not know whether this was strictly true or not.

The first thing that impressed me upon sitting down in the yearly meeting was the deep solemnity that settled over the congregation. One felt that each was engaged in prayer, trying to get in touch with God for himself. The silence was real. God was with His people, and they were learning from Him first-hand. How different from some other yearly meetings where it appears to some that nothing is going on unless some vocal expression is heard!

I do not wonder that Charles Spurgeon, who had attended all the sessions of a previous yearly meeting, said at the close, as nearly as I can remember, something like this: "London Yearly Meeting is the greatest deliberative body I have ever sat in, and no other religious body could conduct its deliberations in the harmony and unity it does and arrive at satisfactory conclusions without a moderator or presiding officer. To me it appeared to be a practical recognition of the headship of Christ."

Under this feeling it was no light thing to break the silence in their meeting for worship, and when anyone did it was felt that he had something to say, something that was in harmony with the spirit of the meeting, and if others followed, they continued in the same line, and the result was to carry the congregation in the direction of a real spiritual blessing. There was a freedom from overwrought human excitement, no endeavor to build on the emotions such as is often seen in those who are anxious to make a demonstration in the audience, the object being to carry the mind and heart in unison, so when the decision in the soul was reached it might be real and lasting.

In the business portions of the yearly meeting my mind was impressed with the freedom given in discussion. While in our American yearly meetings one or two will give their opinions rather freely, and

> One felt that each was engaged in prayer, trying to get in touch with God for himself. The silence was real. God was with His people, and they were learning from Him first-hand.

the great body of the meeting will be satisfied with simply saying, "I unite with that," or "I do not unite with it," here each one took time to explain his views, and sometimes at considerable length.

Another feature of the discussion which rather shocked me at first was the perfect freedom with which they gave their views without regard to the views of others. Sometimes it would appear as though there was some warmth of feeling towards those who differed from them, but when an individual had said what he had to say, he was done, and as a rule did not speak again without the consent of the clerk. Another thing I noticed was that the speakers were expected to speak on the subject or be reminded as to what the matter was before the meeting, and when the clerks at the table had consulted and the clerk had prepared his minute, it was very rare that anything was said.

One of the beautiful things about the whole matter was that when the session closed and they went out and met socially, there was rarely any talking it over again. They acted as though the subject was entirely closed. No one appeared to think that if he did not get his way everything was going wrong.

But perhaps the thing that impressed me more at that time than anything else was the position that the women's meeting occupied in the yearly meeting. The men's meeting was London Yearly Meeting. The women's meeting held a subordinate place. Their business was confined to matters pertaining to women's affairs in a great measure. Belonging to a yearly meeting where women were on an equality with men, and where any disciplinary matter was not legal unless it had the approval of the women's meeting, it was rather hard for me to be reconciled to the position that the women occupied. On attending the yearly meeting a few years ago I found a great change in this respect. Nearly all their sessions were held jointly with the women, and they were taking part in all the affairs of the Church similarly to our American women.[107]

---

[107] This is an interesting comment, since Friends in Great Britain had been holding separate business meetings for women for at least 200 years at this point. On the other hand, public agitation for women's rights in the U.S. began at the Seneca

It was during this yearly meeting, as I have mentioned in the preceding chapter, that in one of the rooms of Devonshire House I met with the young people, and the Young Friends Christian Fellowship Union was formed. The reports of the same continue to come to me, which I much enjoy. It was the beginning also of my becoming interested in the adult school work through meeting with their workers and hearing them talk over their methods of proceeding in various portions of the yearly meeting. It was a very instructive lesson to visit the work at Bedford Institute and the adult school work at Bunhill Field, where George Fox and many of our early Friends were buried.[108]

Joseph Bevan Braithwaite, Jr., was especially interested in the Bunhill Field work. It was helpful to visit several of these mission stations and mingle socially with them at their tea-meetings and other public gatherings. The adult school work is a great work, and has grown wonderfully. It was started some fifty years ago by Joseph Sturge, and has proven a blessing to those who have come under its influence, and also to those who have given of their time and means in carrying it forward. Through its workers, also, it has had a reflex influence for good on the Church at large.

Falls convention in 1848. Although Allen Jay does not seem to have been involved, the women's rights movement included many Quakers, and he would certainly have known about it. Full voting rights for women in Great Britain were not achieved until 1928, eight years after women in the United States.

[108] Bunhill Field was a large graveyard in Islington, which was used from the 1660s for nonconformist burials. It holds the remains of such famous people as John Bunyan, Isaac Watts, William Blake, Daniel Defoe, and Susanna Wesley. The Quaker Burying Ground is adjacent to it. The Bedford Institute, located at Bunhill Fields, was founded by Friends in 1867 to relieve poverty in the East End of London. The work there included Sunday Schools and literacy classes for both children and adults; worship services and temperance meetings; penny savings banks; a lending library; and direct assistance to the poor and ill. The work is still going on, under the name of Quaker Social Action.

CHAPTER 27

Acquaintance with John Bright

One of the richest blessings that came to me from attending London Yearly Meeting at that time was my meeting and acquaintance with John Bright,[109] and the following sketch of this acquaintance with him I take from two letters written to my wife, one while in the home at "One Ash" and the other three days later while in Manchester. Our conversation was in the nature of a friendly talk between two intimate friends rather than two strangers. I may have said something of my life and experience that I have seldom said to others. We used the old Friends' style of language, which John Bright said he was not in the habit of using with strangers.

Before leaving home I had said to my wife that I hoped John Bright would attend London Yearly Meeting, as I wished to see him. His name then was dear to those who had believed in the preservation of our Union, because he had stood by the Government during the Rebellion. He had lifted his voice in our favor in the dark days of the war at a time when Lincoln feared that the British Government

---

[109] John Bright (1811-1889), British Radical and Liberal statesman. His father, Jacob Bright, built a cotton mill at Rochdale outside Manchester, where John Bright was born. He was elected to Parliament in 1841, and immediately became known as an opponent of the Corn Laws, a series of import taxes designed to maintain the high price of British-produced grain. The Corn Laws were supported by large landowners. They were opposed by the rising class of manufacturers, by supporters of free trade, and by advocates for the poor, since the high cost of grain made bread much more expensive.

would throw its influence in favor of recognizing slavery and dividing our nation.

On the morning of the first session of the business meeting, upon taking my seat by the side of Isaac Sharp, I saw John Bright in the meeting. It was unnecessary for anyone to point him out. His features were familiar, for I had seen them often in our public newspapers. The next thought was that I hoped to hear him speak on business and that in some way I might be permitted to shake hands with him, but I secretly resolved that I would not act foolishly nor put myself forward improperly in order to do so.

Yet I soon had an opportunity to do both and much more than I had dared to hope. The next day a matter came before the meeting in which he differed from some of the speakers, especially Arthur Albright, who was at one time, I believe, also a member of Parliament. He replied in a clear and forceful way. There was no misunderstanding what he meant. Early in the yearly meeting a devotional meeting was held in both rooms. It was my desire to go into the smaller room, which was the women's, for I felt it would be a smaller congregation. While speaking I saw John Bright looking at me. After the meeting, as I walked down the aisle, he stepped out in front of me and offering me his hand said, "Welcome, Allen Jay, to England. I am glad I heard thee to-day." Taking me by the arm he said, "Come and go with me to lunch."

As we were eating he asked a number of questions and kept up the conversation. When the time came to go into the afternoon session, he said on parting, "When thee comes to Rochdale, 'One Ash' will be thy home." The prospect was pleasant to me, yet I could not but feel that amid his many public and private duties he would not think of it again. In this I was agreeably mistaken. During the summer, while attending the general meeting at Ackworth, his daughter reminded me that their home was to be mine when I visited their meeting.

When the word was sent, some time in Eighth month, that I would be there on a Fifth-day, John Bright answered, "I will meet Allen Jay." On reaching the station the door was opened and I stepped out with a small bag in each hand. John Bright was there and took one. As we walked along through the station I heard one man say to another, "I wonder who John Bright has now." The other replied, "An American. Look at his boots."

When meeting time came we walked together to the meetinghouse while the rest of the family rode in the carriage. When we arrived he took me to my seat and then went to his own. At the close of meeting his wife came to me and said, "As thee is tired, remain with us until Seventh-day evening and then on to Manchester that evening so as to be there ready for First-day morning." The plan was very agreeable to me, as I had only taken one day's rest since landing in Ireland the first of Third month.

After dinner was over John Bright took me into the library and after we had sat down he pointed to a picture of Richard Cobden hanging on the wall and said, "There is a picture of one of the best men I ever knew." He then commenced and gave a short history of the Corn Laws, telling how Richard Cobden, just after his first wife had died and while he was sad and lonely, came to him and said, "There are many homes in England that are sad to-day because of the Corn Laws, and I have come to ask you to join with me and let us consecrate ourselves to the work of removing these laws, thereby bringing gladness to many a poor home in England."

I have often wondered why John Bright should have done as he did that afternoon with an obscure American who had no claim upon his time. For about two hours he continued to give a hasty review of his life from childhood, told of his experiences in early life, of his entering into the life of a statesman, his Corn Laws experiences, his position and experiences in regard to the Crimean war, also of the battles he fought in our behalf in connection with the Rebellion in the United States. He told me how President Lincoln sent Henry Ward Beecher[110] over there to help turn the tide of public opinion

---

[110] Henry Ward Beecher (1813-1887), Congregationalist minister, Abolitionist, and social reformer.

away from the South and towards the North. He described a wonderful meeting that was held in a great hall in London, in which Henry Ward Beecher proved himself the master of the situation when, after an hour's interruption from those who opposed him, he rose above it all and carried the audience with him. John Bright added, "I regard him as the greatest platform orator I have ever heard."

As we sat there his mail was brought in. He laid it aside with the exception of one letter, saying, "I will read this one, from my dear friend John G. Whittier." He began and read it aloud. It was a strong letter of friendship and love in reply to one that he had written him. It was a treat to hear how these two men appreciated each other. But the point that claimed my attention was the closing sentence, in which Whittier said something like this: "John Bright, why don't thee come to America? If thee will, we will give thee the greatest ovation that any Englishman ever had." When he read that he turned to me and said, "That is just the reason I don't go. I would rather go to America than any other place I know of, and a few years ago I told some of my friends that I had decided to make a visit to the United States. The newspapers reported this and in a few days I got cablegrams from the leading hotels in New York, Philadelphia, Boston, Chicago, and Washington, each telling me that I could have all the room I wanted when I reached their city. Then a cablegram came from the Pullman Car Company telling me there would be a train waiting for me with parlor and dining cars, to take me wherever I wanted to go, free of charge. Then came a message from the President of the United States, saying I must be the nation's guest and make my home at the Capitol. I saw at once that they were going to make a hero of me and that they would kill me, so I had to give it up." I endeavored to show him why our Government and the Northern people generally appreciated him so highly. His simple reply was, "I only did my duty, and our people now begin to see that I was right."

Among the experiences of which he told, connected with his public life, were one or two in connection with the Queen. When appointed to a position in the Queen's Cabinet he had this experience:

It was customary for those appointed to go in before the Queen and kneel down to receive their commission, afterwards kissing her hand. The day before he was to go in for this purpose he received a note in her own handwriting saying, "The members of your Church do not believe in bowing the knee to any one but God. Therefore you may come in to-morrow and receive yours in a way consistent with your profession."

In this way the afternoon was spent, he giving reminiscences of his political life and I sitting listening, completely enrapt as he told of various incidents in his experiences and incidentally brought out the religious side of his character. He said that he believed that he was called to his work as a statesman as distinctly as I had been called to the work of the ministry, and added that he believed it would be good for the United States if more Christian men would give themselves to a political life in our country, for he thought that the Lord had led him in the course that he had pursued.

It was a rare occasion for me. He told of some incidents in the life of Gladstone and of their work together. He also alluded to others of the leading men in England and gave his opinion of them, but what he had to say of our own statesmen was far more interesting to me. He spoke of President Lincoln, Secretary Seward, Charles Sumner, and others of our statesmen with a freedom and frankness that caused me to appreciate my own countrymen. He was especially full of praise for our martyred President and for the great work which he did.

He was a warm friend of our Government. He spoke of its faults and weaknesses, yet he believed that it would become a great nation, one of the great powers of the world, though he felt that we would not reach the climax of our greatness for many years to come. He felt that Friends in our country should study our government more and take a greater interest in the political work of the nation. In one of the last letters I had from him, while I was superintendent of Earlham College, he expressed a desire that our young men should prepare themselves for important positions in the government service and cultivate a love of country, thereby purifying the political life of the nation.

The next day we went out to take a ride over the old road leading out among the hills. We came to where the road wound round a hill in order to reach the top. He asked the driver to stop, and getting out of the carriage he suggested that we walk directly up the hill and see which of us would first reach the top. We started. My plan was to walk by his side until near the end and then forge ahead. When I began to go ahead of him he laughingly sat down and said, "I give it up." With a laugh I said, "John Bright, it is not the first time that John Bull has had to give up to young America." It is a picture in my mind yet how he looked as he shook his finger at me and with a forced expression of seriousness replied, "Naughty! it was bad enough to whip us without laughing about it."[111]

On reaching the top of the hill he pointed out a spot where George Fox had preached and added, "George Fox was the greatest reformer that this world has known since the days of the apostles. He saw more clearly than any other reformer what the spirit of the gospel would do and the changes it would produce in the world when it shaped the lives of men. He spoke of oaths, war, slavery, religious liberty and of the position it would give women in the church and in the ministry, and of other great reforms such as temperance and freedom of the gospel. In its beginning the Quaker Church was the greatest missionary society that has ever been since the days of the early church. He saw all these things and to-day the world is beginning to catch glimpses of what he saw clearly."

> "George Fox was the greatest reformer that this world has known since the days of the apostles."

In was a spiritual uplift to listen to John Bright reading the Bible at the morning devotions. There was a tenderness that came into his voice as he read some of the psalms that was genuine. At the close of one of these services, during which I had engaged in vocal supplication, he spoke and said, "Some say that there is no God, but we know

---

[111] Allen Jay would have been forty-four years old at the time of this story, while John Bright would have been sixty-four.

there is and it is sweet to know that He is with us and strengthens us for His service. He does not leave us alone."

Speaking at one time of his public service he said, "If I have achieved any success as a public speaker, I owe it more to the Bible and to Milton's *Paradise Lost* than to any other books." He remarked that all true poetry is more or less inspired. Milton's *Paradise Lost* was his favorite outside the Bible. I have heard others say that he could repeat a large portion of it from memory.

In parting from me at the close of the quarterly meeting at Liverpool, just before I sailed for home, he said, "Some of us have loved thee because thee has been thyself and not tried to imitate others, but has gone ahead and delivered the message as thee has seen it." These were the last words I ever heard him speak. When I was in London in 1885 he was sick but sent word for me to come and see him. I had made other engagements and did not go. Often since I have regretted that I had not let those other things go and had gone to see him.

While he lived we occasionally corresponded. He was a wonderful man and I have always felt that it was a great privilege to have known him. He was modest, retiring in his disposition, shrinking from publicity. Once while I was walking with him he overheard some one say, "There goes the Honorable John Bright." He turned to me and said, "That is what I have to suffer on account of my position. If I could only go along as a private citizen, how much more pleasant it would be!"

While in England eight years ago with my wife, we sent an appointment to attend Rochdale meeting on a certain evening. John Bright's son, who lived in the old home, was absent with his family, if I remember rightly, in France. When he learned of our appointment, however, with a feeling that I greatly appreciated, he wrote me saying that he was sorry they were away and that the servants had the house very much torn up cleaning and repairing, but remembering his father's feeling of friendship for me, he wanted us to go to the home, get our supper and rest a little before meeting. He said he would order his carriage to meet us at the station on our arrival and drive directly to "One Ash." He hoped we would feel at home and enjoy ourselves.

When we reached the house and had prepared ourselves for a meal, I went into the library and sat down in the chair that I thought he sat in twenty-five years before, and gave myself up to meditation until called to supper. It was the same library and some of the same pictures on the walls. The afternoon's conversation twenty-five years before came up vividly in my memory and I lived over again those hours which were among the richest in my life. When supper was ready I took my wife and led her out to the seat where his wife had sat. I took the chair that John Bright sat in and our young English Friend who was with us sat at the side between us. For me it was living over the past.

We went to the meeting a little early and visited his grave, then went into the meeting-house and sat down until the Friends had come in. When meeting had gathered I took my place and after a while stood up and delivered the message I felt called upon to deliver on that occasion. At the close we went to Manchester, where we were to be the next day. I wrote the son and expressed our appreciation for his thoughtfulness in opening the way for us to visit "One Ash."

CHAPTER 28

Some Prominent English Friends

Our friends, Deborah Thomas, of Baltimore, and Mary R. Haines, her companion from Philadelphia, were also in attendance at London Yearly Meeting in 1875. They boarded where I did, at Joseph Bevan Braithwaite's. They were at the yearly meeting the year before, and during the yearly meeting one day Deborah Thomas requested the privilege of visiting the men's meeting. In the course of her communication she spoke very directly to some one whom she believed was in that meeting and who had felt a call to extensive religious service. She believed the time had come when he should surrender himself to the service and make preparations to enter upon it, as there was not much time to spare if he finished the work.

Our dear friend, Stanley Pumphrey, was present on that occasion, and believed the message was meant for him, as he had long felt a call to visit the meetings of Friends in America. During the year he arranged his affairs and secured the endorsement of his monthly and quarterly meetings, and came to the yearly meeting prepared to lay the matter before the meeting of ministers and elders for their endorsement. On Fifth month 18, 1875, he was liberated by the yearly meeting to pay a religious visit to all the meetings of Friends in America. He expected that it would require four or five years to accomplish all that he had on his heart.

There was much unanimity in the meeting with his prospect, and he was encouraged to be faithful. He was about to engage in a work that was greatly blessed to the various American yearly meetings and that brought him into close touch and sympathy with Friends and their needs in this land. Perhaps when he closed his labors in our country no English Friend of that day was as fully posted on our conditions as he was. I will not speak more of Stanley Pumphrey now, as I shall have occasion to dwell more fully upon his labors in America later.

The same day the meeting liberated Isaac Sharp, Robert Doeg, and myself to attend the yearly meeting in Norway, beginning on the 14th of Sixth month. We were also liberated to perform any other service we thought best in Norway, Denmark, or Germany.

Caroline E. Talbot, of Ohio Yearly Meeting, and her husband were also at the same yearly meeting. She found an open door for service among Friends. We traveled and labored together considerably during the summer in different parts of England.

Isaac Brown was a dear Friend whom I had met in Ireland during Dublin Yearly Meeting, who manifested a great deal of kindness, and opened the way for my service in the yearly meeting. Afterwards at his own home in Kendal he and his wife opened their house, which was called "Brantholme," and I stopped with them several days. It was of great benefit to me in my future work to become acquainted with this dear Friend. We kept up a correspondence until near the close of his life, and his many letters were very instructive, especially in my religious work.

He was a man of deep spiritual experience. He had been a teacher for fifty years, and told me that he had never been late to classes during that time. He was for many years head of the Flounders Institute, which was established near Ackworth, and where many went to complete their higher education and to prepare themselves for teachers and for other useful occupations. He had a large library, and had given much attention to biblical study and research, and had spent much time in writing commentaries on the Bible—withal a very modest and unassuming man. He deeply impressed me with his humility.

Especially was this manifest in his public ministry, there being nothing dogmatic or dictatorial in his communications.

I was sitting one day in his library reading when he came in and sat down. At once I felt it would be a good time for me to find out the meaning of a certain portion of Scripture that I had heard explained in different ways, so, turning to the passage, I said, "Isaac Brown, what is the meaning of this passage of Scripture?" With a smile he said: "If thou hadst asked me that question forty years ago, I would have given thee an answer in a minute, but after forty years' investigation I do not know what it means."

How different from many I have met, who cannot read it in more than one language, yet I have heard them explain it without any hesitation, asserting revelation, while others assuming the same high authority would give a different meaning to it, each declaring that he was right! It is altogether probable that Isaac Brown knew as much about the meaning of the Spirit as any of them. My observation is that it is not very safe to follow those who can explain everything and tell you just what you must believe and what you must not believe. It may be safer sometimes to listen to the man who is able to say: "I do not know."[112]

While with Isaac Brown, I spent a day in visiting one of the lakes in the Cumberland region, about ten miles away, and some of the old abbeys, attended their meeting of ministry and oversight and their monthly meeting. On Sixth-day I went to Swarthmore Hall and visited the meeting and the hall where George Fox lived after he married Judge Fell's widow,[113]

> It may be safer sometimes to listen to the man who is able to say: "I do not know."

---

[112] We have no idea what the debatable passage of Scripture was, but this observation is another classic quotation from Allen Jay. It ought to be engraved in stone and placed over the door of churches and seminaries everywhere.

[113] Margaret Fell (1614-1702) was in many ways the mother of the Quaker movement, who set up women's meetings all over England, nurtured Quaker prisoners and was herself imprisoned three times for her faith. Her first husband, Judge Thomas Fell, was sympathetic to the Quaker movement and gave protection to the early Friends in his home at Swarthmore Hall. She married George Fox in 1669, eleven years after Judge Fell's death in 1658.

and spent First-day at Kendal, attending their morning and evening meetings.

Others who were very kind to me were Isaac Sharp, the great missionary traveler, and Isaac Robinson, who had been in our home in North Carolina, both of whom did all they could to make my visit to London Yearly Meeting a time of blessing. I shall ever look back with great satisfaction upon the days that I spent at London Yearly Meeting in 1875. It was a "school of the prophets" to me, and while there were many things new and different to what we have in our country, yet I feel that in many respects we might learn useful lessons from them.

Being the only man minister present with a minute outside of their yearly meeting, I found ample time for all the service I felt called upon to perform. I became especially interested in the young people of that yearly meeting, and felt that there was an awakening among them which would result in their taking greater interest in the Church. Especially was this being shown in the adult school work, and the First-day school work, so that I left that yearly meeting with a feeling of encouragement in regard to the future.

English Friends give closer attention to the great moral questions connected with their government than we do, such as the temperance question, the educational question, looking after the poor, and making the laws. It was remarkable to me to find so many members of the Society of Friends in Parliament. While their numbers would not have entitled them to more than two or three, they had at that time eighteen members of Parliament, several of them ministers.

The yearly meeting having closed, I visited a few meetings on my way up to Hull, from which place we sailed for Norway.

CHAPTER 29

With Friends in Norway

After the close of London Yearly Meeting I attended several meetings around London on my way up to Hull, from which place Isaac Sharp, Robert Doeg, and I were engaged to sail across to Stavanger, Norway, on the 12th of Sixth month, 1875. Isaac Sharp had visited Norway several times, and Robert Doeg, who was to be my interpreter, had lived seven years in Norway, and was familiar with the language and the people. He was himself a minister of the Gospel, so that I regarded it as providential that these men had minutes for religious service in that country.

We went on board late at night, and went to bed. The vessel passed out of the harbor about midnight, and the next day the weather was fine. In crossing the North Sea it is not unusual for passengers to suffer from seasickness, but I did not find much inconvenience. The second day, Seventh-day, the fourteenth, we reached Stavanger. Six Friends in a little boat came along the ship's side, and as soon as the custom house officers were through with our baggage we were rowed ashore.

We were met at the wharf by a large number of Friends, who carried our baggage through the town to the meeting-house. This was a three-story building, the cellar floor being occupied by Endre Dahl for a store-room.[114] He was one of the leading men of the place,

---

[114] Endre Dahl (1816-1885), was one of the best-known Norwegian Friends of his generation.

had considerable influence with the government and helped Friends when they were persecuted for their religious principles. The second floor was occupied by a family who had the care of the house and kept two spare rooms for ministers who were traveling. One of these fell to my lot, with a narrow bed, there being two beds in the other room for my friends.

We were soon called to tea, having fresh fish, crabs, butter, and bread—everything nice and clean. After tea we walked up to Endre Dahl's house and around his grounds and gardens; they were very nice. His wife was very feeble. We remained until 9:30 o'clock, which was about sundown. This is certainly a sea-girt and rock-bound town. It numbers about 17,000. The fjords run all around among the hills, and there are a large number of rocky islands in view. It was beautiful to see the sun go down behind the mountains.

Sixth month 13 was First-day, and at about ten o'clock we went upstairs to the meeting-room, which was on the third floor, and found a large room crowded to overflowing. We sat down in silence, which was soon broken by an aged woman, who spoke in the Norse language, which I did not understand. Many were in tears when she was through. Isaac Sharp followed, and Endre Dahl translated for him. I engaged in prayer, and Robert Doeg translated for me. I then spoke from the text, "What shall I do to be saved?"[115] Robert Doeg followed, speaking in Norse.

I was so thankful that he was with me, for we had been together in England, and I felt that he was a good man and knew how to help me. He was a pleasant minister, and we became much attached to each other. He knew how to enter into sympathy with my message, and delivered it with an unction that added to its spiritual power rather than detracted from it; for he had spiritual discernment. It is a good thing for the interpreter to be a clean vessel, for he in one sense makes the message his own. Such an interpreter is better than one who simply translates the message from one language and clothes it

---

[115] Probably Acts 16:30; possibly Matthew 19:16, Mark 10:17, or Luke 18:18.

in another. May we who are ministers endeavor to be clothed with the Spirit and with a sense of the importance of "Be ye clean that bear the vessel of the Lord."[116]

At the close of the meeting they gathered round us, and, with tears running down their faces, putting their arms around our necks, manifested their joy. It was a time long to be remembered. There was a meeting again at 4:00 P.M., and a tea-meeting that evening at Endre Dahl's, both of which I hope were a time of spiritual blessing to many. Returning to our rooms about 11 o'clock, with a thankful heart I drew the curtains over the window to shut out the light, and lay down to rest.

Next morning the yearly meeting proper began, and after about one and a half hours of worship, in which much freedom was felt in preaching, the business was begun by Endre Dahl reading the opening minute. The representatives being called, our minutes were read and many warm expressions were given to welcoming us to their meetings and homes.

It was an interesting day. The business sessions both in the forenoon and afternoon were harmonious, nearly all the members taking part in speaking to the subjects that came before the meeting. I sat beside Robert Doeg, who kindly kept me informed about the business that was before the meeting. Among other things, they had under consideration some changes in their discipline. They discussed the proposed alterations with great freedom, and arrived at conclusions with but little difficulty. It was certainly an interesting yearly meeting, one that it was a great privilege to attend. The closing hour was one of the most solemn and impressive closing sessions that I have ever sat in. We separated from these dear people in much love and tenderness of spirit.

During my stay in Norway I was much impressed with their earnestness in their meetings for worship. Even before a word was spoken we could see the tears falling freely and dropping on the floor. Well

---

[116] Isaiah 52:11

do I remember walking down the aisle after meeting, and on looking each way seeing the floor wet with tears between the seats. Although having read of such things when a boy, it was hard to realize. Here now my eyes saw it demonstrated not once, but several times.

At the close of the yearly meeting we arranged to start out to visit the meetings of Friends in this land, and many of their families. Our traveling was done on the fjords by steamers and row-boats, and on land by public conveyances. These conveyances sometimes consisted of two-wheeled carts, the passengers sitting in a box on the axle, and the driver sitting behind on a seat nailed on the shafts, which ran back beyond the axle far enough for him to sit there, his feet hanging down, holding the lines with one hand on each side of the box. Sometimes each passenger had his own conveyance and driver.

In one of these rides I was taught a lesson about traveling that I have not forgotten. There were five passengers of us one morning setting out from our hotel. Being pointed to my box, doubling up my traveling rug I placed it in the bottom, and with my Irish ulster overcoat on I got in and sat down. Soon the five drivers appeared, one of whom was a young woman. She was assigned to the American. All started in a row, one behind the other. It was up hill for two or three miles, and we went along engaged in watching the scenery, but when we reached the mountain top I was suddenly aroused from my musing by the driver's saying something and dropping the lines. Immediately the horse laid back his ears and started in a run down the mountain. On one side of us the rocks towered still higher, and on the other a deep canyon lay, hundreds of feet below. My first impression was that the horse was running away, and that we would be thrown over the bank and dashed to pieces on the rocks far below.

Grabbing the reins, I began to pull and to shout "whoa." My whoa was English, and it did not trouble the horse; but my pulling was Norse, and interfered with his running. My driver caught me by the shoulders and began to shake me and to talk in an excited manner. Thinking she was frightened and wanted me to exert myself more, I pulled harder and called "whoa" louder. About that time she left off shaking me and gave me a slap on my right ear that was English. I could understand that language.

There was no mistaking what she meant. Letting go of the reins, I took hold of the sides of the box and stopped saying "whoa." Looking on ahead and down in the road winding before us, I saw all the other horses running. So I came to the conclusion that that must be the orthodox way to go down hill in Norway. While it was an orthodoxy that was hard for me to accept, I made up my mind to do so, and quietly sat back in my seat and behaved myself the rest of the way down the mountain; but I drew a long breath of relief when we reached the valley below.

As soon as we started up hill again the driver got out and walked along by the side of the cart, looking at me with a smile as much as to say that she was in a good humor. I replied in the same language as best I could. We understood each other. But when we came to the station where all stopped to change horses, she went forward and told my interpreter what she had done, and refused to go any further until he came and explained the danger there was in holding the lines tight while the horse was running; for they are trained to run down the hill with a loose line. My action was liable to cause the horse to fall, and the result probably would have been disastrous to us. We had a great laugh over it, and I told him to thank her for acting so promptly and efficiently.[117]

While engaged in this work in Norway I did not keep any diary. Consequently what I have written has been mostly from memory and form letters written to my dear wife. But our dear friend, Isaac Sharp, who was one of our company, was pleased to say something in his diary about my part of the work, and my dear friend, John F. Hanson, in his book entitled "Light and Shade from the Land of the

---

[117] It may seem that Allen Jay is spending a great deal of time to tell about this incident, but remember that he was writing at a time when horse-drawn travel was still very common. It would have been of great interest to his original readers.

Midnight Sun"[118] has inserted the following from Isaac Sharp's diary, which he introduces with these words:

> Allen Jay, a minister of Richmond, Indiana (who at that time resided in North Carolina), made a most valuable visit to Norway in 1875. His service is yet spoken of "as savor of life unto life to many." We cull the following account from the notes of Isaac Sharp, who accompanied him on the visit:
>
> "On Third-day, Sixth month 15, 1875, we left Stavanger by the steamer *Haukelid*, and on arriving at Sand about noon, a boat was in waiting to convey us to Sovde. For about two hours it rained heavily, then cleared up and rained again. The waterfalls were very beautiful, and the grand old mountains, wrapped in green and fringed at their base with ferns and flowers, arrested the attention of Allen Jay, who gazed with admiration on our surroundings of beauty and grandeur, but wondered how it was possible to provide for the wants of a family from the produce of the tiny farms, many of which we passed in the course of the journey.
>
> "In rather less than four hours we reached the head of the fjord, and walked to the meeting-house, over which were two rooms, each having two beds, for the accommodation of the traveling Friends. A storm arose with great violence and the rain descended heavily as we gazed from the window on the white wreaths of cloudlike vapor spread over the fjord we had so recently left. The violence of this thundery tempest soon abated, and at 8 o'clock, sixty came together from their several homes. Soren Olsen, from America, now on a visit to his native land, was

---

[118] *Light and Shade from the Land of the Midnight Sun*, by John Frederick Hanson. (Oskaloosa, Iowa: Western Work Publishing Association, 1903)

agreeably with us, and interpreted for Isaac Sharp. All four were heard in testimony and prayer. It was a good meeting, and the people were in no haste to leave at its close.

"Our young friend, Thorstein Bryne, from Stavanger, also bears us company, and proves a kind and willing helper. In the early part of last year he was the companion of John Frederick Hanson in his visit to Denmark. Considerably after 10 o'clock it was still light enough for Robert Doeg to read a portion of Scripture; a uniting sense of brotherly love was present with us, as also the directing and protecting care of our Heavenly Father, to which expression was given by Allen Jay in prayer and thanksgiving.

"About 10 o'clock the following morning we set out for a few calls from house to house. After our first visit we had an opportunity of seeing that the real wants of man are in small compass; the living room or family room in which we entered was about fourteen feet square. In one corner was a bed, on which the father of the family was resting from the fatigue of his early morning toil. The mother and three or four healthy-looking children were also present; all were dressed in very ample costume, each one wearing a pair of light wooden shoes. In one corner was a cooking, drying, and warming stove, in another the spinning-wheel, and in the remaining corner a table, on which the sleeves of a garment, with knitting needles attached and a ball of worsted, were lying. There were also two benches, a chair or two, and a few shelves, sundry articles of domestic use were hanging from the walls, the whole presenting a picture of rigid simplicity. They appeared thankful for the visit and what was communicated to them, as well as for the prayer offered up in their behalf.

"After two more visits, pelting rain came on; in the brightness between showers the rocky crags and surrounding mountains were very fine to look upon, and the snow still resting upon some of their summits bore evidence of their altitude. The isolation of this place is in part relieved by the arrival of the steamer now and then, thus affording facility at an easy rate for proceeding from place to place, or for the transport of goods to be sent away or received.

"A second meeting was held at Sovde on Fourth-day evening satisfactorily. On the following morning, the 17th, we rose early, and after breakfast enjoyed our reading. The spirit of prayer was present, and found vocal utterance. With calm and peaceful quiet we took leave of Sovde and its grand surroundings, which brought to remembrance the passage, 'As the mountains are round about Jerusalem,'[119] etc. We set off at 8 o'clock, and in walking to the boat Allen Jay remarked: 'We have had a nice visit, a very nice visit; I shall not soon forget this place.'

"Four hours were occupied in rowing to Sand, whence we proceeded in the *Skjold*, one of the local steamers, to Naerstrand. We were kindly met on the quay by Rier Oveland, to whose house we walked in the evening and had a religious sitting. The next morning at 11 o'clock a meeting was held in the house of a ship carpenter who, though not connected with the Friends, kindly gave the use of a good-sized room, which was well filled with a solid and attentive congregation. The same day, a few miles distant, another meeting was held at the house of Cecilia Tedneland, a well-esteemed Friend, a widow, who evidently has a real pleasure in arranging for visits such as these. On Seventh-day, the 19th, we set out

---

[119] Psalm 125:2

by carriole, and afterwards took a boat for Slogvig, where reside Anders and Berta Slogvig, at whose house we had a family sitting, and were hospitably entertained by them.

"Anders Slogvig is well acquainted with the district, and an open air conference was held with him. Visitors and visited sat down together on a rocky ledge, commanding a diversified view of great beauty. Bright-green glades in the near surroundings were in striking contrast with the rugged outline of the snow-flecked distant range. Just below us the patches of corn and potatoes, with bright-green grass not yet ready for cutting—all smiling in the noon-tide sunlight—were in harmony with the thrush-like song borne upward from the grove of birch and fir and oak and other native planted forests which have adorned the little domain of Slogvig from one generation to another.

"We left Slogvig between 3 and 4 in a boat, and subsequently proceeded by carrioles, which came for us to the water's edge and brought us nearly to Stakland, to which place we walked, arriving there after a journey of altogether three hours. Robert Doeg and Soren Olsen were kindly entertained at the house of Erik Stakland; Allen Jay and Isaac Sharp lodged at Elias Stakland's, who was five times imprisoned in Bergen for refusing military service. The father of these brothers was a valuable Friend, and suffered severely from ecclesiastical distraint—his faithfulness in this respect, it is believed, was blessed both to himself and family.

"Two meetings were held on First-day, the 20th, at 11 and 4 o'clock, in weather damp and unfavorable. The voices of the four stranger Friends were heard.

Allen Jay quoted the text, 'Choose ye this day whom ye shall serve.'[120] He appeared to be much impressed with a sense of the value and responsibility of parental influence, and said very feelingly: 'I thank my God for a mother's prayer.' Both meetings ended solidly. An evening sitting with the Friends here, after a social meal, peacefully concluded our service at this place.

"The next morning, Second-day, the 21st, we proceeded to the seaport of Hougesund, calling at the house of Torbjorn Aareg on the way, with whom and his family a religious sitting was held, which proved a time of refreshment. About 11 in the evening we went on board the *Motala*; all the berths were taken, so we lay down in the sofa seats without undressing. Allen Jay was much indisposed, and had severe pain in the head, but greatly improved in a few hours. Six or seven Friends were on the quay between 11 and 12 at night to take leave of Allen Jay. After midnight the steamer continued her course, and about 9 the next morning we landed at Flekke Fjord. The weather was now bright and beautiful, and soon after 11 o'clock we set off on our journey to Kinnesdal. 'Wonderful! Wonderful!' exclaimed Allen Jay, as we rode along this valley of diversified beauty and grandeur. The graceful birch was waving in the wind on the rocky banks of the Kvina, along which we rode; from whence, ascending upward, an altitude of 1,200 feet was gained. The air was bracing and the views were fine.

"Our worthy friend, Tollag Roisland, met us on the way and forded the river on horseback. He and his daughter narrowly escaped drowning some time ago, owing to the rapidity of the current. We went

---

[120] Joshua 24:15

over in a flat-bottomed boat, and about 8:30 in the evening we reached our destination. In the upper story of the meeting-house two of our number found comfortable accommodation for the night after our social evening reading. These seasons have proved especially refreshing and comforting to us, as, sensible to severance from home and home ties, our loved ones have been commended, with our own souls, to the protecting care and guidance of the Lord. Punctually at 10 o'clock on Fourth-day, the 23rd, about forty assembled, including fifteen who are in membership. On First-day from twenty to thirty usually sit down together. Tollag Roisland is not the only Friend whose voice is heard acceptably among them. We met again at 4 o'clock, and both these meetings were, we believe, owned and blessed of the Lord.

"On Fifth-day, the 24th, we set out before 8. The weather continued bright and beautiful. Some of the mountain ranges are from 1,500 to 2,000 feet high. At Rafos the River Quina, alluded to above, rushes through a narrow chasm of rock, over which it tumbles in broken water and spray, producing a fine effect. We reached Aamot about noon for a meeting there. About fifty assembled in the room wherein we met, which, added to those in the adjoining rooms and outside the house, made altogether a considerable company. Allen Jay had a good service here, earnestly pressing upon the people that 'now is the accepted time, now is the day of salvation.'[121] The voices of the other Friends were also heard.

"From this place we passed on to Flekke Fjord to lodge, and the following morning about 9 we went

---

[121] 2 Corinthians 6:2; Isaiah 49:8.

on board the steamer, and passing the well-known Lindesnaes of Norway about 2 o'clock, we landed at Christiansand in the evening, and found comfortable quarters at the Britannia Hotel.

"After having labored together in great harmony and brotherly love, we took leave of our dear friend, Allen Jay, on board the *Hero*, which vessel left her moorings about one o'clock on the 26th of Seventh month."

In parting with my dear friends, Isaac Sharp and Robert Doeg, at Christiansand, I was made to feel how closely we had been united in this work in Norway. They were going to Denmark, and I was returning to resume my labors in England. I have always felt that English Friends were very kind in arranging for us to travel together.

Since that day I have often met Isaac Sharp in his own land and in ours. He has been in our home, and we have talked over those days of traveling together. Dear Robert Doeg I never saw again, except when I was in England in 1885, when he was on his bed in his last long illness. His wife said that he had so often spoken about me that she would like me to have the privilege of seeing his face. He was too feeble to see me, but while he was asleep she took me to his bedroom door, and I was permitted to look upon his face for the last time. He died the following year at Scotby, at the age of seventy-eight years.

CHAPTER 30

Religious Service in England and Scotland

Having returned from Norway to England, I had a little over three months to devote to work in England and Scotland before sailing for home on the 22nd of Ninth month. Immediately after the close of the yearly meeting, in company with a number of other Friends, we spent a day of blessing and enjoyment going out to visit Jordans and holding meetings morning and afternoon in the old meeting-house where William Penn, Isaac Pennington, and Thomas Elwood used to meet to worship. We had a picnic in the grove between the meetings, which we enjoyed very much. The graves of William Penn and his wife Gulielma and of other noted Friends were interesting places to visit, not only for Friends, but for other American tourists. We saw the homes of Isaac Pennington, Thomas Elwood, and the house where John Milton wrote "Paradise Regained." I sat down in the chair that he was supposed to have sat in as he dictated this wonderful poem.

I had been among meetings in the south of England before going to Norway. Now, it was my desire to spend my time visiting the middle and northern portions of England and the meetings in Scotland. Several letters came from Ireland inviting me to come back there and attend some series of meetings, and there were also calls to return to the south of England, but my feelings were to attend as many of the other meetings as I could during the remaining time. Consulting with some of my friends, a program was made out for me, which closed at Liverpool with the quarterly meeting which was to be held there the day before my vessel sailed for Philadelphia.

Much might be said of my visits to many of the interesting meetings and the dear Friends I met with, but others have written and spoken so much of our English Friends that they are becoming more or less familiar to us. It is a cause for thankfulness that we are coming more and more to know each other, and as this progresses there has also grown up a stronger bond of Christian fellowship with each other and the work we are all engaged in. I trust that this feeling may continue to grow as years go on.

I wish only to add that while some have said that the English Friends are a little more reserved and harder to get acquainted with than some others, I was welcomed into as many homes and received with as warm Christian greetings as in any place where I have ever labored; and now, after thirty-four years, those days of service are bright and pleasant to live over in memory. Many of the older ones have passed beyond, but the precious young people of that day are joyfully taking their places and carrying forward the work.

During those months there were some experiences that I wish to dwell upon as I pass. Prominent among these was the general meeting at Ackworth Boarding-school.[122] The three days spent there with the young people were days of blessing. A large number of them were open to hear the Gospel, and several expressed a desire to lead Christian lives. Frederick Andrews and wife were the right persons to fill the places they held as heads of the institution. Much might be said of the workings of the school and the good that it has done, but others have written its history, and all over England, Canada, and many places in this land are those who remember Ackworth with pleasure.

---

[122] Founded in 1779, Ackworth School is still in existence.

It was my purpose to visit all the educational institutions under the care of Friends. It was a rare treat to visit Flounders Institute[123] in company with Isaac Brown, who was so long at the head of it. At the time we were there William Scarnell Lean was the principal. It was also a treat to spend several days at Darlington, where my home was with Theodore Fry. His wife was a daughter of John Pease, who at one time paid a religious visit to Friends in the United States.

While we were there they were engaged in making preparations for a celebration, it having been fifty years since the first railroad in the world was completed, from Darlington to Stockton, a distance of twenty miles. It was built and owned by Edward Pease, a minister among Friends. I saw the first locomotive that was made and the shop where it was built.[124]

Newcastle-on-Tyne was a meeting in which I found good service. At that place I visited the grave of William Hunt. He was the father of Nathan Hunt, grand-father of Asenath Clark, and great-grandfather of Dr. Dougan Clark, all of whom visited England on religious service as ministers afterwards. I went on to North Shields, then to Scotland, stopping in Edinburgh at the home of William Miller, the father of Ellen Clare Miller, who traveled with Eli and Sybil Jones in the Holy Land.

I visited the castle of Edinburgh, saw the Highland regiment, and heard the far-famed bagpipes for the first time. Next in course we went to Aberdeen, passing by Ury, the home of Robert Barclay. We attended the general meeting for Scotland in Aberdeen, which proved to be a satisfactory time. The city is built of granite, and is sometimes called the "Granite City." Next we went to Dundee, where we had a good meeting, and then on to Carlisle, and so on, south, taking in the principal meetings on the way.

---

[123] Flounders Institute was a teacher training college operated in association with Ackworth School. It was established in 1848 by a bequest from Benjamin Flounders, a Quaker industrialist and railroad developer who left what was then the tremendous sum of £40,000 for educational purposes.

[124] The Stockton and Darlington Railway opened in 1825, with a locomotive built by inventor George Stephenson.

On the way up to Scotland I had the pleasure of seeing Her Majesty, Queen Victoria, in the station at Perth. She was going to her Scotland home. Our train stopped for a short time, and as the guard opened my door he asked me if I would like to see Her Majesty. Of course I answered "Yes." He said, "Follow me," which I did. Our train was standing on the far side of the station, and she had gone upstairs on the opposite side to take luncheon. Carpet was laid down across the station, and a line of soldiers stood on each side from the train to the door where she would come down.

My guard took me and placed me between the soldier and the wall by the side of the door. I thought it was rather a bold act, but took the place. On the opposite side of the door was the mayor of the city in his official uniform. We had to wait only two or three minutes until John Brown, her noted servant, came down, soon followed by Leopold and his physician, then by several ladies in waiting. They were followed by her daughter Beatrice.[125]

When Her Majesty came down, she stopped in the door and reached out her hand, when the mayor, bowing down on one knee, took her hand and kissed it. She then entered into conversation with him about some matters in regard to the welfare of the city. Standing so near that I could have laid my hand on her gave me a good opportunity to see and hear. To me she appeared to be a noble woman with a large, motherly heart and while not handsome, yet pleasing to look upon. I greatly appreciated the opportunity which I thus enjoyed, which, however, lasted only a few minutes, until she passed on to the train and it pulled out of the station.

Especially did I enjoy my visit to York, attending that meeting where so many influential Friends lived, and also visiting the two large schools there, one for girls and one for boys. They are excellent

---

[125] Queen Victoria (1819-1901) was fifty-six years old at the time of Allen Jay's visit to England. Her consort, Prince Albert, had died in 1861, so Victoria had been a widow for fifteen years. Leopold (1853-1884) was their son, a student at Oxford at the time of Allen Jay's visit. Leopold suffered from hemophilia and had to have a physician in constant attendance. Beatrice (1857-1944) was Victoria's youngest child, just eighteen at the time.

institutions, and have been a great blessing to the Church. York is the center of a great Quaker influence. My home there was with Henry and Marla Richardson, at "Cherry Hill" house, and I also had the pleasure of visiting in a number of other homes.

I also visited Scarborough, where I made my home with Daniel Pryor Hack. Isaac Brown went with me. It was at the time when Robert Pearsall and Hannah Whitall Smith[126] were having a great holiness conference, held in the Corn Exchange, which could seat a large number of people. It was said that there were 600 ministers in attendance from England, Ireland, and the continent of Europe. There was certainly a great interest manifested among the Christians, and, being acquainted with our dear friends, who were from Philadelphia, they arranged for me to sit upon the platform, so that I had an opportunity to see and hear. These meetings were greatly blessed to many, and our dear friends were very popular.

I was very much interested in visiting the meeting and Friends at Bristol. This was one of the places where, in the beginning of our society, when the parents were all in prison, the children under fourteen years of age met on the ruins of the meeting-house that had been pulled down by the soldiers and held their religious meetings.

Here was where our friend, Joseph Storrs Fry, lived, who was clerk of the yearly meeting at that time, and who was at the head of the firm of Frys who manufactured cocoa. It was instructive to go with him to visit the factory. It was the custom at a certain hour in the morning for a large bell to ring, then the workmen, 2,000 in number, went directly to a large room, and there religious services were conducted for about thirty minutes, consisting in singing hymns, reading a chapter, and prayer. Then they returned to their work. These workmen were paid for this half-hour as for any other half-hour during the day. It is hardly necessary to add that in such a manufacturing company they never

---

[126] Hannah Whitall Smith (1832-1911), of Quaker background, was a holiness preacher and one of the founders of the Women's Christian Temperance Union. She is best known today for her book, *A Christian's Secret of a Happy Life*, which is still in print.

have any strikes. I am glad to say that the Cadbury Cocoa Company does the same thing now at Birmingham, except that they have such a large number of workmen that only the women can go one morning and the men the next morning. The same thing is true of the Rowntree Company, York. In addition they are interested in the physical comfort and welfare of their workmen, providing playgrounds, libraries, and other things which add to their physical and religious welfare.

Thus I visited the leading meetings throughout England, coming finally to Liverpool, where I attended the quarterly meeting and did some other religious work in and around the city, closing up on the 21st, the night before I sailed for home.

Having thus hastily reviewed my labors in England, Ireland, Scotland, and Norway in 1875, I hope it will not be considered improper to close this account with the returning minute sent to North Carolina Yearly Meeting by the English Friends after my return home. They say:

> Our thoughts have at this time turned toward our beloved friend, Allen Jay, who a year ago was in attendance at our yearly meeting in the prosecution of his religious engagements on this side of the Atlantic. We desire to convey to you our warm appreciation of his acceptable services and our thankfulness to the Lord that the labors of His servant were extended to this land. Alley Jay was diligently engaged in His Master's work while here, and also during the two weeks in which he visited Friends and others in Norway. We would make a special allusion to the warm acceptance of his ministry amongst the young people of this yearly meeting, many of whom, as well as other older Friends, hold him in loving remembrance. Signed on behalf and by direction of the yearly meeting of ministers and elders of London Yearly Meeting, held the 3rd of Sixth month, 1876. W.D. Sims, Clerk.

CHAPTER 31

With Stanley Pumphrey in America

It was a bright day when Stanley Pumphrey and I went on board the steamer *Illinois* at Liverpool, bound for Philadelphia. Our dear friend, Stanley Pumphrey, had been liberated by London Yearly Meeting to visit the meetings of Friends in America and he came home with me for the purpose of entering upon this extensive work. He did not know what lay before him, but expected it to require three or four years to complete the task.

A number of Friends came to see us off. We occupied the same stateroom. Our voyage was a rather pleasant one, but my friend suffered with seasickness during the first half of the voyage, while I enjoyed freedom from it and took pleasure in waiting on him and endeavoring to make him comfortable. The first thing he could eat was a piece of a good ripe American watermelon.

It was a happy feeling that came over me as we entered the mouth of the Delaware River one beautiful morning and sailed up towards the city of Philadelphia. My dear friend Stanley Pumphrey thus alludes to it in his *Memoirs*: "Sailing up the Delaware, my dear brother Allen Jay sat by me on the deck. We said but little to one another for the hearts of both of us were full. Allen Jay was returning home from a service in which the Lord had greatly blessed him. I was entering upon one the responsibility of which I felt exceedingly, but in which

I was trusting to the help and blessing of God. My thoughts went back to other years as I pictured William Penn sailing up that same river with a band of men and women driven from their own land by persecution, resolved to try on this virgin soil the 'holy experiment' of founding a state the corner-stone of whose policy should be liberty of conscience and in which the endeavor should be made to carry out the divine precepts of the Saviour in His sermon on the mount, of peace and good-will towards all men."

I had been engaged in preparing my things in readiness to go ashore immediately upon arriving at the dock when suddenly I remembered my friend with a feeling that I had neglected him, for I recalled my feelings when landing on the other side as a stranger several months before, with a burden resting upon me as I looked forward to a service among strangers in a strange land.

Immediately going upon deck, I found him sitting on the hindmost part of the ship, hidden from view and weeping. Sitting down by his side in silence I hardly knew what to say. Finally I ventured to say that I remembered my feelings when landing in Ireland and could sympathize with him, but now I was returning with the reward of peace and with thankfulness that the Lord had been with me and strengthened me for the work, and that I trusted in course of time he might be permitted to do the same when his work was done in this land.

Never shall I forget his look of sorrow as he turned to me and said: "Allen Jay, that is not the trouble. I could give up home and friends and joyfully enter upon the work in this land, but I am overwhelmed with sorrow because the Lord has given me a message for Philadelphia Yearly Meeting and I have seen clearly that many of the Friends will not receive it."[127]

---

[127] John Wilbur (1774-1856) was an Orthodox Friend from New England who opposed many of the innovations advocated by Joseph John Gurney, including involvement in broader Christian activities such as mission work. In 1845, New England Yearly Meeting suffered a new separation. Philadelphia Yearly Meeting, already divided by the Hicksite/Orthodox separation of 1827, avoided further separation by refusing to read the travel minutes of ministers from other yearly

When in coming months he met with opposition in various meetings in the limits of the yearly meeting, that scene on the *Illinois* that beautiful morning would come before me—this servant of God weeping because they would not receive the message that God sent him to deliver. I have known most of the leading ministers in our Society during the last fifty years. To my mind few have been his equal in spiritual life and insight into the deep things of God.

So my heart was pained and dipped into deep feeling of sympathy with him when he was met by Friends and told that it would not be acceptable for him to sit in the gallery. At another place the first thing that was said to him was, "Well, Stanley, I am not glad to see thee making the appearance thou dost." He says: "I sat down near the end of the gallery and as far as human sympathy went I never felt so lonely in my life, but my gracious Master drew near to me and encompassed me with His love and I prayed out my soul before Him with many tears. After the close of the meeting a leading elder pursued me and told me that I ought not again to sit in the gallery and that I was setting a bad example."

Similar propositions met him at a number of the meetings within the yearly meeting; but we turn from this to the other side of the picture. He tells what great comfort he met with in the attendance of other meetings. At Twelfth Street, Philadelphia, Germantown, Burlington, Haverford, and many others they received his message, and he spoke especially of the comfort he enjoyed being in the homes of John B. Garrett, Robert B. Haines, Eliza P. Gurney, and also many other homes and meetings. He says: "I attended Twelfth Street Meeting far oftener than any other and I always received the warmest of welcomes there, and in many other places in and around Philadelphia the Friends were generally willing to listen to me, and I have faith to believe the seed was not sown in vain."

---

meetings. Stanley Pumphrey found a warm welcome from some Orthodox Friends in Philadelphia, but faced opposition both from Wilburite-leaning Friends and from Friends who feared that Pumphrey's ministry might lead to another separation.

Those of us who have known Philadelphia for the last forty years and who have had the privilege during the past few years of coming in contact more or less with the earnest and faithful body of younger and middle-aged Friends as well as some who are older, and witnessing their devoted labors in building up the Redeemer's Kingdom in various lines of Christian work are forced to say that that which was sown in tears is bringing forth abundance of fruit to the glory of the Master of the Vineyard.

Pumphrey was a man who had understood the signs of the times and knew what Israel ought to do. During the four years that he was in this land he labored to unite the Society in this country in their work on foreign missions. It became a real concern and he wrote and spoke on the subject in nearly all of our yearly meetings, and when he returned home he was disappointed, saying, "I shall not see it, but it will come to pass before many years." We now see it accomplished in the American Friends Board of Foreign Missions, which was adopted by the last Five Years Meeting.

Friends of America owe much to the visits of our dear English Friends, not only those of the older class who visited us years ago, such as Jonathan and Hannah Backhouse, William and Josiah Foster, Joseph John Gurney, Joseph Bevan Braithwaite, Sarah B.S. Clarke, and a number of others who have attended our conferences and Five Years Meetings, but among the younger class such as John Wilhelm Rowntree, Stanley Pumphrey, Henry Stanley Newman, and Harriet Green. The three latter visited the Society more generally, went into the study of our needs and wants, entered many homes not only along the Atlantic shore and on the prairies of the West, but went down into the South also. They knew how to sympathize with the meetings which held their religious services in sod houses, and with the homes where Friends lived in log cabins, driving for miles over the prairies, through snow and mud and over the difficult roads of the South.

I have spoken of my unity and sweet fellowship in labor with Stanley Pumphrey. It was equally precious to sit by the side of Henry Stanley Newman and hold up his hands while he proclaimed the

Gospel. It was in our own home that I had the privilege of preparing a program for his four years' labor in America, and so closely were we united in labor in some parts of the work that we received the appellation of David and Jonathan.[128]

It was also our privilege to have dear Harriet Green in our home and to follow her in sympathy and prayers in her labors and journeyings in our land, from the Atlantic to the Pacific coasts and also down in the South, and to be present when the dear Friends of North Carolina laid her to rest under the spreading oak in the cemetery near Guilford College which she had learned to love so well. I am glad that these have lived and labored among us and rejoice that I have known them all and labored with them. I am a better man to-day and have a wider vision of God's love and goodness because I have known such servants of His.

After reaching home our monthly, quarterly, and yearly meetings came on in the three following weeks. I returned the minute granted me one year before with accounts of my journeyings and labors. A review of the work brought a sweet and quiet rest to my mind. The report was received kindly by the meeting. Our dear friend, Stanley Pumphrey, attended Baltimore Yearly Meeting and then came on to North Carolina Yearly Meeting. It was pleasant to have him in our home. He was a welcome member of the household and quite a favorite with the children.

During the spring and summer of 1876 I was much with him in visiting the meetings of Friends in North Carolina and Tennessee and we closed our labors together at Hampton, Virginia, where we made our home with George Dixon and visited the colored school under the care of General Armstrong and spoke to the students several times.[129]

---

[128] 1 Samuel 18:1

[129] The school referred to was the Hampton Institute, which began in 1861 as a school for escaped slaves. It was the site of the first Southern reading of the *Emancipation Proclamation*. In 1868, it became a school for the training of African-American teachers, with former Union general Samuel Armstrong as its first principal. In 1870 it was chartered as the Hampton Normal and Agricultural Institute. One of its earliest students was Booker T. Washington. It became Hampton Institute in 1930, and Hampton University in 1984.

When through here we separated. Stanley Pumphrey says: "I felt sad at parting with dear Allen Jay, to whom my heart had become closely bound in brotherly love. 'We shall neither of us ever forget these weeks of associated service,' he said, and then knelt down and prayed with me once more. I had a comfortable voyage up the Chesapeake Bay back to Baltimore."

Having alluded to the interest taken by Stanley Pumphrey and Henry Stanley Newman in organizing the American Friends Board of Foreign Missions, I propose to give a brief statement of this Foreign Mission Board among Friends in America.

CHAPTER 32

The American Friends Board of Foreign Missions

My lifetime has compassed the whole time of the work of American Friends in foreign missions, so far as organized work goes. We have always been known for our active sympathy and Christian labor for the Indian aborigines of our country and for the oppressed negro race as found amongst us; but we were not among the earliest of the American Churches to reach outside of our country in efforts to carry the Gospel to needy nations beyond.

The earliest, so far as I know or recollect, of missionaries going forth from us to other lands were Joel and Hannah E. Bean, of Iowa (Friends of Iowa being then a part of Indiana Yearly Meeting). In Tenth month, 1860, information was laid before the meeting for sufferings of Indiana Yearly Meeting that Joel Bean had been liberated according to the order of Friends "to visit in the love of the Gospel the inhabitants of the Sandwich Islands and to stand resigned to reside for some time among them."

The meeting for sufferings united with his concern and appointed a committee of leading Friends to render him necessary assistance, to correspond with him, while so engaged, and report to that meeting. The committee was also authorized to draw upon the treasury of the yearly meeting as they thought necessary. Later it was decided that his wife, Hannah E. Bean, and their infant daughter should go with him.

Of this companionship, after experience in the work on these islands, Joel Bean wrote to the committee: "Nothing has appeared clearer than the wisdom of my dear wife's accompanying me. Her company has all along been one great means of opening my way, and together we can go and labor where I could not go without her." Now that she has so recently passed from earth (First month 31, 1909), it is grateful to my feelings to make record of the esteem in which she was held on those islands by natives and missionaries alike.

But to return. They sailed from New York, Sixth month 21, 1861, and delaying a short time in San Francisco, they reached Honolulu on the 19th of Eighth month. They spent a part of their time on each of the three largest islands of the group, and remained until the next spring, distributing Bibles and tracts, preaching the Gospel, visiting many in their homes, teaching in the mission schools, and part of the time having evening schools of their own.

Joel Bean in one of his letters said: "It has been my privilege to address a very large proportion of the native population in their religious meetings." (The native population numbered then about 71,000.) They were warmly invited by some of the missionaries to remain there and help them, especially in the work of female education, but they felt that the work to which they were called was completed, and sailed homeward from Honolulu on the 24th of Fifth month, 1862. The knowledge of their work was but little diffused among Friends, being confined pretty much to the members of the meeting for sufferings, antedating as that work did the formation of any foreign missionary board in any yearly meeting of Friends.

But the spirit of foreign missions was beginning to start again among Friends. Three years later, in 1865, Friends in England organized an association or board for foreign mission work. To this board Louis and Sarah Street, then of Richmond, Indiana, applied to be sent as missionaries to Madagascar. They were accepted, and went out in 1867 and labored there successfully for about ten years.

Two years later, in 1869, Elkanah and Irene S. Beard, also of Indiana Yearly Meeting, went as missionaries to India under the care and support of English Friends, and between these dates, 1867 and 1869, Eli and Sybil Jones, of New England Yearly Meeting—who had visited Liberia on a missionary tour as early as 1851—made their religious visits in Syria and became in fact the initiators of American Friends mission work in Palestine, though in the beginning it was connected with the work of English Friends.

In 1868 some members of Indiana Yearly Meeting formed a foreign mission association with the twofold object as set forth in their statement of the subject, *i.e.*, "First, to present to those who may feel called upon to go abroad among heathen nations in the love of the Gospel, an organization that can aid, counsel, and advise. Second, to be a channel for the gifts of the willing-hearted in this direction and thus provide means for the necessary expenses of those men and women who shall enter upon this service." They invited the correspondence of any who might feel it their duty to engage in this class of Christian work.

From the first this association was in correspondence with Louis and Sarah Street for their help and encouragement in their work in Madagascar. Before it Elkanah and Irene S. Beard laid their concern to go to India, and it recommended them to the English board. To it Samuel A. Purdie, the veteran missionary of Mexico, soon applied, and he and his wife were sent out under its care and support in 1871.

Samuel A. Purdie was a native of New York State, but for some time previous to the above date he had been teaching in North Carolina, at the same time struggling with a sense of call to go to Mexico as a missionary, and was even then studying the Spanish language in preparation for that work. I will say here that, when the Baltimore Association called me to take charge of the work in North Carolina, I found that one of the teachers, Samuel A. Purdie, of New York, had caught the missionary spirit and was feeling that Mexico was calling him to come over and help.[130] He was not enjoying the work he was engaged in, for his mind was in Mexico.

---

[130] Acts 16:9

The second year I was there this was impressed upon me so clearly that I never doubted it again. Driving up to the schoolhouse at Back Creek one day at the noon recess, I found him out in the woods, sitting on an old log with a big Spanish miner sitting by his side, engaged in studying the Spanish language. When I came up he said: "Excuse me, for I must obtain a knowledge of Spanish," and in a serious manner added, "Some day the Lord will open a way for me to use this knowledge to His glory."

So a few months after this time, when Charles F. Coffin,[131] of Richmond, Indiana, wrote for my opinion about Samuel A. Purdie's going to Mexico as a missionary, I was prepared to give my approval. There was no doubt but that he was filled with the true missionary spirit. His mind and heart were there, and he longed to be there in body. It was not home to him anywhere else. He rejoiced when the time came to leave all and go, and when he received the word that he was accepted by the committee, it did not take him long to be on the way.

He came to our house one evening with his youthful wife. It was a night long to be remembered. We talked until a late hour of the work ahead of them. Neither of us knew much about what foreign missionary work meant, but the way looked bright before him. To him it was the way of duty. His wife, who was leaving all her people, was nevertheless cheerful in the prospect of the work before them.

Next morning in family worship we all knelt together and commended each other to Him who putteth forth His own and goeth before them. We loaded what few goods they had into the spring wagon and drove to the depot at High Point, where they took the train. As I watched the train go out of sight, I turned away feeling that it was carrying a man who was going cheerfully at the call of the Master. He believed the Master had other sheep who were not of his fold,[132] and he was going in the name of the Shepherd to bring them in.

Samuel A. Purdie continued at the head of this mission about twenty-five years, organizing and developing it successfully on three main lines: Gospel preaching, publishing, and schools. When he left

---

[131] Charles F. Coffin (1823-1916), served as clerk of Indiana Yearly Meeting from 1858-84.

[132] John 10:16

it he left six native Friends, recorded ministers, at work, also many trained teachers and other native helpers, and the printing press, doing a large business for its small resources and limited field, and more than 500 Mexicans brought into the Church.

The time came when he heard the call to another portion of the vineyard. There was no hesitation on his part. He hastened on and entered this latter field, and when the Master called He found him faithful unto death. He laid down his life in the field. Thus lived and died Samuel A. Purdie. Others may have been just as devoted, may have done a greater work, but none have been more loyal, none possessed a truer missionary spirit.

This Indiana Association found its work increased on its hands beyond its ability to support, and in 1874 the yearly meeting accepted it and adopted as her own both the association and the Mexican work. For some years after the opening of this Friends mission in Mexico, nearly all of the yearly meetings gave it more or less encouragement and support, but most of these, one after another, chose each a field, organized a board, and started a mission of its own. Each of these missions had a constituency larger or smaller of attached and devoted supporters, and much good work has been done by them. But as for grasping the idea that "the field is the world," these yearly meetings ran all over the world almost in selecting their mission fields, with little reference to the location of one another. They were generally not even co-operative, but isolated and independent.

In this initiative period Stanley Pumphrey, of England, visited Friends in America, and during the four years of his visit he looked carefully into the condition of foreign mission work in the different yearly meetings. He saw, as he thought, that American Friends would dissipate their strength by division into small independent boards whose separate missions, often meagerly supported, must perforce be weak, and to make their work more effective he earnestly advised the union of all American Friends in one general mission board.

> ... to make their work more effective he earnestly advised the union of all American Friends in one general mission board.

His proposition met with some favor. While he was here Ohio Yearly Meeting adopted a minute in accord with his ideas and sent it to the other yearly meetings, inviting them to join in forming one general board; but Friends did not fall in with the plan. Indiana Yearly Meeting appointed a committee on the subject when the Ohio minute was laid before it, but released its committee the next year. In 1885 Iowa Yearly Meeting presented a proposition to the yearly meetings (under the pressure brought to bear by one Levi Johnson, for united work in Africa) that American Friends form a union foreign mission board. The plan was favorably considered by several yearly meetings to the extent of appointing committees to join with others in considering the subject, but not enough united in it to accomplish the purpose.

Indiana Yearly Meeting appointed a large committee to take the subject into consideration and report the next year. This committee reported in 1886 so far favorably as to recommend the appointment of a committee of five to consult with committees of other yearly meetings, and if the way opened, for it to enter into the formation of such a board. They nominated for this committee Mahalah Jay, Lilburn White, Allen Jay, Timothy Nicholson, and Ellen C. Wright. Their report was united with and those named appointed. This committee stood, doing what it could for the cause, until a plan of union was adopted by the General Conference of Friends in 1892, and the yearly meeting appointed members of the American Friends board instead.

In 1888 this Indiana committee, aided by Henry Stanley Newman, of England, a brother-in-law of Stanley Pumphrey and sympathizing fully with his views of the need of united work in the missions of American Friends, being in America and in attendance at Indiana Yearly Meeting that year, this committee with his assistance (in reality Mahalah Jay, the secretary of the committee, and he did the work) framed a plan or constitution for a union board of missions and laid it before Indiana Yearly Meeting. The yearly meeting approved it and sent it forth to the other yearly meetings, asking their concurrence therein, only to meet the same fate as came upon the preceding efforts. So much time and effort did it take to educate our people to the idea of a union board, and that too although the women of the yearly meeting had united in a foreign mission union for work in the home field to promote foreign missions, and their success had demonstrated the possibility and advantage of such a union.[133]

At the General Conference of Friends in Indianapolis, in 1892, a member of the above committee, Mahalah Jay, urged the business committee of the conference, of which I was chairman, to make way for this subject of a union foreign mission board to be brought before the conference and discussed there. It was done, and how fully it was discussed may be seen in the stenographic reports of the conference. After this discussion, showing about how far Friends were prepared to go, the subject was referred to a committee, and a plan for a union board, drafted by William P. Pinkham and Mahalah Jay, which was equally a board of reference and advice and for gathering and disseminating missionary information, was reported to the conference at a later session and by it adopted.

It was directed that the plan be laid before the American yearly meetings as they came in course. The requisite number of yearly meetings united in it and appointed their members of such a board. The board was organized in the summer of 1894, at Wilmington, Ohio, at the time of Wilmington Yearly Meeting; Mahalah Jay was appointed secretary and Ellen C. Wright treasurer, and the American Friends Board of Foreign Missions was launched.[134]

---

[133] This is not the first (or last) time that women Friends have led the way, in this as in many other areas of concern!

[134] Why it took eighteen years, from 1874-92, for such an eminently sensible idea as a united mission board to be accepted, needs some explanation. As Allen Jay points out, all of the yearly meetings had their own missions, and there was no doubt a certain amount of protective feeling on the part of each yearly meeting towards its own turf. Many yearly meetings were expanding rapidly during this period, and there may have been some unwillingness to make an ongoing commitment to fund such a new organization. Although communications and travel were improving, going to the ends of the earth to preach the Gospel was still a new idea to many Friends who lived their whole lives in their own small communities. When the first proposals were made, large parts of the South were still recovering from the Civil War. For all these reasons, it took nearly a generation for the idea of a united mission board to be accepted and supported by American Friends.

The board entered at once upon its duties, opened correspondence with all of the American Friends mission boards and collected and published in the following year an eight-page report, partly historical and partly statistical, as complete as could be secured, of all the foreign mission work of American Friends, and it has continued to report annually on these subjects since then.

The uniform discipline adopted in its plan of a general foreign mission board most of the features of the plan on which the American Friends board was organized and added the function of authority to engage in field work. The American Friends board, in its reorganization for the second term of five years, placed itself in line with the proposed plan of the uniform discipline and prepared to take up field work in Cuba.

At the close of the Spanish War[135] the pressure was great upon the people of the United States to carry the Gospel to the West Indies and other Spanish islands. The American Friends board, having been applied to by one or more yearly meeting boards and by different individuals who felt that in some way Friends must take part in this work, submitted to the yearly meetings in 1899 the suggestion of united work in this island. A number of the larger yearly meetings, embracing more than half of the Friends in America, promptly approved the plan and pledged financial support. Others joined in later.

Early in the next year Zenas L. Martin,[136] of Iowa, was sent to Cuba to survey the field and recommend a place to begin. The north side of the province of Santiago, now Oriente, was selected. In the next fall, 1900, four missionaries were sent and the work begun, a work on which the blessing of God has rested and from which desired results have been rapidly reaped, comparatively speaking. Under the wise and faithful management of the superintendent, Zenas L. Martin, who still remains in the field, three principal mission stations have

---

[135] Spanish-American War, 1898

[136] Zenas L. Martin (1851-1931) served as superintendent of Iowa Yearly Meeting before going to Cuba, where he headed the mission work for thirty years.

been opened and provided with the necessary buildings for mission residences and meeting purposes as well as schools.

Through the diligent labors of godly missionaries, a monthly meeting, with Sunday school, Christian Endeavor Society, etc., has been gathered from the native population at each place, also a day school at each place, which is partly self-supporting. An out-station or village work is kept up at several other places. Wilmington Yearly Meeting's work in Cuba, joined by organic affiliation with the American Friends board, also North Carolina's, ready for the same affiliation, have been prospered under the same superintendent. Thus all the Friends work in Cuba, employing some ten or sixteen missionaries working effectively and harmoniously under one superintendent, makes an excellent showing of what may be expected from a judiciously appointed union board.

When the Five Years Meeting was organized in 1902 it adopted this American Friends board, already organized and incorporated in accordance with the plans of the uniform discipline, as its board of foreign missions, extending and defining more particularly its scope and function. One of these specifications was that it should be the duty of this board to represent American Friends in matters pertaining to the interdenominational aspects of foreign mission work, thus settling by authority the propriety of the board acting in such cases, for almost from the first this board has been applied to in such cases as there was no other general missionary board among American Friends.

It has represented Friends in missionary publications and periodicals of a general character, in general missionary conventions, conferences and boards, both national and international, including the student volunteer and young people's missionary movements, and it has usually, upon invitation, appointed delegates to these as they have occurred. Upon request Friends appointed two members of the general committee of arrangements for the great ecumenical conference held in New York City in 1900,[137] and gave credentials to the twelve delegates to the conference which were allotted to American Friends.

With much labor, because the information had not before been collected and put into shape, it furnished the promoters of that conference the information they requested concerning Friends and their foreign mission work, for their reports and general tables, and brought its own statistical reports into line with the form that the conference adopted for the world of missions. The American Friends had then and have had since then a recognized and creditable place, for the size of their denomination, in the great councils and other general forces that make for the evangelization of the world.[138]

Having attained a small measure of union in missionary work, there was a widespread unrest among American Friends and a desire that this union should be more comprehensive. The American Friends board was applied to by four yearly meeting boards and from other sources to call a general conference of American Friends to consider this subject. It called the conference, notifying all the foreign mission organizations of American Friends to send delegates to it, which they did.

The conference met in Tenth month, 1906, in Richmond, Indiana, and with unexpected unanimity agreed on a basis of union that would in the end make the American Friends Board of Foreign Missions the sole agent of the various yearly meetings for the administration and control of their foreign mission work. The board was reorganized at the Five Years Meeting in 1907 with this end in view, and appointed as general field secretary Charles E. Tebbetts,[139] who is now taking

---

[137] The Ecumenical Foreign Missionary Conference, held at Carnegie Hall in New York City in 1900, drew representatives from 162 mission boards and organizations.

[138] Here may be yet another reason why some Friends resisted the idea of a united mission board—the necessity for mixing and cooperating with mission workers from other denominations. With his great heart and ecumenical experience, Allen Jay would not have seen such cooperation as a danger, but many Friends would have felt this way.

[139] Charles E. Tebbetts served as founding president of Whittier College from 1900-07, and general secretary of the American Friends Board of Foreign Missions from 1908-15.

hold of the work vigorously, being located at Richmond, Indiana. He sailed on the 24th of Second month on a visit to Jamaica, Cuba, and Mexico, returning by way of California, Oregon, and other Western yearly meetings.

But *all* does not depend on union. The successful work of independent yearly meeting boards and other foreign mission associations of American Friends is matter for sympathetic and joyful congratulation of the faithful workers in those organizations. The aggregate results and their steady growth may be shown in a few statements.

The first twenty-five years were like most years of beginnings. Since 1895, when the American Friends Board of Foreign Missions collected its first statistical report, the annual home contributions of American Friends for foreign missions has risen from $32,500 to about $78,000;[140] that of the native Church membership, gathered through the missions, from $793 to $4,190. The pupils in mission schools have increased from 728 to 2,736; the number of missionaries from 43 to a full 100. Other comparisons equally encouraging might be made.

Our American Friends missions, in ten different countries, seem to engirdle the earth. A number of them and their tried and faithful missionaries appeal strongly to me for special mention in this account, but time and space forbid. We really have done commendably since we began to work at foreign missions, but we have not come up to our ability in this line of service for our Master. Let us be of good cheer, and in whatever way we find it best for us to work, let us not fail our Lord, but do our part of the work that He intends for our generation.

---

[140] The equivalent in 2008 would be an increase from about $700,000 to $1.6 million.

CHAPTER 33

Albert K. Smiley and the Providence School

In the autumn of 1876 my wife and I attended the Centennial Exposition, in Philadelphia, taking our son William with us, and while there I took him to Providence, Rhode Island, and entered him as a student in Friends Boarding-school, located in that city, now called "Moses Brown School."

During the winter of 1876–77 I found much to claim my time in finishing the work in North Carolina that I felt it right to do before leaving. In the spring I attended New York Yearly Meeting, and while there Albert K. Smiley, principal of Friends Boarding-school, Providence, asked me to take the position of treasurer of the school, and also to exercise my gift in the ministry in the meetings of the school and to have general oversight of the religious work of the institution.

This offer, after some consideration, my wife and I felt it right to accept, believing that the time had come to leave the yearly meeting that was dear to us, for a fear rested upon my mind that Friends paid too much attention to my judgment. In other words, I was having more influence in the yearly meeting than was best for any one man to exercise for his own good or for the good of the Church. It leads the Church to depend too much on one individual and may result in injury to the individual who exercises such influence.

The parting was a day long to be remembered at old Springfield meeting. We left on Second-day morning, and on the First-day before a great concourse of people were at the meeting. However, as I have returned again and again to visit that yearly meeting, and have witnessed the way that the young men and young women who have now grown up are carrying forward the work of the Church, I am more and more convinced that it was the leading of the Spirit that took us away at the time we left.

So, when school opened in Providence that autumn, we were comfortably located in the building at the school and our three children were entered as students. We had our rights of membership transferred to Providence Monthly Meeting, and became members of New England Yearly Meeting. I settled down to my work in the institution, work which I greatly enjoyed, as those four years were years of great blessing to me. Our association with Albert K. Smiley, the principal, and his wife, Eliza P. Smiley, together with his twin brother, Alfred H. Smiley, and his wife and family, who were generally there in the winter time, were such that it always brings up pleasant recollections as we look back to those days.

It was a pleasure to speak to the dear young people twice a week, to be with them in their First-day school work, and to attend their prayer meetings. It was a cause of rejoicing to see some of them giving themselves to the Lord and growing up to become useful members of the Church. New England was different from North Carolina, and yet we found an open door there for service.

The Origin of the Moses Brown School

It may be well to stop and give a little sketch of the school. I quote from the catalogue of 1904: "It was founded by Moses Brown, Providence, who was also a founder of Brown University and the first president who suggested the removal of the university from Warren to Providence. He was one of Rhode Island's most eminent citizens, a founder of literary and benevolent institutions, as well as of great manufacturing industries which have been of vast and perpetual benefit to the whole country. Isaac Lawton opened a school at Portsmouth, Rhode Island, Eleventh month 8, 1784. It continued for four years, and then for want of funds was discontinued until 1819, when it was opened in Providence, and has continued with slight interruption until the present time.

The school was in successful operation during the last seventeen years of the life of Moses Brown, and claimed his constant watchful care. He gave to it annually during this period $100, and in addition to many small donations he gave another lot of land and $15,000 in money in his will. It is probable that his example influenced his son, Obadiah, who had a great regard for his father, to give to it the sum of over $100,000 in his will, which the school received in 1822. John G. Whittier wrote of the school:

> Not vainly the gift of its founder has made,
> Not prayerless the stones of its corner were laid;
> The blessing of Him Whom in secret they sought
> Has owned the good work which the fathers have wrought.[141]

Albert K. Smiley

My remarks, I feel, would be incomplete without some allusion to the principal, Albert K. Smiley, who had been in charge seventeen years when I went there, and remained two years longer. Perhaps I cannot do better than to make a few quotations from his own remarks made at Lake Mohonk on the day of his golden wedding, Seventh month 8, 1907:

> When my brother and I were fourteen years old, the principal of the academy we were attending had a fifteen minutes' talk with us and told us that

---

[141] From "The Quaker Alumni," poem by John Greenleaf Whittier, first published in 1860.

we ought to prepare for college, and advised us to study Latin. We had to leave the academy in a week or two to chop a year's supply of wood, and while chopping we went through the declensions and conjugations and read the Latin reader through. That fifteen-minute talk took us from the farm, sent us through college, and made me an educator for thirty years—four years an instructor at Haverford College; four years at an English and classical academy, which my brother and I started at Philadelphia to fit boys for college; two years head of a large boarding-school established close to my own home; and nineteen years as principal and superintendent of a semicollegiate school at Providence.

I will just throw in here that I am still in the educational field, and not entirely in hotel life. For thirty years I have been a trustee of Bryn Mawr College, and I am a trustee of Brown University and of Pomona College, California, and president of the board of trustees of the State Normal School, New Paltz. So I am not fully a hotelkeeper.

When my brother Alfred and I were born we were so much alike that our mother tied ribbons on either our arms or legs, I don't remember which, to distinguish us. None of our neighbors or teachers knew us apart. We always worked together, walked together, slept together, had measles, mumps, and whooping cough together, never had a single article of clothing, money, or anything else separate for twenty-seven years. In the morning we jumped into the first suit of clothes that came in our way, no matter who wore it the day before. Until we were twenty-seven years old, when my brother married, we never had anything to be called "mine," but always "ours."

In 1856 he became acquainted with Eliza P. Cornell, and they were married Seventh month 8, 1857, in Twentieth Street Meetinghouse, New York, after the manner of the Quaker ceremony. His wife has proved a great blessing and strength to him during the years of his active life. They had one child, a daughter, who died in early life. I wish to bear my testimony to Eliza P. Smiley's noble Christian character, a life that has been devoted to the good of others. Many a homesick boy and girl at Providence can look back and remember her loving sympathy and Christian counsel, and in later years strong men and women who have visited Lake Mohonk have borne away in loving remembrance her self-devotion in making their stay at Mohonk a pleasant one.

To quote again from Albert Smiley's own words:

> I bought Mohonk with the idea of making it a home, expecting the hotel to be conducted by an agent, planning to live a mile or more from the hotel and devote my time to developing and beautifying the property. My brother Alfred conducted the hotel for ten years, while I remained in Providence to earn money to pay off the debt and to enlarge the hotel. When he built Minnewaska and left Mohonk, I resigned from Providence and came here. I desired to have some member of my own family to assist me, and secured my brother Daniel for the summer of 1880. He was at that time chief assistant in the Penn Charter School, Philadelphia. In the winter of 1881 I visited him there and found him about to publish a Greek grammar, and, furthermore, about to get married. I persuaded him to leave his literary career and join me in building up Mohonk. He and his wife came here in June, 1881, and have been here ever since.
>
> Mohonk has afforded me intense pleasure in its development. I have treated this property, the result

of twenty-six purchases, as a landscape artist does his canvas, only my canvas covers seven square miles. I never take a walk or a drive over the property but I find some ugly trees to be removed, a new path to be built, a group of trees or shrubs to be set out, a vista to be opened, groups of trees to be planted to give seclusion to a too open view, a summer house to be built, bright flowers to be set out or dead flowers to be removed. I am confident that the outdoor life at Mohonk has added years to my own and my wife's lives.

More than forty years ago my wife's health broke down, largely in consequence of the loss of our child, and two of the best physicians in New England declared she could not live three months. A little later I too suffered as severe a case of nervous prostration as I have ever known as a result of overwork in the Providence school. We both consider that Mohonk air and outdoor life have brought us through many years in a very fair degree of good health.

My intense interest in the welfare of the Indians and in international arbitration, which has resulted in thirty-eight Mohonk conferences, has afforded me the greatest satisfaction. Would that I might live to see the greater number of international difficulties settled by peaceful arbitration! Any suggestion about naming a price for this estate has met the instant reply that Mohonk is not for sale, and no money can ever induce me to part with my home, which I love as fondly as a mother her child.[142]

---

[142] Mohonk is still in operation as Mohonk Mountain House in New Paltz, N.Y. The conferences on Indian affairs ran from 1883-1916, while the Lake Mohonk Conferences on International Arbitration, which led directly to the creation of the Court of International Arbitration at the Hague, ran from 1895-1916. Minnewaska, built in 1879, stayed in the family until 1955, and was closed in 1972 and burned in 1978. It is now a New York State park.

Associations and Reminiscences of Providence and New England

The committee having charge of the school was composed of a number of leading Friends of New England Yearly Meeting. Among them were Tabors, Howlands, Chases, Tobeys, Bufkins, and other family names of New England. It was a pleasure to me to associate with these noble men. That yearly meeting had been held at Newport, Rhode Island, almost from its origin, but while I was a member it was held for the first time at Portland, Maine, and as Friends had no accommodation there sufficient, they were invited to hold it in the City Hall.

The hall was pretty well filled, and I can call to mind some of the leading men who were present at that time, among them John G. Whittier, Neal Dow,[143] Eli Jones, and others who have done noble work for the cause. One day during the yearly meeting, going down into the basement I found the officers of the law engaged in pouring 100 barrels of whisky that they had captured into the mouth of the sewer that ran out into the bay. It had been shipped into the city under some false name and disguised in such a way that it was not expected to be detected, but the authorities were on the watch, and where there is a disposition to do so there is generally a way to find out those who are violating the law. It is often said that prohibition did not prohibit in Maine. I remember, on one day of my excursions down into Maine, in two days' drive in the carriage I found three jails. One was converted into a barn, another into a cow stable, and the third into a hay barn. They said that since prohibition had gone into effect there were no prisoners to occupy them.

After I had been at Providence two years, A.K. Smiley resigned and went to Lake Mohonk, and Augustine Jones, who was a lawyer in

---

[143] Neal S. Dow (1804-1897) was born of Quaker parents. He was one of the founders of the Maine Temperance Society in 1827. He became mayor of Portland, and sponsored the Maine prohibition law of 1851. He served as a colonel of Marines in the Civil War, rising to become a brigadier general. He was captured by Confederate troops and spent eight months in prison, later being exchanged for the son of Robert E. Lee. He ran for President on the Prohibition Party ticket in 1880.

Boston and an active member of New England Yearly Meeting, was selected to fill the place. He was a man of literary taste, fond of study, and at once took a deep interest in the welfare of the institution. My connection with the institution under his administration was pleasant and agreeable. He encouraged me in my department of the work, but soon after this time I began to get letters from the managers of Earlham College, Indiana, making propositions to me to come to that institution and take the position of superintendent and treasurer of the college, and my wife to take the place of matron.

At first it did not present itself as very attractive, for my relations at Providence were pleasant and without any very great responsibility in regard to government or control. Yet, after being separated for more than a dozen years from all of our relations, the proposition had something attractive in it, and in view of our sons' growing up, there was an inclination to return to the West.

So, after considerable correspondence, I accepted the position of superintendent and treasurer of that institution, but my wife, who was not very strong, preferred to be a looker-on for one year at least before assuming the office of matron. So I resigned my position at Providence, to take effect at the close of the second year of Augustine Jones's administration and the fourth year of my labors at Friends boarding-school.

Again we felt the severing of the ties of Christian fellowship that had grown up towards our dear New England friends. We had formed many warm attachments and I had found an open door for labor in the Gospel in the limits of the yearly meeting, visiting all the quarterly meetings, attending conferences of various kinds connected with the yearly meeting work, finding comfortable homes to rest in during the summer vacation in Maine, Lynn, Nantucket Island, New Bedford, and many other places. Especially do I wish to mention the home of the Swan sisters, Boston, where many weary laborers have found a resting place. I shall ever look back with deep interest on the four years spent with the Friends of New England Yearly Meeting, and I trust that my feeble efforts have not been in vain in strengthening the work there.

Four years ago my wife and I attended New England Yearly Meeting, held within the walls of the old boarding-school. It brought up many memories of the past. They gave us my old room to sleep in, the same place in the dining room at the head of the table, and as I met from day to day those who, more than thirty years before, were boys and girls in the school, but had now grown up to be fathers and mothers, and brought their children up to introduce them, it made me feel that I was growing old. But as I saw these same people taking active part in the yearly meeting, and heard their names called on various committees, I felt that the dear old Friends boarding-school had not existed in vain and that the labors of other days had not been lost.

CHAPTER 34

Earlham College Past and Present

At the close of the boarding-school at Providence, Rhode Island, in the summer of 1881, after four years' service in that institution, my wife and I, with our three sons, left for Earlham College. We went directly to my old home at Marion, Indiana. It was pleasant to have our faces turned towards our friends in Indiana, whom we had left more than twelve years before with the prospect of being gone one year, little realizing what lay before us. Our experience had been varied, and yet we could see the hand of the Lord in it all, and now we were returning with our family to Indiana Yearly Meeting, where I had been a member until I was twenty years old.

After nine years' experience in North Carolina and four in New England Yearly Meeting, many friendships had been formed and a rich experience in Christian work had been ours to enjoy, and we had no doubt but other doors would open as we came to them. Changes had taken place in the home circle. My father had passed away a few months before, and a brother-in-law and sister-in-law had entered the Beyond, besides many dear friends who had fallen here and there, leaving work for others to take up. It was with a desire to find our place that we came, not to rest, but to enter the open door that presented itself. We found one, as those who are willing to work in the Master's service will always find. We could exclaim that the hand of the Lord had been good upon us during these years.

The next morning I went to Richmond to attend the commencement of Earlham College and to get a view of our future field of labor. Little did I realize what lay before me in connection with my work in that institution. It will soon be twenty-nine years since I entered its doors as superintendent and treasurer, and I have been connected with it in some way all these years, as superintendent, treasurer, solicitor, trustee, serving on the board of managers and on the various committees connected with its management. I have spent months and years in visiting meetings, homes, and individuals within the limits of nearly all the yearly meetings in America, also spending three months among the dear Friends of England, soliciting funds for the building up of the institution and increasing the endowment fund. Many and varied have been my experiences with meetings and individuals, public and private, in this arduous labor.

The day I reached Earlham is one not to be forgotten. It was a hot summer day. The commencement exercises were held out in the grove between Earlham Hall and where Lindley Hall is now located. I remember well the sun shining through the trees and blistering my bald head. I had just left an institution where the buildings were in good repair, with plenty of room, and with sufficient funds to run it in a creditable manner, with its enrollment of between two-hundred and three-hundred students.

Here was a college with one building for everything—cooking, living, sleeping, eating, laundry work, study, recitations, lectures, library, reading room, museum, laboratory, meeting room, society halls, etc., etc. The treasurer's office and the president's office were both in the same room. The treasurer's office was used for selling books and stationery, keeping accounts, post-office, and everything connected with the superintendent's office. The president, Joseph Moore, had his office and little desk in one corner by the old clock, and what made it still more disagreeable, this building was in very poor repair. The heating apparatus had given out, the cooking and laundry departments had to be torn down and rebuilt, barns and stables had to be repaired. After dinner I walked around and looked the situation over and then went out in the boys' grove and found an old log back in the far corner, and sat down, and for more than one hour, meditated. I have never told anyone my feelings, and I will not try to do it now, yet they are very vivid. But I am still alive, and the scene has changed.

Now, as I sit at my desk, I can look out and see six new buildings, which have cost, with their furnishings, something over $200,000. The endowment fund, which was then a little over $50,000, is now nearly $340,000. The number of students in all departments the year before I came was 196, 48 of whom were college students and 148 in the preparatory department. This last year we have had 525 enrolled in all departments, including music, and have no preparatory department at all.

But it is just to say that the trustees had decided that something would have to be done towards improvement in and around the buildings, and they had selected that grand old man of Earlham, Walter T. Carpenter,[144] to assist me in carrying out the plans and improvements proposed. Walter T. Carpenter had been superintendent at Earlham College some fourteen years in all, having been there at three different periods. At times when the college was in a close place financially he went in and gave it a start again. I hope some pen better than mine will say the right thing in his memory some day. He still lives, in his ninety-ninth year, and is loyal to Earlham. Let others be false who will, his is always a word of cheer to those who are bearing the burdens of today. Such a man is a tower of strength.

We went forward with the improvements, he taking the lead and I following with a good, hearty will. We put in an entirely new heating plant, building a new cooking and laundry building and boiler house; we divided the large sleeping rooms up into rooms for two students in each, and arranged for the students to have their trunks upstairs, rather than in the basement, where they had been in the habit of going

---

[144] Walter T. Carpenter (1811-1910) served as superintendent of Earlham from 1858-63 and again from 1868-72, and for many decades was on the management committee. Carpenter Hall on Earlham College's campus is named after him.

to wash and dress. We made changes all through the entire building, and made additions to the barn and stables. It was a pleasant autumn, so that we were able to complete the work before cold weather set in.

This work done, the trustees selected Nathan Pickett to go over the financial accounts with us and see where we were. We sat down, and one night about midnight, when we had finished our accounts, found that we were $27,000 in debt and only had $1,000 subscribed to pay it with. When we had finished our figuring, dear Nathan Pickett, who recently passed away at the age of 91 years, said: "What shall we do?" After a little silence Walter T. Carpenter spoke in his positive way and said: "Allen Jay must go out and get it."

During the next few months I went among the meetings and the homes of Friends in Indiana and Western yearly meetings, when I could leave the college, and before next commencement day it was all subscribed and nearly all paid in.

Thus I have given a short synopsis of the conditions of Earlham at the time of the college commencement in the summer of 1881. And now, taking into consideration the impression that Earlham College has made upon the Society, and the positions its students have occupied and are occupying to-day in the various yearly meetings, and the positions they are taking in religious, moral, and educational spheres, I have felt it might be the proper thing to pause and give a little historical sketch of the origin and growth of the college up to the present time, as such a history has never been prepared.

CHAPTER 35

The Founding of Earlham College

In 1832 Whitewater Quarterly Meeting, in its report to Indiana Yearly Meeting, stated that it had for some time had the subject of a boarding-school at Whitewater under its consideration, and had united in laying it before the yearly meeting. The matter was referred to a large committee, which reported favorably on the subject and proposed that "a committee of men Friends be appointed to receive contributions from such benevolent individuals as may be disposed to help in the concern by donations or legacies, and with a view to keep alive and increase the interest therein, and that any contribution which may be made by them be so managed as to continue to accumulate, and while we desire not to press forward more speedily than our resources will admit, we think the mind of Friends will become more and more prepared for it as our information advances and means increase, so that in the course of a very few years an institution so desirable may be brought into operation; and in order to extend the concern as much as practicable, we propose that the yearly meeting recommend the subject to the attention of the subordinate meetings to endeavor to promote within their respective limits a lively interest in the concern and contributions of funds to carry it into operation."

This report was deliberately read and considered, was united with by the meeting, and the subject was directed to the subordinate meetings as proposed. A committee was appointed to receive contributions for the boarding-school, and the incorporation of such an institution was referred to the meeting for sufferings.

The above is the first record made on the subject. It was the beginning of what is now Earlham College. In 1833 this committee reported that they had received $137. In 1834 they reported $11.50 received; in 1835 they reported nothing received; in 1836 they reported $7.00 received. Some additions were made to the committee this year, and the quarterly meetings were recommended to open free subscriptions for the promotion of the concern.

Another committee was also appointed to propose to the next yearly meeting a plan and regulations for the contemplated boarding-school. In 1837 the committee on plans and regulations reported: "We are united in sentiment that the location of the school proposed within our limits shall be on the farm belonging to the yearly meeting. In reference to the building, it is the opinion of the committee that males and females may both be instructed in the same building, as at Providence, Westtown, and New Garden; that a house and the requisite buildings suitable for the accommodation of 300 scholars should be erected, the cost of which may be about $16,000. It is proposed that the length of the house be 150 feet and the width 50 feet."

The minute made on the occasion says: "The report, being read, was united with and adopted by this meeting, and the subordinate meetings are affectionately encouraged to raise the amount proposed in the report by voluntary subscription, and report to the next yearly meeting."

In 1838 the quarterly meeting reported that $5,640.65 had been subscribed. The committee reported that they had 713,000 bricks, burned at a cost of $2,189, and "they are considered of a good quality." They had also contracted for a sufficient amount of lumber, but the contract had not been entirely fulfilled. This year the yearly meeting made a plea to what it was pleased to term "the middle class, as respects their circumstances in outward affairs." "It is from this class that we have our main expectation in regard to the funds for this institution. Leave out these and we cannot succeed. But let them contribute their $5, their $10, or their $20 per annum for three or four years, and our funds will be abundant. That this class is able, without the least oppression, so to contribute we have not the least doubt. It would be ingratitude to undervalue our blessings and to permit a sordid, worldly spirit and the love of gain to prevent the exercise of that Christian liberality which should distinguish the members of our religious society."

As we continue to follow the history of raising money to build and complete the boarding-school that Indiana Yearly Meeting had now on hand, we are impressed with the long and continued effort required to succeed, and learn that it finally became necessary to complete a portion of it and begin the school, waiting for some time before finishing the entire building.

In order to judge our Friends of that day correctly, it is but right to take into consideration the long-depressed condition of money affairs which followed the great panic of 1837,[145] which became a potent factor not only for one year, but for several years. There was plenty of produce in the land, and the Friends, who were mostly an agricultural people, depending almost entirely on the production of their farms and home-made manufactures, lived in a comfortable condition, and as land had greatly advanced in value, might be said to be in prosperous circumstances; but many of them had contracted debts in the preceding years of speculation, and now the small amount of money in circulation, the low price of all farm produce and the expense of getting it to market all combined to make it very difficult for them to raise sufficient money to pay their debts, taxes, and their small necessary money expenses for a living.

---

[145] The Panic of 1837 came after a long boom of economic and population growth and tremendous land speculation. Almost half the banks in the U.S. closed and a five-year depression began which affected the entire country. Money in circulation fell by more than thirty percent and crop prices fell by more than fifty percent.

The prosperous farmer who wished a better coat for his son just reaching manhood could not get the material for it for less than 100 bushels of oats or corn, after the expense of hauling it to market. Pork, that in the fall of 1836 sold for $7.00 per 100 pounds, in the year that followed would bring but $2.00 per 100 after being made into bacon. An illustrative anecdote of these times used to be told of a man who was watching his pile of bacon on the wharf at New Orleans, whither he had conveyed it in a flat-bottomed boat, when a wag passing by told him he need not watch it as there was no danger of it being stolen. "Oh," said the man, "I am not afraid of that. I am only afraid some one will put more to it."

I remember hearing my grandmother say that in the autumn of 1836, when pork was so high, a number of Friends had driven their hogs to market one day and sold them at $7.00 per 100. The next day a traveling Friend had a meeting appointed at Randolph Meeting-house. After the congregation had sat in silence for some time, this dear Friend rose with great solemnity and broke the silence by saying: "Pork is worth $7.00 per 100." This he repeated three times with impressiveness, after which, taking it for a text, he preached a long and searching sermon.

In 1839 the committee said that they had contracted for the digging and walling of the cellar, and a committee of 49 men Friends was appointed to collect subscriptions during the year. They reported next year that $291.75 had been secured. In 1840 the building committee reported the foundation was completed, and a committee was appointed to consider the propriety of adopting a manual labor system for the government of the school. In 1841 the committee reported in favor of adopting that system for the management of the school, but the meeting was not ready to accept the proposition, but appointed a large committee to take the matter under consideration, and, if they thought best, digest a plan for carrying it on that way, and report next year. The boarding-school committee this year proposed that the west wing be completed, which would be about two-fifths of the whole, and would accommodate from fifty to seventy students.

As the demand for such a school was so urgent, the meeting directed them to go forward with this portion of the building. In 1842 the committee on a manual labor system reported that they were not prepared to propose any plan, but urged the importance of getting the school started and advised leaving the details to be worked out as time advanced. This appears to have been the end of the proposed manual labor system.[146]

There had been formed previous to this a Young Friends Association, the object of which was to assist in raising funds and help in starting the institution. They reported this year $555, and they continued after this to help in various ways to advance the work.

In 1843 the building committee of the boarding-school reported that no progress whatever had been made with the building for the want of funds. In 1844 the report of the building committee was not encouraging, but the matter was continued, and in 1845 the report showed that they had received $1,343.09, and a subscription of $566 was taken in the meeting.

The meeting was united in directing the committee to proceed with the work and propose to [the] next yearly meeting a plan for putting the school into operation. In 1846 the committee reported they had contracted with John B. Posey to finish the part now up for $3,300, he to use the raw material on hand, and the following plan was proposed for the opening of the school: "The principal features of the plan for the boarding-school which were submitted and agreed to were to have the school open about the 1st of Fourth month, 1847; that $1,500 be used to provide the school with necessary articles for use; that the yearly meeting appoint a general boarding-school committee of men and women Friends, some from each quarterly meeting, to have general charge of the school; that the general committee appoint

---

[146] The "manual labor system," which allows students to come for free in exchange for work they do for the school, was in line with many of the communitarian movements of the times. It was adopted by a number of colleges, notably Berea College, Ky., founded in 1855, which continues to offer this style of education, tuition-free, to this day.

an acting committee of suitable men and women Friends from their own members to visit, to provide officers for, and to have at all times charge and oversight of the school; that the acting committee report to the general committee, and the general committee to the yearly meeting each year."

Both sexes were to be admitted. The teachers and scholars were to be members of our religious Society and to conform to plainness of dress and language, and meetings for worship to be held on First and Fifth-days of each week in the school, under the care of the acting committee. A general boarding-school committee was appointed, consisting of 62 men and 47 women, their names having been brought in by a nominating committee. The general boarding-school committee in 1847 reported that the school was opened early in Seventh month, under Cornelius Douglas and wife as superintendents, and Lewis A. Estes and Huldah C. Hoag as teachers, and continued fifteen weeks with an average attendance of about 36 scholars.

It was proposed to divide the scholastic year into two terms of twenty-three weeks each, the winter term to begin just after yearly meeting and close about the middle of Third month, and the summer term to immediately succeed it and close the latter part of Eighth month. The expense for board and tuition was to be $70 per year, or $35 per term.

In 1848 the general boarding-school committee reported to the yearly meeting that they had received an additional donation from Friends in England of $491.11; from women Friends of Indiana Yearly Meeting, $5.57; and from the quarterly meeting, $542.08, which with the balance from the previous year, made $1,301.08.

During 1848 the school made satisfactory progress under Barnabas C. Hobbs and wife as superintendents, and Lewis A. and Huldah C. Estes as teachers, and averaged about 75 scholars. They also proposed that the midweek meeting at the school be omitted the week of preparative meeting and of monthly meeting. The committee was enlarged by the addition of five men and four women, making the whole number 118.

In 1851 a proposition was made to build a house for a teacher, which was united with, the house not to cost over $600. In 1852 the proposition was made to appoint a special boarding-school committee, which would have the special care and oversight of the institution, consisting of 12 men and 12 women, and the proposition was made to try to raise $16,000 to finish the main building. In 1854 the building committee reported it had entered into contract with John B. Posey for the putting up and finishing of all the unfinished portions of the building for the sum of $19,445. In 1855 the proposition was made to sell off some lots of the meeting-house ground and also to sell and appropriate to it that part of the school farm lying north of the turnpike road, together with such other portions of the land as could be spared, and pay off all the indebtedness of the institution, finish the building and furnish it as above described. This report was very fully united with by the meeting, and the trustees of the boarding-school farm and land were authorized to make the sale and apply the proceeds as recommended.

Without going into further detail, it may be sufficient to say that from year to year the building committee and the boarding-school committee continued to report progress, and the subordinate meetings were encouraged to raise money to carry on the work. In 1857 the yearly meeting directed the trustees to sell the land on the north side of the turnpike and apply the proceeds to paying the debt. We find the whole amount of money expended while it was a boarding-school and before it became a college was $73,639.04, as nearly as can be obtained from the minutes of the yearly meeting. The entire building was completed in 1855.

The following proposition was received from the committee at the yearly meeting in 1859: "In order to enable the institution to meet more fully the wants of many students, both young men and young women, who are looking to it for a complete education and desire to obtain college advantages without going to institutions outside our Society, the committee have, after much consideration, adopted regulations establishing a faculty and authorizing, with the approbation of the yearly meeting, the granting of regular college degrees (excepting all unnecessary forms and ceremony which we do not approve) to such students as go through either the college or scientific course, and the issue of diplomas properly executed. We propose that the name of Earlham College be adopted as the future name of the school."[147] The minute made by the clerk of the yearly meeting with reference to the report of the boarding-school committee on this occasion says it "has been read and is satisfactory to the meeting and the new regulations proposed by the committee are adopted." So the Friends Boarding-school became Earlham College, Tenth month 1, 1859.

Financial History of Earlham College

Having given a hasty review of the history and struggles of the Friends Boarding-school financially until it became Earlham College, I will leave the financial growth and development from that time to this for other pens to write down, after simply adding that the same struggle has been continued all these years.

The first permanent endowment fund was raised in 1870 and 1871, our late friend, Charles S. Hubbard, giving much time and effort in the matter, and being assisted more or less by Joseph Moore. In 1872 the report to the yearly meeting stated that the amount of subscription was $50,000, which added to that previous raised made $53,000, and steps were taken to collect the same and have it placed on interest.

In 1887, after much labor, funds were secured for erecting Lindley Hall and Parry Hall, the former as a recitation hall and the latter to accommodate the chemical laboratory. Several years later funds were solicited and the present gymnasium erected and Reid Field secured for athletics. During the spring of 1907 funds were secured for erecting

---

[147] Earlham Hall, near Norwich, England, was the family home of Joseph John Gurney, one of the best-known leaders of the Orthodox Quaker movement. Choosing this name for the college was a clear statement of where its Quaker loyalties lay.

Bundy Dormitory Building for boys, Zenas Bundy and wife giving $25,000 on condition that the college secure that much more and put up a $50,000 building. Thirty-thousand dollars was also secured from Andrew Carnegie towards putting up a library building on condition that the college raise a similar amount, the interest of which was to be used in the upkeep of the library. These buildings were completed ready to be occupied in the autumn of 1907.

These additions to the college buildings made it necessary to erect an additional heating plant, which was done in the autumn of 1907 at an initial cost of $20,000. During these years also the endowment fund has been increased to $340,000[148] through the efforts of the friends of the college, and the school has increased in numbers so rapidly that at the present time all available space is occupied.

Leaving now the financial side of the college and its equipment, I will review the share it has taken in educational and religious work and show its influence on the Church and the world.

---

[148] Equivalent to about $7.4 million in 2009.

CHAPTER 36

Educational and Religious Influence of Earlham

We have seen that the beginning of Earlham was a religious concern for an institution where the young Friends could have a guarded and religious education. This deep-seated concern had enabled them to overcome all opposition, and now at the opening it was meet that they should read a psalm of rejoicing in which they gave God all the praise for what He had wrought. As we look back from our present standpoint we are impressed with the thought that our fathers built better than they knew. The hand of their God had been good upon them,[149] and their labors had brought forth a rich harvest of blessing to the Church and to the world.

He who takes a list of those who have been at the boarding-school and at Earlham College and traces their lives and marks their influence in the Church must be at once impressed with the wisdom of those who built for the future of the Church. Indeed, the student of history must see that no Church will live long or impress itself upon the world that does not have its educational institutions, and in proportion as these institutions are strong educationally and religiously will that influence be felt. As I have said before, it is when the head and the heart are trained together that the greatest and truest results will be seen.

This, I believe, is what Earlham has stood for in the past and is striving for at the present time even to a greater degree. I trust that there

---

[149] Nehemiah 2:18

is no disposition on the part of those who have the care of Earlham to boast and, above all, to compare her with other Friends institutions or try to build her up by pulling others down. If she cannot live on her own merits, she had better die. In all my pleas for funds or students for Earlham I have never felt at liberty to speak unkindly of other Friends colleges. Let her records speak for her. The church or college that boasts of its merit by finding fault with others and boasting of its superiority over sister churches or colleges in educational or religious lines is on the way to its own downfall.

I know all the colleges among Friends in this country; they all have their good qualities and all have God-fearing men and women in their faculties who are doing God's work in training the young men and women for the work that is before them. So, while I review a little of the influence that Earlham has had in the educational and religious world, it is with no feeling of boasting, but of thankfulness for what God has helped her to do, and with a desire to encourage her sister colleges to go forward with their good work, that they, together with Earlham, may labor and make the Quaker Church what it should be to meet the demands which will be made upon it during the twentieth century.

Talking several years ago with a president of one of the denominational colleges of our State, he remarked that the "teachers that come from Earlham graduates stand high among our schools. They do good work educationally and their moral and religious influence is good." From the statistics it appears that a larger percentage of the graduates have entered the profession of teaching in the past than of some other institutions, and perhaps a larger percentage do so at the present time. The explanation of this may lie in the fact that they were trained to a religious feeling that it was their duty to do what they could for the good of the Church and world, and that the calling of a teacher was the open door to directly influencing the world for good.

> ... the calling of a teacher was the open door to directly influencing the world for good.

The need of an education for a minister, missionary, or any other direct worker in the Christian field was not so apparent then as it is to-day. Now, however, they are entering a greater variety of fields of usefulness. It is more and more felt that to fill any position in the Church or State requires our best. To be a farmer, a good business man, or a useful citizen of any kind, one needs a well-trained mind. Consequently more of our college graduates are now found in these various avenues of usefulness.

In a previous chapter reference was made to a religious awakening which took place in the summer of 1865. One who took an active part in this spiritual awakening, and who is still living, has given the following information: "It was so pronounced among the students that a concern originated among the students themselves to hold a prayer meeting. It was decided to lay the matter before Walter T. Carpenter, who at that time was superintendent. He gave his consent, and manifested his interest by being present when he could. They had some remarkable meetings. At times several would take part, and much tenderness was manifested. Indeed, a revival spirit broke out in the school, especially among the young men. These young men, upon their returning to their homes, carried the spirit of religious awakening with them into [their] home meetings, and may have had much to do with the revival that took place about that time in various centers throughout the Society here in the West."

The prayer meeting started at that time has never been laid down. From that day to this it has been kept up through all the years when the college was in session. Many of the old students have come to remember the "Earlham prayer meeting" as being the time and place where they received a spiritual blessing. The boys now have their meeting in Bundy Hall on Fifth-day evening, and the girls have theirs in Earlham Hall at the same time. On First-day evening they all meet together in the association room in Earlham Hall. In addition to these, during the series of special meetings which are held in both halls during the winter term of each year, "floor prayer meetings" are held for five or ten minutes each day, each of these meetings including only the students who are grouped on one floor or one hall of the building. I have never found more satisfactory prayer meetings, among all those I have attended, than those at Earlham College on First-day evening, that had their origin in 1865 in one of the rooms of Earlham Hall.

I wish to describe the manner of conducting them. They are under the care of a joint committee of the Young Men's and Young Women's Christian Associations, the chairman of which is usually a senior. This committee selects a leader for each evening. This leader takes his or her position at the table in front of the meeting, generally calls for a hymn, and then reads a portion of Scripture bearing upon the subject that he wishes to bring before the meeting. This is usually followed by a season of prayer at the commencement in which all drop into silence. No one is called upon, but each one is left to engage in vocal prayer as he may feel led. This generally lasts for several minutes, during which very often twenty or more are heard in vocal prayer.

When the season of prayer is over the leader then speaks on the subject that impresses his mind for about ten minutes, after which another hymn is sung and the meeting is again thrown open for each one to take such part in prayer, testimony, or song as he may feel called upon to do. No one is urged and no one named, but it is conducted as a real Quaker meeting. During this time generally one comes out who has never spoken before. It is good for those of us who are older to go in and sit among these young people and feel that the Spirit is leading them in their devotional exercises and that God is in their midst.

As a result of this religious atmosphere in the institution there are a number of volunteer Bible classes, both among the girls and among the boys, which are kept up throughout the year. There is also a branch of the student volunteer organization for foreign missionary work which includes several of the students, both boys and girls, and there are several mission study classes along general lines of mission work which meet weekly.

Some two years ago Professor Murray Kenworthy, of the Biblical department of Earlham College, collected some facts relating to the religious life of the Church and college, extracts from which were printed in the Earlham College Bulletin of November, 1907, and which have been placed at my disposal for use. They are as follows:

> It appears that in the twelve yearly meetings of Friends in this country there is on an average one minister to every 69 members, while among the former students of Earlham College the proportion is one to every 40, and among the graduates of Earlham there is one minister to every 13 members of the alumni. From 1885 to 1895 inclusive the total number of students enrolled in the Biblical department was 123. During the years from 1896 to 1906 inclusive the total number was 479.
>
> During the last year, 1906–07, there were 34 ministers, prospective ministers, and missionaries enrolled as students of the college. The following Earlham missionaries are and have been in the foreign field. In Mexico, 14; West Indies, 2; Alaska, 4; among the Indians, 9; Japan, 7; China, 5; Palestine, 1: making a total of 42. The largest number from any other Friends college is 26. The total number of American missionaries in the field is 95, of whom a large percentage are former Earlham students.
>
> Even this, however, is not an adequate criterion of the religious life of the college, since these missionary statistics are confined exclusively to Friends, who have constituted for years an average of not much over 50 per cent of the total enrollment of the college. We are thankful for the opportunity to make even a slight contribution to the progress of the Church of Jesus Christ.

The above figures do not include the records of the last two years, which would increase the members in both Earlham and in other institutions. The above facts are given with a feeling of thankfulness to our Heavenly Father for his blessings upon Earlham, and with a prayer that He may continue to bless her and all her sister colleges among Friends.

CHAPTER 37

Filling Various Offices at Earlham

The six years during which I held the position of superintendent and treasurer of Earlham College were active years, calling for much labor and activity to meet the demands. Many changes were made, not only in the buildings, but also in the working of the institution and in its internal management. Among these was the changing of school rooms into dormitory rooms, in each of which two students studied and slept. Instead of all the girls studying in one school room under the care of an officer, and all the boys at the other end of the building under similar care, they now did this studying in their own rooms, which was productive of much good.

Another move, which was made with considerable trepidation on the part of those who had long had the care of the institution, was permitting the scholars to have their trunks taken to their rooms on the various floors in place of having them all in the basement where they had to go to wash and dress. Hot and cold water was introduced on each floor, and bath-rooms were put in for those living in Earlham Hall.

A small organ was placed in the superintendent's parlor, and the practice of allowing students to meet and play the instruments and sing Gospel hymns for one hour on First-day afternoons was introduced[150]—a practice that has been kept up all the years since to the help and benefit of many of the young people in cultivating their gift of singing, which has added comfort and refinement in many homes to which these people belonged. This was before a music teacher was employed and the study of vocal and instrumental music was introduced into the college.

More opportunity was granted the young men and women to walk together at proper times and proper bounds, and other social privileges were granted that have had the tendency to make the government of the institution easier and much more pleasant by removing much of the friction that existed under the old *régime*.

While my wife and I were looking after these things, I found time to visit all the quarterly meetings in the limits of Indiana and Western yearly meetings, and those of some other yearly meetings, soliciting funds for building and endowment. I also visited many homes and private individuals in various portions of our country, from Maine to the far West. This was especially laborious work and added much to my cares.

In 1885 the college found itself with a heavy debt resting upon it, originating from various improvements and other sources, and the trustees were anxious for me to go to England and Ireland to solicit funds. Our Friends on that side of the water had taken an interest in the early history of Earlham, and as we have already seen, manifested it at times in giving of their means.

So, in the summer of 1885 I went over and spent three months in going among the dear Friends of London and Dublin yearly meetings. My work was mostly done privately, although I attended the yearly meeting and a few of the quarterly meetings and several other meetings. I did not feel at liberty to speak of my mission publicly except to answer such questions as might be asked and to give such information as was desired.

---

[150] This would still have been a radical idea to many Friends in the 1880s.

The trustees, in their report to the yearly meeting in that year, make the following allusion to this visit: "At our request Allen Jay visited England in order to present to our Friends there the educational interests of Friends in America, not so much with a view to receiving present contributions as to impart definite information which might in the future result in larger additions to our endowment fund. He was very kindly received by our English Friends, who unexpectedly invited him to address London Yearly Meeting upon educational matters in this country. He subsequently attended several of the quarterly meetings, in some of which he was requested to speak on our educational affairs and, as shown in his report, a considerable amount of money was subscribed to promote the educational interest of Earlham, which is very valuable to our material prosperity. From information received by some of our board through private correspondence, we believe his visit was opportune."

Friends received me kindly and gave an amount sufficient to wipe out the debt and to add a few thousand dollars to our endowment fund, for which the college authorities were thankful. But I wish to say here that my acquaintance with English and Irish Friends and the great work they are doing in home and foreign mission work, educational and general philanthropic work at home and abroad, has led me to the conclusion that the time has come when Friends in America should cease calling upon those in England for financial aid in carrying on the work we are engaged in, in our own land. It was all right when our country was new and our Friends were largely farmers, clearing their land and laboring to get a start in the financial world, for our English brethren to assist in building meeting-houses and starting schools, to give of their abundant means to help us in this country to lay the foundation for the work that was resting upon us. But has not the time now come for us to freely use our own means? I think so, except in rare cases or special circumstances that may occasionally come up out of the ordinary course of events.

Another phase of the work at Earlham which I have already alluded to became regular while I was superintendent. Each year we held special religious services for all those who made their home in Earlham Hall. It was a privilege to take an active part in providing for this work and to take a leading part in carrying it forward. The meetings were productive of much good, and many date the beginning of their Christian life to these special meetings. The most remarkable of these was the series held in the winter of 1885. The meetings were held immediately after supper and before study hours commenced. Then those who desired to remain could do so for a while, when they were more definitely encouraged to decide for the Master.

Some idea of the result of this effort may be gained from the following extract taken from President J.J. Mills' report to the yearly meeting at the close of that school year: "Probably no former year in the history of the college has been characterized by greater religious interest than has the year just passed. From the opening of the school year it was comparatively rare for a meeting for worship to close without one or more testimonies from students to the power of Christ in their hearts. In the students' prayer meetings the spiritual awakening was even more earnest, resulting in numerous professions of conversion. Before the close of the winter term all but about fifteen of the large number of students in attendance had professed faith in Jesus Christ. The new converts as a rule remained firm until they left for their homes at the close of the college year. All of the senior class left their alma mater to enter upon their lifework as earnest, consecrated men and women."

In 1884 a special course of study was organized for the benefit of ministers, Bible school teachers, and other Christian workers which was the beginning of what now is the Biblical department of instruction at Earlham College.[151] The establishment of this special course was an attempt to meet what was believed to be a need of the Society

---

[151] The Biblical department was first headed by Dougan Clark, a well-known Evangelical Quaker holiness preacher and revivalist, who came under fire for advocating water baptism. He was replaced at Earlham in 1895 by Elbert Russell.

of Friends in this day of rapid development of evangelistic, pastoral, Bible school, and missionary work.

On account of my wife's failing health, her strength was not sufficient for the duties devolving upon her as matron, and we felt it to be right to resign our positions and retire to our home near the college.

Solicitor for Earlham

We left Earlham on account of the failing strength of my dear wife. The trustees had entered into an arrangement with me to give much of my time to soliciting funds to build and equip two buildings, which are now called Parry Science Hall and Lindley Hall. The former received its name from Mordecai Parry because this friend had agreed to give $5,000 for its erection. The latter was called Lindley Hall from the fact that Dr. Alfred Lindley and his wife, Eliza H. Lindley, gave $10,000 towards the building.

I have no desire to enter into any detailed account of the soliciting I did during the next few years. It is done, and the results speak for themselves. We can only say that greater funds had been secured both for building and [for the] endowment fund. Those who have not passed through similar experiences will not realize what a drain it makes upon the mental and physical life to go from meeting to meeting, home to home, and individual to individual, persuading them to give of their means to religious and educational work.

Some of those experiences are pleasant to look back upon. Others are not. One instance of the former kind I will mention. While at Friends Boarding-school, Providence, a dear Friend living near Fall River, Massachusetts, gave $1,500 to help that institution. Thinking the matter over one day, I said to my wife: "I am going to see Sarah Slade and ask her to give me as much for Earlham College as she gave to Friends Boarding-school."

Next day I started. When I reached her home they were preparing to go to meeting that night. After supper she asked if I would go with them to meeting. I told her I would, but that I would like to lay my business before her before going. I called her attention to what she had done for the boarding-school, told her what we were trying to do at Earlham College, and in about fifteen or twenty minutes laid the whole subject before her. She turned to the friend having charge of her account and asked if there were enough money on hand to pay that amount. He replied there was. She added: "Give Allen Jay a check for that amount and we will go to meeting." The next morning I was ready to return home.

It was not always so. I remember another time going to Massachusetts to see a man whom I hoped to interest in Earlham. That was a failure. He did not give anything. After years of soliciting funds I am convinced that a large amount of the money given for benevolent work comes from what may be termed the middle class—those who are neither rich nor poor. I am glad to say that there are some noble exceptions to this rule. If a man has been prospered and has made money by saving, but has lived to be fifty years old without learning to give, he rarely gives much. He may possibly give it in his will, when he can no longer hold it.

It is a cause for thankfulness that we are now training the children to give in our Bible schools, Christian Endeavor and missionary societies, and in some places in the Church also. When church members give on the first day of the week according as the Lord has prospered them, then there will be money to carry on Christian, educational, and philanthropic work. Then the occasions for public appeals will be more rare and be confined to special work and special occasions.[152]

While the work had its unpleasant features, it had also its pleasant side. It opened the way for me to go into many Friends homes and become acquainted with them and with their children, which resulted not only in my obtaining financial help, but also in increasing the

---

[152] Many Friends meetings at this time did not take up a collection or offering during worship, preferring to send funds directly to the meeting treasurer. This would have been universal during Allen Jay's younger years, and his comment shows how much local meeting practices had changed in his own lifetime.

number of students in the college. Looking back over those years, we see that the number in attendance has increased. The growth has been in proportion to the work done.

Religious Visits

In addition to this I often obtained minutes from my meeting liberating me for religious service in the monthly, quarterly, or yearly meetings where I went. In this way I visited most of the quarterly meetings in Indiana, Western, Ohio, and Wilmington yearly meetings, besides many of the other meetings, and up to 1898 I attended all the yearly meetings in the United States and Canada with which we held epistolary correspondence, and several of them a number of times, my wife going with me on a number of these visits.

I attended the opening of Wilmington Yearly Meeting,[153] and in 1895 the opening of California Yearly Meeting as a delegate from Indiana Yearly Meeting, the other delegate being our late friend, Mary A. Goddard. Others have written of the setting up of California Yearly Meeting, so I pass it by, simply saying that it was a satisfactory occasion and I believe it was opened in the ordering of our Heavenly Father. My wife being with me on this occasion, we held a series of meetings in a number of the meetings composing California and Oregon yearly meetings. We returned home by way of Oregon and attended that yearly meeting, which had been opened two years previously.

These two new yearly meetings on the Pacific coast are occupying important positions in regard to the future welfare of our Church, especially along our western coast. Whittier and Pacific colleges should claim a special interest and sympathy, for the welfare of California and Oregon yearly meetings largely depends upon the maintenance and success of these two colleges.

---

[153] Wilmington Yearly Meeting was set off from Indiana Yearly Meeting and held their opening sessions in 1892.

Superintendent of the Evangelistic and Pastoral Committee of Indiana Yearly Meeting

Besides the above claims upon my time, I was a member of the evangelistic and pastoral committee, a member of the executive committee of the Peace Association of Friends in America, also a member of the associated executive committee on Indian affairs, all of which demanded more or less of my attention.

Especially was this the case during the six years in which I acted as superintendent of evangelistic and pastoral work of Indiana Yearly Meeting. This was an opportunity that opened a wide door for great usefulness. The evangelistic and pastoral committee was appointed twenty-eight years ago by Indiana Yearly Meeting.[154] It has done much towards strengthening the yearly meeting. Its duties are to superintend the evangelistic work, look after pastoral work, and enter in and possess new territory that may present a promising field.

It was first called the committee on the ministry, then the evangelistic and pastoral committee, but now is known as the evangelistic, pastoral, and Church extension committee. It is necessary for this committee to be acquainted with the different meetings and the different workers, and to be able to help locate the pastors and evangelists, and have a general superintendence of the work and the workers. It has never been the policy of the committee to dictate who should go to certain meetings to act as pastors, but where a meeting desired the assistance of a resident minister, to introduce them to each other and then let them decide between themselves as to the call being of the Lord. In the evangelistic work it was highly important that the

---

[154] The Evangelistic and Pastoral Committee of Indiana Yearly Meeting was formed in 1881. Allen Jay served as superintendent from 1890-96, and as chair of the committee from 1902 until his death in 1910. It is difficult to overemphasize the explosive growth which Indiana Yearly Meeting experienced during this period. At least sixty new monthly meetings were set off, in places as diverse as Indiana, Ohio, Michigan, Arkansas, and Florida. Most were in small, rural communities, but some were in the growing industrial centers. At least fourteen meetings which were founded between 1890 and 1910 during Allen Jay's period of active involvement with this committee are alive and well today, forming almost a quarter of Indiana Yearly Meeting.

one who went in to the field was able to do the work required in that particular place.

It has been of great importance to be able to prevent those who are introducing disturbing elements, calculated to divide and scatter meetings, make contention and dissension, from coming into the limits of our yearly meeting. It has been the course of our committee to say but little about this class except when they came among us and actually produced trouble by their wild and extreme hobbies and fanatical doctrines. It is then their policy to quietly advise the closing of our meeting-house doors against them, Indiana Yearly Meeting having given this committee this power a few years ago in order to avoid this fruitful source of trouble.[155]

It is a cause for thankfulness that to-day in nearly every portion of Indiana Yearly Meeting love and harmony are prevailing, and the present prospect is that our next annual report will be one of the most satisfactory we have had in a number of years. It is a cause for thankfulness to have had the privilege of being so closely associated with the leading church workers and the vital interests of the Church's welfare both present and future; to look back and see the changes that have taken place in the active work in the Church during the years we have lived and labored, and to feel at times that perhaps we have added our mite to the spreading of the Redeemer's kingdom in our day.

But at such times it is safe to remember our infirmities, to bear in mind the language of Paul where he says: "Lest by any means when I have preached to others I myself should be a castaway."[156] It is not our work for the Church nor our activities and zeal for the cause of Christ that save us and give us an inheritance with the saints in light, but faith in Christ. Here I am reminded of an incident in my life.

---

[155] A major concern of the Evangelistic and Pastoral Committee was maintaining Friends' traditional position on outward sacraments. This was a special problem during a time when ministers were recorded by the monthly meeting, rather than the yearly meeting, and when little or no formal training for ministers was required. A review of the successive Books of Discipline during this period shows an increasing level of concern on this topic, and increasingly explicit directions to disown members and ministers who violated the discipline in this area.

[156] 1 Corinthians 9:27

In the year 1873, after visiting the meetings in Canada Yearly Meeting,[157] on my way home I stopped and attended a general meeting held at Winthrop, Maine, in a tent located on the grounds of Moses Bailey. It was a wonderful meeting. The power of the Lord was manifested and many were converted. The meeting closed on First-day night. Our friends, Eli and Sybil Jones, attended the beginning of the meeting. Then Sybil Jones was taken dangerously ill, so much so that her friends almost despaired of her life.

On Second-day morning, before leaving, I called to inquire how she was. She requested that I should come in, and pointed to a chair near where she lay propped up in bed. Her voice was weak. She referred to the wonderful reports she had heard of the meeting the day before, and then went on to say, as near as I can remember, something like this: "Yesterday I was on the border of the river, looking across. All looked bright and I began to rejoice that the life battles were over and that I had been faithful, but while reviewing the years spent in the Master's service and counting the sacrifices that I had made in His behalf, a cloud came over my vision and I exclaimed, 'Lord, what does this mean?' The answer came back, 'Not by works of righteousness thou hast done, but by my own precious blood have I saved thee.' Immediately I looked to Jesus. Again all was joy and peace."

Looking at me, she raised her finger and pointing it toward me slowly said, "Go, Allen Jay, but wherever thou goest in the world, preach salvation through the Lord Jesus Christ. Farewell." These were the last words I ever heard her speak. She died not long afterwards.

---

[157] Canada Yearly Meeting (Orthodox) had strong ties to its neighbors in the U.S., and joined Five Years Meeting in 1907. The present-day Canadian Yearly Meeting was formed in 1955 by a merger of Canada Yearly Meeting (Orthodox), Genessee Yearly Meeting (Friends General Conference), and Canada Yearly Meeting (Conservative).

CHAPTER 38

Origin of the Five Years' Meeting

A Brief Review of the Origin of the Five Years' Meeting, the Preparation of the Declaration of Faith, and the Adoption of the Uniform Discipline

In preparing this short history of these facts, I wish to acknowledge that I have drawn largely from a lecture given by Timothy Nicholson before the Christian Endeavor Society of Friends Church, Indianapolis, and later before the one at Fairmount, Indiana. I have also had access to all the published proceedings of the various quinquennial conferences and of the Five Years' Meeting up to date.

In all ages of the Church, God has had men who, as some in the tribe of Issachar in David's time, have had understanding of the signs of the times and knew what Israel ought to do. Such men have had ideals sometimes so far in advance that they have had to wait for the mass of people to be educated up to the visions God had given them before it was safe to proclaim them. I have seen it stated that John Woolman said that he waited some years before he was at liberty to tell Philadelphia Yearly Meeting all he had seen of the evils of slavery and the position that God called that yearly meeting to take on that great issue. Perhaps Barnabas C. Hobbs, of Western Yearly Meeting, had understanding of the signs of the times when he wrote the proposition, an extract from which was sent to all the other yearly meetings in a postscript to Western Yearly Meeting's epistles in 1870:

"This meeting has been introduced into a desire for a more perfect union among the different yearly meetings of Europe and America. There are many departments of Christian labor of common interest that call for united counsel...We apprehend that a general council, composed of representatives appointed by the several yearly meetings, would have a harmonizing and unifying effect upon our common Society and render the whole and its parts more truly supportive of each other; whose conclusions and recommendations shall only be advisory in their nature. Should this proposition meet with general approval, we would suggest that the first meeting be held in the State of New York, immediately after Canada Yearly Meeting, in 1872."

Indiana Yearly Meeting, which occurred the following week, referred this proposition to a committee to report in 1871. The report was in substance that "the way did not open to accept the proposition at this time."

Similar action was taken by several other yearly meetings. Therefore no general conference was held. Widely separated as American yearly meetings were, and there being no permanent bond of union between them except that of epistolary correspondence, there grew up a spirit of independence and neglect of co-operation.

This independence on the part of certain prominent members in one or more yearly meetings was manifested in some of the epistolary correspondence. Differences of opinion in these epistles sometimes led to earnest exhortation, now and then bordering on criticism. This kind of correspondence was the basis of the proposition of Western Yearly Meeting in 1875. In that same year, 1875, Indiana Yearly Meeting adopted the following as the united judgment of the meeting: "We feel called upon at this time to reaffirm the views always held by Friends upon the subject of baptism and the supper. We believe that the baptism which essentially pertains to the present dispensation is that of Christ, who baptizes His people with the Holy Spirit, and that the true communion is a spiritual partaking of the body and blood of Christ. Therefore we believe it to be inconsistent for any one to be acknowledged or retained in the position of minister or elder among us who continues to participate in or teach the necessity of the outward rite of baptism or of the supper."

Again, in 1885, the following minute was adopted by Indiana Yearly Meeting: "Having learned with sorrow that certain individuals holding the position of ministers of the gospel in one of the co-ordinate bodies of the Society of Friends have partaken of the rites of water baptism and of the bread and wine in the so-called communion of the Lord's Supper, some of whom have administered these rites to others and have been holding meetings within limits of Indiana Yearly Meeting, and advocated publicly and privately their views, which are contrary to the testimonies which the Society of Friends have always maintained as to the spiritual nature of Christ's kingdom, and to the declaration of faith in our book of discipline, and to the united judgment of our yearly meeting in 1875; now in order to protect our membership from such influences and teaching, all of our meetings are refused to receive as acceptable ministers of the gospel, whether members of other yearly meetings or of our own, those teaching doctrines or practicing rites contrary to the above declaration of faith and minute of the yearly meeting. Their minute or certificates should not be read in our meetings, nor should meetings be appointed for them in our meeting-houses, nor should they be encouraged to labor within our borders."

For the foregoing reasons and some others, the concern of Western Yearly Meeting in 1870 and 1875 was still a living concern with several of the leading Friends of Indiana and other yearly meetings. One evening during yearly meeting, in 1886, at the table of Timothy Nicholson were seated William O. Newhall, of New England; Mary Underhill, of New York; William L. Pearson, then of North Carolina; Barnabas C. Hobbs, of Western; Isom P. Wooton, of Iowa; and Francis W. Thomas, of Indiana Yearly Meeting. During the meal the host introduced the subject of a conference of delegates from all the yearly meetings. The matter was discussed with much interest and with entire unanimity of judgment that the time had come for such a meeting, and Francis W. Thomas was requested to introduce the subject to the yearly meeting the next day.

This was done, and the following minute was united with by the meeting: "The subject of a conference of committees from the different yearly meetings in America with which we correspond, having been introduced into this meeting, after deliberate consideration it was believed that the holding of such a conference to consider matters pertaining to the welfare of our branch of the Church would strengthen the bond of Christian fellowship amongst us and tend to promote unity in important matters of faith and practice in the different bodies into which Friends in a manner are divided. We are therefore united in proposing to our sister yearly meetings in America that such a conference be held, and that it be composed of delegates appointed by the different yearly meetings, its conclusions to be only advisory, but at least five yearly meetings must unite in it or the conference not be held. We also propose that such a conference be held next year, 1887, in Richmond, Indiana, beginning on Sixth-day, following the close of Western Yearly Meeting, at 9:00 A.M." Then followed the names of twelve delegates.

"And we further propose that a cordial invitation be extended to London and Dublin yearly meetings to send delegates to this conference. This minute is directed to be appended to the epistles to the different yearly meetings with which we correspond."

All the yearly meetings in the world with which we corresponded accepted the proposition of Indiana Yearly Meeting, and the conference was held at the time and place proposed. Those who had given the most thought to the conditions in our several yearly meetings, and who advocated the holding of such a conference, hoped that in this way one declaration of faith or Christian doctrine and one uniform discipline for all the American yearly meetings could be agreed upon, and that ultimately the advisory committee would result in a permanent body with certain delegated powers.

It is not my purpose to give a detailed account of the various quinquennial conferences and the discussions which finally resulted in the declaration of faith, in the uniform discipline, in the formation of the American Friends Board of Foreign Missions, and the establishing of the Five Years' Meeting in 1902, for these discussions are matters of history and are published in the minutes and proceedings of each meeting, and will be interesting reading for the future historian of our Society. Our young Friends should read and study them, that they may know how all these conclusions were finally reached.

A few facts about the writing of the declaration of faith may be interesting and worth preserving. After the organization of the conference the first question proposed for discussion was: "Is it desirable that all the yearly meetings of Friends in the world should adopt one declaration of Christian doctrine?"

One entire session was devoted to the discussion of the question, more than twenty delegates from nine yearly meetings taking part, and all but one in the affirmative. A committee of twelve was appointed to draft the said declaration of faith, which was, after free discussion, approved by the conference and subsequently adopted or approved by all the American yearly meetings except Ohio.[158]

The committee met, and different ones were appointed to prepare certain sections of the declaration, but the greater portion of it was prepared by our late dear friend, Joseph Bevan Braithwaite, of London Yearly Meeting. It was written at the desk where I am now sitting. When he left home, thinking that something of the kind might claim the attention of the conference, he put in with his baggage several books and manuscripts that were prepared by the earlier writers among

---

[158] It was no surprise that Ohio Yearly Meeting did not approve the Richmond Declaration of Faith, which strongly reaffirmed the traditional Quaker position on outward sacraments. In 1885, two years before the Richmond conference met, Ohio Yearly Meeting had allowed "liberty of conscience" in the matter of outward observance of baptism and communion. It must have grieved Allen Jay terribly that two Friends who he respected and worked with, David B. Updegraff and Dougan Clark, led the way in Ohio for this departure from Quaker tradition. A firm believer in moderate change and evangelicalism himself, this was one line which Allen Jay could not cross.

Friends and had not been changed by Friends of more recent date in this country or anywhere else. His remark was: "We want the original Quakerism free from the influence and thought of some of our Friends who have imbibed some of the spirit and practice of other denominations or have been influenced by their environments."

Our dear friend worked early and late when not in the conference. I remember lying on the lounge until he quit writing near midnight, and then taking him to the dining room and getting him something to eat before he retired. Then in the morning he was up before anyone else. This was the case for two nights. Before it was presented to the conference it was gone over carefully, Joseph Bevan Braithwaite sitting at the desk reading carefully what had been written; Dr. James E. Rhoads, of Philadelphia, looking over the quotations from Friends writings to see that they were correct[ly] quoted; and Dr. James Carey Thomas, of Baltimore, watching the Scripture quotations to see that there were no mistakes made there. They have all three passed away, but their work remains. Next morning, after it was adopted by the conference, Joseph Bevan Braithwaite handed me the pen he wrote it with and said: "Thee may have that to keep." I have it yet.

The subject of establishing a conference of yearly meetings with certain delegated powers, to meet at stated periods, was ably treated and agitated in a paper written by Dr. William Nicholson, of Kansas Yearly Meeting. He pointed out the importance of it, and with a perfect insight he portrayed what we now have in the Five Years' Meeting. There was no time to discuss it, but the yearly meetings were requested to consider the subject.

While there was no time to enter upon the consideration of this important matter, it was interesting to notice that the opposition to this and other advanced steps, such as the uniform discipline and the American Friends Board of Foreign Missions, came from those occupying extreme views, conservatives or radicals. The extremes met in opposing movements calculated to unite the Church. People who have extreme views either way as a rule are not safe leaders. They can see but one side of a question. Indeed they would have people believe there is but one side, and that one their side.

A friend of mine who was a great educator once remarked to me: "Only a few men can see both sides of a question," but Dr. William Nicholson read the signs of the times and knew what Israel ought to do. Such men are born leaders, but have to wait sometimes. He said: "Such a meeting will be organized some day and will have a beneficial effect in strengthening and unifying the Church." He saw the finger of God pointing in that direction. Such men labor, and other men enter into their labors.

To-day our branch of the Church needs men who have "understanding of the signs of the times and know what Israel ought to do": men whose vision is forward, and not backward; men who see good and not evil in the future for the Church; men who are laboring to unite rather than to divide the Church; men who tell us that the hand of God is good upon us. So that Friends may say to one another under their leadership: "Let us arise and build."[159]

> People who have extreme views either way as a rule are not safe leaders. They can see but one side of a question.

---

[159] Nehemiah 2:18

CHAPTER 39

The Origin of the Bible Institute

The beginning of the Bible institute came about in this way. While acting as superintendent of the evangelistic and pastoral committee of Indiana Yearly Meeting, I was impressed with the importance of our ministers giving more time to the study of the Bible. While our First-day school conventions and Christian Endeavor assemblies and ministerial conferences had their places and were doing a great work in stirring up an interest in these various fields of labors, yet this interest was too superficial and temporary to meet the needs of our ministers and Christian workers.

This was fully demonstrated when the Bible institute was started and the study of the Bible was more thoroughly introduced through lectures that required thought and research to follow and enjoy. It was nothing unusual to hear those who had been accustomed to the excitement of revival work and who had listened to the addresses and lectures given before the Bible school assemblies and Christian Endeavor conventions, which were filled with anecdotes and exciting illustrations intended to move the emotions and stir up the feelings for the time, to say: "We do not enjoy these Bible institutes. We want to be out 'saving souls.' We want to do something more practical. These studies are too dry for us."

This is the same argument often heard from the college boy when his father wants him to remain in college: "I want to get into business. I want to make money." It was the same hurry for visible results that first prevailed in regard to going into the foreign mission work. If some missionary had the zeal and wanted to go, the Church laid its hands on him and sent him forth, but after many failures and a great waste of time and money, no foreign mission board to-day that is worthy of the name will accept a candidate for the mission field who has not, along with the zeal, a trained mind, and who has not studied to prepare himself for the field where he is to go. And if, in addition to his religious training, he has some medical knowledge, so much the better. Yes, and the subject of bodily health is now included in the curriculum of the more advanced foreign missionary board[s].

The future minister of the Gospel in our branch of the Church must recognize the fact that along with his call and zeal there must be a knowledge of the Bible and of Christian work that he will only obtain by thorough work and real study and research that will fill his mind with "things new and old"[160] that the Spirit can draw upon when he stands before the congregation.

> Our congregations are being filled more and more by persons who know more than the minister ...

Our congregations are being filled more and more by persons who know more than the minister, who weigh him and decide wherein he is wanting. They have their spiritual experiences as well as the minister, and know that which feeds the soul and builds up the spiritual man. The minister who ignores these facts may satisfy for a season, but soon he will find he is not wanted. The congregations may be kind to him and treat him gently for what he has been, but when the opportunity offers he will find himself in the rear. Others will be put forward. If we have neglected the preparation we must not murmur. If they have grown tired of our oft-repeated sermons and turn to fresher ones with new thoughts and fresh life in them, we must not complain.

---

[160] Matthew 13:52

It was this view of the future of our Church that impressed me with the idea of making an effort to call as many ministers and Christian workers together at Earlham College as I could. Our evangelistic and pastoral committee had no money, but they were willing that as superintendent I should try my plan. I wrote an appeal, explaining what we wanted to do and the object we desired to accomplish. One hundred of these letters were sent to my friends, asking them to send whatever amount they felt it was right for them to give. The trustees were asked to let us have the use of the buildings and grounds at Earlham.

Notice was sent to the various monthly meetings of Indiana, Western, and Wilmington, inviting the ministers and workers to come. When the time arrived, between thirty and forty of this class were present, and the twelve days' program was carried out to the satisfaction of those present. Money enough came in to pay the board and all other expenses of those who came, and $100 was left after the entire expenses were met. That $100 was turned over to the Biblical department of Earlham College.[161]

Such was the beginning of this work, which I believe has been greatly blessed to many who have come under its influence. The following year the yearly meeting was requested to assume control of the movement. This resulted in an invitation to Western and Wilmington yearly meetings to unite in the control of the same. While there have been those who have found fault, as is the case with all onward movements, yet as those who have availed themselves of its benefits are the ones who are in demand for teachers and religious workers of various kinds in the different yearly meetings, the wisdom of the movement is demonstrated.

---

[161] The summer Bible institute ran from 1897-1909 at Earlham College under the leadership of Elbert Russell. Russell began teaching at Earlham in 1895 with only ten weeks of study of the Bible at the Moody Bible Institute and at Chautauqua. He quickly added more formal study of the Bible at the University of Chicago, and became widely known among Friends for his liberal understanding of the Bible.

CHAPTER 40

The Opening of California Yearly Meeting

During the next few years I attended several of the yearly meetings and engaged in such religious work as appeared to be right. In 1888 I attended Ohio and Iowa yearly meetings. In 1889 I attended Canada Yearly Meeting, my wife going with me. In 1890 my wife and I attended Baltimore Yearly Meeting and the opening of Wilmington Yearly Meeting in 1892. During the latter year, as yearly meeting superintendent, I visited the Friends in Florida belonging to Indiana Yearly Meeting.

In 1895, when Iowa Yearly Meeting set up California Yearly Meeting at Whittier, California, Indiana Yearly Meeting donated $1,000 to assist them in the beginning of their work, and appointed Mary H. Goddard and myself to attend the opening as delegates representing our yearly meeting. A number of Friends from Ohio, Indiana, and Western yearly meetings also went as visitors to the yearly meeting. According to the arrangements made, twenty-two of us left Chicago in the same tourist sleeper on the Sante Fé Railroad. My wife went with me. We had a minute from our meeting at home liberating us to attend the meetings of California Yearly Meeting, and also Oregon Yearly Meeting and the meetings belonging to it.

We had a very pleasant trip. There were several ministers in the company. It was customary, after breakfast was over and things were straightened up, to have a season of divine worship, which consisted in reading the Bible, singing hymns, and prayer, in which nearly all took part. After the first morning others requested the privilege of coming in from other cars in the train. The conductor entered into the arrangement, and the time selected was the one most convenient for him. Walking on the platform at a station while the train was taking water and making some changes, the engineer came up to me and inquired: "Do you belong to that car that has religious services every morning?" He added: "I wish I could attend them, but we men do not get much opportunity for anything like that." The last morning the car was full. It is pleasant to look back to those occasions and the company that met, but we are widely separated now. Perhaps some may have been blessed. We are commanded to sow seed by all waters.[162]

Pasadena was safely reached, and our train was on time. We were met by Friends, who kindly cared for us. The next day a company of ten or twelve of us were driven across the country in a tallyho to Whittier. It was a beautiful day, and we enjoyed the scenery very much. A warm welcome awaited us. The next morning the yearly meeting opened. I need not dwell much on that, for its history is known, but there were some features of it that were interesting.

> ... upon taking my seat and looking over the company, I recognized nearly half as Friends that I had met in the various yearly meetings along the Atlantic coast and the yearly meetings in the middle West, and a few from London.

When we met in the college building it was a great surprise to see so many that I knew. On the way my wife had remarked that when we reached California we would be among strangers. On the contrary, upon taking my seat and looking over the company, I recognized nearly half as Friends that I had met in the various yearly meetings along the Atlantic coast and the yearly meetings in the middle West, and a few from London. A larger proportion were

---

[162] The reference is unclear; possibly a conflation of Psalm 1:1-3 with the parable of the sower, found in Matthew 13:3-9, Mark 4:3-9, and Luke 8:5-8.

from Indiana, Western, and Iowa, the latter having more representatives than any other one. It was an intelligent and earnest body of Friends, many of them having come from meetings where they had been active members in Church work; so they were prepared to do their part in forming and organizing a strong yearly meeting and in carrying it forward, there being, however, one element of danger in this unique situation.

The strong men and women had their own idea of the proper manner of conducting the business of a yearly meeting, each being guided by the way in which it was done in the yearly meeting from which he came. Those who are acquainted with all the yearly meetings in America, each having its special territory, widely separated from each other, know the peculiar characteristics belonging to each one. Each differs from the other in some respect, and there is nothing to bring these different methods into harmony except epistolary correspondence and the visiting of ministers traveling in "truth's service," these latter being much more beneficial than at the time was recognized.

These visits were undertaken by the minister under a "religious concern" to preach the Gospel and to build up the Church, but as we look back to-day we can see that they did much to unify the meetings, draw the bond of Christian love tighter, and keep the spirit of separation down. It was beautiful, from session to session, though they had strong opinions of their own, to witness their yielding to one another and uniting in love and harmony in the transaction of the business that came before them in the organization of this yearly meeting, which was destined to play so important a part in the growth of Quakerism on the Pacific coast.

As the time has rolled on the same spirit has enabled the dear Friends of that yearly meeting to assimilate the various elements that have continued to flow into its borders from other yearly meetings. Perhaps there is a greater variety of opinions and shades of belief entering into the membership of that yearly meeting than of any other, yet they have continued to labor together with more or less harmony,

Whittier College[163] has done much to make it a center of great influence in the field it occupies, and as its membership becomes more united in the college its strength will increase and its stability will be assured. California Yearly Meeting has also been permeated with a real missionary spirit, which always has a reflex influence upon the meeting that is engaged in reaching out into new fields. So we must believe that the opening of this yearly meeting was in the ordering of the great Head of the Church and has been instrumental in the building up of His kingdom.

After the close of the yearly meeting my wife and I visited most of the meetings belonging to it, holding a series of meetings in several places, especially in Whittier and Pomona. Having finished our work in that yearly meeting at Berkeley, we then went on to Newberg, Oregon, where we had a pleasant time and found an open door for preaching the Gospel while attending Oregon Yearly Meeting, which was the first one established on the Pacific coast, having been set up in 1893. Here again we found many Friends from Eastern yearly meetings, though not in such great variety as in California.

The dear Friends here had shown great enterprise and liberality in starting Pacific College and building a good and substantial meetinghouse for the yearly meeting. Here again at the close of the yearly meeting we visited the meetings belonging to it. In looking back at the Friends of Oregon we feel now, as we did then, that they should have the sympathy and help of other Friends in the Eastern yearly meetings. Certainly Pacific College is located in an important field and is fulfilling a real mission.[164] I trust the day is not far off when they will receive more financial aid.

From there we returned home.

---

[163] Whittier College was founded in 1887 as Whittier Academy. Its first buildings were put up in 1893, and it received its charter as a college in 1901.

[164] Pacific College (now George Fox University), was started as an academy with fifteen students in 1891, and became a college in 1895; it changed its name to George Fox College in 1949, and merged with Western Evangelical Seminary in 1996 to become George Fox University. It is affiliated with Northwest Yearly Meeting and is located in Newberg, Oregon.

CHAPTER 41

Winter in Alabama and Florida

My dear wife, who had been failing in health for several years, now became so feeble that we decided to try a warmer climate during the winter of 1897. After some inquiries we decided to go to Evergreen, Alabama, located on the Louisville and Nashville Railroad, about fifty miles north of Mobile. We reached there and went to the leading hotel to board until we should have had time to look around and find rooms where we might set up housekeeping for ourselves.

There were a number of boarders, and on the second night there was a move to have a dance and a general good time. With true Southern politeness, I was invited to take part in the dance. When I pleaded ignorance in that line, an elderly gentleman took pity on me and invited me to take part in a game of cards. When I told him I did not know one card from another he looked surprised. At this stage an old gentleman came to my help with a look of real sympathy on his face and asked me to drink some wine with him and have a smoke, and when I replied that I neither drank nor smoked, he looked at me for a moment and exclaimed, "Well, what do you do?"

When we had watched for a while their proceedings, until they finally got the ball started and all appeared to be enjoying themselves, we retired to rest, impressed with what trash they were willing to feed upon and call it enjoyment. What poor food for either mind or body! It was continued until a late hour, and some had to be carried to bed, and the next day they were a sorry looking set, little prepared for real lifework. It is sad to see life wasted in such manner. Such people do not know what true living is.

We were soon nicely located in a couple of rooms, where we did our own housekeeping. Evergreen was a town of some 3,000 inhabitants, with an institution of learning located there to which they gave the name of "academy." My wife, being feeble, did not get out much. I attended a Methodist Bible school and their meetings on First-day, which were held every other First-day, and on the day that there was no service at the Methodist Church I went to the Baptist service and attended their Young People's Society in the afternoon. The Baptist was the largest congregation and the richest and most influential denomination in the place.

The Methodist leader, who had a class of older persons in their Bible school, was taken sick about three weeks after we reached there. The superintendent invited me to take the class, which I did. It soon got rumored through the town that we were Quakers and that I was a minister. We were curiosities. From that time I became a "speckled bird" in the town, and had many opportunities to discuss theology. I never enjoyed splitting hairs on doctrine, but felt the deep need of living Christ before the people, who were very friendly and came often to visit us and ask questions. We prayed that the Lord would make our stay a blessing to the churches, for religion was at a low ebb in all, the churches having but few members.

My class in the Bible school increased so that we had to have a larger space to meet in, and when the teacher returned he went into the class and told me to go ahead. I did away with reading the questions and the class reading the answers, and our class hour became a time of much interest. The Baptist Young People's Society called upon me several times to address them, which I gladly did, for their meetings had a large number of young people.

One First-day evening the Methodist minister asked me to preach for him, which I did, my wife saying, "I have been praying that the way might open to preach the Gospel to them." The name of Quaker brought a crowded house. A few days later, meeting the Baptist minister, he said, frankly, "Brother Jay, I would be glad to invite you to preach in my pulpit, but the officers of my church do not believe that anybody can preach the Gospel unless they have been immersed, and I understand you have not been." I simply told him that I was getting all I wished to do among his young people and in the other church.

Time rolled on, and between preaching occasionally, my Bible class, and the Baptist Young People's Society, I was kept busy. My wife occasionally got out to the prayer meeting, and when she took part it was a great surprise, and the women invited her to their missionary meetings and other special occasions and requested her to lead in vocal prayer.

About one month before the time for us to leave, the Methodist minister asked me how I would like to occupy his pulpit the next Sunday while he was away at his other appointment. I told him it was just what I had been wanting. So it was announced in the daily papers that the service would be held by a Quaker preacher. The house was packed morning and evening. It was a good day, and it was easy preaching. At the close of the night service the wife of the presiding elder, who lived at Evergreen, came to me and said: "Brother Jay, you made a mistake to-night. You ought to have called for an altar service. The congregation was ready for it." I told her that I had no disposition to take advantage of the pastor's absence.

The next evening the minister came to our home, and laying his cigar down on the porch rail, came in and asked me to take a moonlight walk with him. He said that the leaders of the church felt that the time had come to hold a revival service, and that they believed I should hold it. I told him that my wife and I had been praying for the way to open, and that I was ready. I wanted him to take charge of the singing and the opening prayer service, and then I would take charge of the meeting after that. He said, "Next Wednesday night, being prayer meeting night, we'll begin."

It was thoroughly advertised in the daily papers, and handbills were posted all over the town, so that the house was crowded from the beginning. The day before we were to begin, the minister came, with the Baptist minister with him, and said they thought it would be right to tell me a little about the conditions which surrounded the church in that place—that I must be careful not to say anything against card playing or dancing, and that I had better let the theater alone, as most of their people attended it. My reply was, "We will try and let the Lord direct the preaching."

The meetings went on eight or ten days, when one night, after I had closed preaching, I stepped down to the altar rail and said something like this, "Now, while they sing another hymn, if there is anyone in the house who wants to give his heart to God and live a Christian life, let him come and take my hand." Scarcely had the hymn begun when one of the wealthiest, most influential young ladies, theater-going, card-playing, and a leader in the ball-room, rose, about half-way back, and walking up the aisle with her face bathed in tears, came forward and grasped my hand, exclaiming, "Pray for me," and fell on her knees at the altar. Soon the altar was full, with some twenty or thirty persons. It was the beginning of a wonderful revival. The whole town was shaken.

My dear wife wrote a little account of the work to *The American Friend*, which was published in that paper Fifth month 6, 1897, and is as follows:

> Dear Friend: We have just returned to our home from Evergreen, Alabama, and I believe it will be right to tell a little of the work my husband has been engaged in since the note he wrote to thee a few weeks ago. He continued to teach the Bible class on First-day morning, which increased in numbers. He was called upon to address the Epworth League in the

Methodist church, and the Sunbeam Society in the Baptist church. He was also called upon to conduct the devotional exercises in the academy, which has over 300 students, besides being often called upon to tell of our religious views in private circles.

On First-day, the 4th of this month, the Methodist minister went to his other appointment, and my husband asked the privilege of holding meetings that day, both morning and evening. The house was full. On Second-day, when the minister returned, his official members called on him and requested that a series of meetings be held and my husband be invited to conduct them. He united with the proposition and began at once to make the arrangements, which were soon made. It was what we had been praying for, and the meetings began on Fourth-day, the 7th of Fourth month, continuing eighteen days, two meetings each day, one in the afternoon and one at night.

In addition there were five prayer meetings each day, at the same hour, in different parts of the town in private houses, where those living in the immediate vicinity attended. Many were reached in this way and thereby induced to attend the meeting. The merchants and other business men closed their places of business during the last week and came with their clerks to attend the services both afternoon and evening.

The meetings have been occasions of great blessing. The house has been full, and at times some went away, being unable to get in. Generally from fifty to one-hundred came forward seeking salvation or a better experience, manifesting much brokenness of spirit. Many of these were members of some one of the churches, having been baptized with water, but continuing in card-playing, dancing, theater-going, and other worldly amusements. Many confessed that they had never heard the Gospel preached before. They had not thought of a self-denying life as so essential to a real Christian character.

They were told plainly that they must deny self, take up the cross, and follow Jesus daily. The baptism of the Holy Spirit was held up as the only saving baptism. The doctrine of a full and free salvation was proclaimed without reserve. I think I never heard my husband more favored in proclaiming the Gospel. The prejudice among the churches gave way and they all joined in, many who were converted, to praise the Lord. Even the women's voices were heard in prayer and praise in public, which was a wonderful revolution among their churches.

At the last meeting my husband asked all who would promise to have family worship in their homes to come forward and shake hands with him. A large number did so, with tears and solemn promises. The meeting was closed by singing "God be with you till we meet again." The parting was in much love. It has been the Lord's work. To Him be all the praise. Sincerely thy friend, Martha A. Jay.

With the above I close my account of the winter spent at Evergreen. The newspapers said a great deal of a flattering nature, which is better forgotten. The Methodist and Baptist ministers each wrote a very full account of the work and addressed it to our monthly meeting, but it was so full of flattery that I never felt like presenting it to the meeting. I do not remember now that I ever showed it to any of my friends. It is enough to say that the remembrance of those days brings a feeling of thankfulness. Many came to the train to see us off the night we left.

Winter in Florida

My wife continuing poorly, we felt that it would be right to spend the following winter where the climate would be mild and healthful. After some inquiry, and having some friends staying in Melbourne, Florida, we decided to go there. It was a pleasant little town, located on the banks of the Indian River, and several Northern people were in the place, spending their winter there on account of its pleasant climate. It contained several churches. I found work in the Bible schools of the Methodist and Episcopal churches, and was frequently invited to preach on First-day and take part in conventions and Sunday-school work.

It was interesting to observe the simple faith of those Southern people. While I do not know that Southern people as a class are any more religious than people in the more northern portions of our country, yet there is this difference: Among the great masses of people in the South you find comparatively few who express any doubt about the Bible or the facts it contains. Even those who pay but little attention to living a religious life will acknowledge the facts of Christianity as taught and believed by the various Churches. They may rarely go to church or Sunday-school, yet they will admit it is the right thing to do. They may seldom look inside their Bibles, yet they hold them in more reverence and would not think of disbelieving the doctrines set forth there as they understand them. To them the Bible is a sacred book, never to be repudiated.

My experience and observation has led me to believe that it is easier to preach the Gospel to them than it is to preach to the masses in our Northern States. While this is the case, I am not prepared to say that the moral and religious life of the people is, on the average, any higher than that of the same class of people in the northern and western sections of our country. They are perhaps more emotional, and will accept the truths of the Gospel more quickly and make a profession of faith more easily, but they may not hold out as long as those who have found it harder to get rid of their doubts.

During the winter I made a few excursions with the purpose of finding a few scattered Friends who had located in Florida. Among these I found one dear Friend whose father I had known in England. My visit at his home was one that I shall long remember. He did what he could to get up a meeting for me on First-day morning among the people where he lived. It proved a favored occasion.

Bereavements

We spent the winter very comfortably, going out nearly every day in a little boat on the water, which proved beneficial to my wife. Early in the spring, however, we learned of the declining health of our son, Dr. William C. Jay, who lived near Oskaloosa, Iowa. So we hastened home, and I went to help them close up their home in Iowa, bringing my son, his wife, and their son to our house. Soon afterward he went entirely blind, and I gave my time to the care of him and his mother until First month 10, 1898, when his life peacefully closed.

My wife gradually grew weaker until Fourth month 27, 1899, when she also sweetly passed to the Beyond. Her end was a beautiful example of how a Christian may die. Her advice and counsel to me during her closing days has been a strength and has enabled me to continue the work that I have found to do. Thus passed away a loving and devoted wife and mother. We had walked together over forty-four years. She never hesitated to give me up when I felt called to leave home to preach the Gospel or labor in religious work of any kind. Indeed I have often felt that her sacrifice was greater than mine, and that she was the one who should receive the greater reward. It may be sometimes that in expressing our sympathy and giving encouragement to the minister, the faithful wife at home with the children is forgotten by the church and its membership.

It was a lonely day when she left me. I felt indeed that the light of the home had gone out. None but those who have gone through it know what it is. I have tried, in a measure at least, to remember her advice, given the day before she died, when she said to me: "Now, when I am gone, don't sit down and mourn, but rise up and go to work and finish the service the Lord has for thee to do, and when it is done, come home and we will be together." She then told me some of the important things that it would be right for me to do, such as paying another visit to London and Dublin yearly meetings, helping to get Earlham and Guilford colleges out of debt, and some other labor. She certainly had a prophetic vision of what lay before me. I pray it may all be completed when the end comes.

Visits to Baltimore, New York, and New England Yearly Meetings

During the next year I felt it right to attend to some religious service in Baltimore, New York, and New England yearly meetings. During this journey I spent several days in the city of Washington, D.C., laboring among the Friends in that city and making my home with my dear friend, Robert Warder and his wife.

While in New England I went across to Nantucket Island and spent several days resting and looking over some of the old records to be found among those of the Historical Society on that island. My grandmother having been a Macy, and her father having come from that island, I felt more than ordinary interest. Seeing the name of Macy over a grocery store, I stepped in and told the owner that my great-grandfather Macy came from that island. He simply exclaimed, "You have 500 cousins here."

I visited the old meeting-house, where once there was a large meeting of Friends. It is said that at one time there were more than 2,000 Friends on the Island, but they are gone now, and there are only a few left. Those remaining belong to what they call the Wilburite party. I am not sure that there is any meeting held on the island any more.

It is a sad commentary on the vitality of Quakerism. We must believe that it is through no fault of the principles of Quakerism, but it is the fault of those who fail to present its living principles to the world around them. How much the separation had to do with pulling down Quakerism on that island and in many other places we may never know, but I believe that division and separation cannot remedy an evil, but always result in weakness and distraction to the Church.

While there I visited many interesting places. Among these was the home of William Mitchel, the father of Maria Mitchel, the astronomer, who won distinction and received a medal for her discovery in astronomy.[165] I enjoyed going up on top of the house where she used her telescope.

From Nantucket Island I went to Amesbury and talked with my dear friends, Daniel Maxfield and wife. The former was connected with Providence Boarding-school while we lived there. I visited the scenes of Whittier's early life and his home in Amesbury, which is now preserved by the Whittier Society and kept open for visitors, so they can see the home as he left it and many relics which were dear to him.[166] In visiting his grave I had an opportunity of witnessing evidences of the esteem in which his memory was held by many who came to look upon his last resting place. At the head of the grave the hedge which surrounds the lot had been cut away by people who had cut off portions to carry home as mementos.

Our English Friends have all along appreciated his writings more than Friends in America. I see that the Yorkshire 1905 Committee, in the belief that Friends have not yet done what they might in making known the "magnificent spiritual legacy left us by Whittier," have prepared a selection of his poems for free distribution.[167]

---

[165] Maria Mitchell (1819-1889), born to a Quaker family, won the gold medal prize for discovering a "telescopic comet" (too faint to be seen with the naked eye) in 1847. She also made important discoveries about sunspots. She later taught astronomy at Vassar College, N.Y.

[166] The Whittier home is still open to the public at 86 Friend Street, Amesbury, Mass.

[167] *A Whittier Treasury: Selected by the Countess of Portsmouth*, 1903.

It was interesting to visit the home of Thomas Macy, whose house has been placed under the care of the Society and turned into a museum where are kept many interesting mementos of the earlier days of Amesbury and the surrounding country.[168] Thomas Macy was persecuted for harboring Quakers. I have seen it stated that perhaps Marmaduke Stevenson and William Robinson[169] stayed over night in his home a short time before they were hung in Boston. He took his family in a boat and went down the stream into the ocean and crossed over to Nantucket Island, and some accounts say that they were the first white people who ever settled there.

After spending most of the summer in visiting many of the Friends and meetings in these yearly meetings, I returned home in time for our yearly meeting.

---

[168] The Macy-Colby House, at 247 Main Street in Amesbury, Mass., was first built in 1654. It still exists and is maintained as a museum today.

[169] Marmaduke Stephenson, William Robinson, Mary Dyer, and William Leddra, the "Boston martyrs," were hanged on Boston Common in 1659-61. Their deaths caused King Charles II to issue an order that all Quakers accused of capital offenses in Massachusetts should be brought to England, effectively ending the worst of their persecution.

CHAPTER 42

Marriage and Visit to England and Ireland

As the year 1900 was advancing, the subject of another religious visit to London and Dublin yearly meetings came up with such freshness as led me to believe that it would be right for me to lay the matter before my friends. So in the Eighth month of that year I presented it to our monthly meeting, and to the quarterly meeting on Ninth month 1, both of which meetings gave their unity and encouragement. I then began shaping matters in order to be ready.

While waiting for the yearly meeting of ministry and oversight to occur, before which it was necessary to lay this concern in order to receive its final endorsement, I was busy in perfecting these arrangements. About two weeks before the yearly meeting, without any previous thought on the matter, my mind was impressed that it would be right to ask Naomi W. Harrison to become my wife and that she should go with me. It was so unexpected that I hesitated two or three days before acting, but when I did mention the subject to her it was pleasant to know that her mind had been directed in the same channel, so that the matter was soon arranged.

We were well acquainted, our homes being close together, and having been associated in church and college work for a number of years. She had been at the clerk's table of Indiana Yearly Meeting for twenty-six years, half that time as assistant and the other half as the clerk.[170] When we informed our friends during the yearly meeting, we found much encouragement from the Friends in different parts of the yearly meeting. We were married according to the good order of Friends, Eleventh month 25, 1900.

The yearly meeting having endorsed my concern to visit Friends in London and Dublin yearly meetings, we proceeded to make arrangements for the journey, my wife having obtained a minute from the monthly meeting to unite with me in the service. We sailed from New York, Second month 2, 1901, my wife's youngest daughter, Miriam A. Harrison, who lived with us, going along. The monthly meeting endorsed her going and gave her a minute liberating her and encouraging her to be faithful to perform such work as she might find to do. We had rather a rough voyage, yet did not suffer much inconvenience from seasickness, my wife going to every meal.

Upon arriving in Liverpool, we went directly to the home of Dr. Thorpe where we received a cordial welcome. The next day we went to Leominster, where we made our home with our dear friend, Henry Stanley Newman, at Buckfield, to rest for a few days before starting upon our work. It was a real pleasure to be with our dear friend in his own home and to talk over the days spent together in America.

Our English Friends have what they call an American Committee, composed of persons who are set apart to kindly look after American ministers who are traveling with minutes for religious service in their country, to counsel and advise them, help them in preparing their program, and give all necessary assistance in carrying out their concern. It was thought best that I should go up to London and meet with this committee before entering upon the field of labor which lay before

---

[170] Naomi Harrison served as clerk of the women's yearly meeting from 1882-94, and again for one year in 1900.

us, which I did upon the following day. We had a very satisfactory conference. They were exceedingly kind and did all they could to help make the necessary arrangements. Having a map of the meetings in London Yearly Meeting, together with the Book of Meetings, I made out a tentative program before leaving home which, at their request, I laid before them and which, with a few slight alterations, they fully endorsed. I returned to Leominster the following day.

After a few days we attended a quarterly meeting in Wales and went to Doncaster, Sheffield, Manchester, and from there crossed over to Ireland, and went almost directly to the limits of Ulster Quarterly Meeting in the north of Ireland, stopping first with our dear friend, Anna Pym, at Lisburn. We then proceeded to visit all the meetings belonging to that quarter, also the schools. Having visited the meetings in the north of Ireland, we then went to Leinster Quarterly Meeting in the south of Ireland, going almost directly to Cork and making our home in that city with Benjamin Haughton. I had made my home with his father, Benjamin Haughton, Sr., twenty-six years before.

We visited the meetings and schools within the limits of that quarterly meeting, after which we spent three days visiting the Lakes of Killarney and their surroundings. Then going into Munster Quarterly Meeting, we visited the meetings and schools of that quarter before the time of the yearly meeting. It would be pleasant to trace our journey from meeting to meeting throughout Ireland and to dwell upon the many kind homes where we were made welcome, but this is not the purpose of this autobiography. It is only my purpose to speak in a general way and perhaps to allude to a few facts more prominent than others in the work.

First among these and one which brings peace when dwelt upon was the universal kindness and Christian love which we met with throughout our entire stay in Ireland. We visited, as far as I can remember, all the meetings of Friends with possibly one exception. Some of them were very small, but these small meetings were specially upon our minds, and our visits to them were occasions of blessing to us, and I trust the dear Friends visited were strengthened by our calling upon them. One of these meetings had only three members. We also visited all the schools under the care of Friends, this being an interesting portion of our labors.

The yearly meeting was a time of enjoyment. It was felt to be a favored occasion in which the Church was strengthened and encouraged. I missed some who were active leaders twenty-six years before, when I first attended that yearly meeting, but it was a great pleasure to receive the warm welcome of others. Prominent among these was our dear friend, Adam Wood, who was still active. We made our home with him and his dear daughters at their lovely home at Dundrum, his precious wife having passed on since I had been there before. There were others who were still in the foremost ranks. It was especially gratifying to see among the younger ones numbers coming forward and filling up the places of those who had fallen out of the Church militant.[171]

After the close of the yearly meeting we crossed over to Holyhead and so on to London, where we went to the home of our dear friend, Joseph Bevan Braithwaite, and once more found a pleasant resting place during our stay in London. During the few days before the yearly meeting commenced we visited a few of the meetings in and around the city. According to previous arrangement, I attended the Young Friends meeting at Stoke Newington and addressed them on the subject which they had selected for me, "The Demand of the Hour Upon the Young."

On Fifth month 22, the yearly meeting opened with John Morland as clerk, and Mary Jane Godlee, clerk of the women's meeting. Here, again, I found changes had taken place in the last twenty-six years. To me London Yearly Meeting has always been an interesting occasion whenever I have been present, and I think never more so than on this occasion. I could say much regarding the kindness of the dear Friends and the work of the yearly meeting, but London Yearly Meeting has been so often described by American visitors and in the English papers

---

[171] For those not familiar with the phrase, "the Church militant" refers to church members who are living and active; "the Church triumphant" refers to those who have died and gone to Heaven.

that I do not feel that it is necessary to dwell much upon it, only to say that it was the same strong, deliberative body that it had been and active in practical Christian work. Many of the younger members were coming forward and taking an active interest in the affairs of the Church. As a yearly meeting they were seeking to know the mind of Christ in the work that they were called to do; upon the whole, a very satisfactory yearly meeting, growing stronger and reaching out to build up the waste places, which it has continued to do until the present time, the last report showing a steady growth until they have reached a membership now of a little over nineteen-thousand.

After the close of the yearly meeting we were engaged very busily attending the greater number of the meetings in the north of England and in the Midland Counties. Here, again, I might find much of a pleasing nature to dwell upon, especially in our visits to Darlington, Kendal, Swarthmore, and Birmingham. Particularly at Birmingham we were deeply interested in the adult school work and other Christian work carried on by the dear Friends there. We were thankful to have the privilege of attending the annual meeting of the adult school workers, who had been organized into a society, and enjoyed taking tea with them. We visited George Cadbury, who has since turned his old home into the center for the Woodbrooke movement.[172]

Perhaps it will not be out of place to add that our daughter, Miriam A. Harrison, found a place for service with us, especially among the younger members of the Church, and she was requested to attend and take part in the young people's societies and the adult schools. Her singing opened a door for her in many places among that class.

Before closing the account of this visit I feel like alluding to a day spent with our dear friend, John Wilhelm Rowntree, who had previously been at our home in America for several days and who requested me to come to his home before leaving England, which I did. Upon arriving there, early in the morning, I found him ready with his

---

[172] George Cadbury (1839-1922) was the second generation of the Cadbury chocolate and cocoa makers. Deeply concerned for the welfare of his workers, he built the model village of Bourneville, where Woodbrooke was founded in 1903.

lunch basket and we soon reached Robin Hood Bay. There, on a cliff overlooking the water, we sat down and talked over the condition of the Society of Friends in England, Ireland, and America. Indeed, we first reviewed the condition of each yearly meeting separately, both in his country and ours. Then we dwelt upon the prospect of the Church's future prosperity and the things to be overcome. In doing this we freely discussed the men and women who were the leaders in the onward movement and those who bade fair to take a leading part in coming years.

This was no idle conversation. It was opened by prayer and the yearly meetings and individuals were discussed with a desire to know what the future would bring forth. This conversation was not for the public. It has never been made known to the public. This dear man, with a prophetic vision, was trying to penetrate the future of our Society. He saw more than many others. He saw some of the things that are beginning to transpire and which the future may more fully demonstrate. He labored, but others have entered into his labors.[173]

We closed our work, and left for home the first week in Eighth month, landing at Boston, and after spending a few days there we returned home.

---

[173] John Wilhelm Rowntree (1868-1905) was another Quaker chocolate manufacturer. He was also an important scholar, educator, and organizer. Rowntree died in 1905, just four years before Allen Jay published his autobiography.

CHAPTER 43

Helping Guilford, Earlham, and Whittier Colleges

After returning from our visit with the Friends of London and Dublin yearly meetings, we settled down in the home at Earlham View, located in front of Earlham College,[174] and found work to occupy our time in the Church and in connection with the college. We attended North Carolina Yearly Meeting in 1902, and Baltimore and North Carolina yearly meetings in 1903. I attended New York Yearly Meeting at Glens Falls in the spring of 1904 and some of the meetings belonging to it.

One day in the winter of 1904 I received a letter from our dear friend, Elihu E. Mendenhall, of Deep River, North Carolina, who had long been president of the board of trustees of Guilford College, and one who had given of his time and means for the good of the institution. Near the close he wrote, "Allen, I had hoped to see Guilford College out of debt before I died, but I never shall unless thee comes down and helps us." Turning to my wife and daughter, I asked, "How soon can you get ready to go to North Carolina and spend the winter?" The reply was, "In a few days." I then said, "We will start next

---

[174] Allen Jay's home no longer exists. It stood directly across from Earlham College, at 790 National Road West. The spot is now occupied by a funeral home.

Fourth-day." Turning to the desk, I wrote Elwood Cox, who had been appointed president of the board in the place of Elihu Mendenhall, who resigned on account of old age, and asked him to call a meeting of the trustees at the college on Sixth-day of the next week. At the time set we closed up our home for the winter and started, reaching the college the night before the meeting.

With the treasurer we went over the books, and found that the debt amounted to nearly $28,000. This was chiefly an old debt which, with the interest, had been growing from year to year. The trustees were all present. The whole matter was gone over, which resulted in the afternoon in my making the following proposition: That I would undertake to raise the amount if they would help, and if one-fourth of the amount could be secured in the limits of North Carolina Yearly Meeting before going outside to solicit. The members of the board showed their interest by subscribing $4,000 before we left the room.

The next day President L.L. Hobbs and I started out, and within ten days we had secured subscriptions amounting to one-fourth of the debt. My wife had a room at the college and was to look after my correspondence, and I started for Philadelphia, hoping to get the remainder of the amount in and around that city and Baltimore. Then began one of the most strenuous efforts in soliciting funds that I ever experienced. Soon after arriving, the weather turned cold, and for several days there was a blizzard, so that one night, after walking a good deal during the day, I had to walk to my home, which was with my dear friend, Asa Wing, when in the city.

Another thing that made it hard was the fact that it was a *debt*. Many felt that they should not have gone into debt, so that I met with rebuffs on that account. Others felt that they would not subscribe unless the whole amount should be raised. On the other hand, many dear Friends lent a helping hand. President Isaac Sharpless, Joshua L. Baily, Thomas Scattergood, Asa Wing, and others encouraged me to hold on. So, for nearly four weeks, in and around Philadelphia, I went into homes, offices, and places of business, meeting with success sometimes and failure at others.

Having done what I felt I could at that time in Philadelphia, I turned towards Baltimore, where I had reason to expect some good subscriptions. Here again things looked discouraging, for on First-day before my arrival in the city the great fire of 1904 took place, so that much of the city was in ruins.[175] However, I stopped over, and going into the home of Francis White, he said, without any solicitation on my part, "I will give $2,500, even if I have lost heavily by the fire."

Returning to Guilford and reporting the results to the trustees, we found, when all was counted up, that there was $4,000 still lacking. They desired that I should return at once to the East and try to secure that, but I told them I would try another plan first. Securing a room, I put in two days writing letters to my friends in different parts of the United States, believing the amount would be forthcoming.

Having a minute for religious service, I had arranged for a month's work among the meetings of Deep River, Southern, Western, and Yadkin Valley quarterly meetings, our daughter Miriam going with me, and her mother caring for the correspondence. It was indeed pleasant to visit the meetings and homes of the dear Friends I had so often labored among thirty years before when a member of that yearly meeting.

When we returned it was a great joy to find the officers and managers of Guilford rejoicing because the debt was all subscribed, a telegram having come that morning from Samuel Hill, of Seattle, saying, "I'll pay the last $1,000," which closed the long-drawn-out effort. It was a glad day for Guilford. She put on new life and has been growing ever since, and is doing a great work.

Buildings and Endowment for Earlham and Whittier

For a long time the trustees of Earlham had talked of making an application to Andrew Carnegie for money to build a library at Earlham. Early in the year 1905, at a conference with the local trustees, I was requested to go East and make the effort. After studying

---

[175] The Great Baltimore Fire took place on February 7-8, 1904, and destroyed more than 1,500 buildings in an area covering seventy blocks.

the matter over I concluded to go to Washington and see if I could secure any help.

Knowing that Joseph G. Cannon, the Speaker of the House of Representatives, was personally acquainted with Andrew Carnegie, and that when a young man he was a student at Earlham, and being myself also personally acquainted with him, upon my arrival in the city of Washington I went to the Speaker's room. We were soon engaged in talking the matter over. At first he did not think we would succeed, but after talking for a while he suggested that I write out an application and come back the next morning.

Going to the hotel, I spent most of the night preparing the application and having three or four typewritten copies put in shape. Next morning at the appointed hour I met him in his room. He took the paper and read it over carefully, then assuming his familiar attitude, with his feet on the desk and a cigar in his mouth, he dictated a very satisfactory letter which, as soon as his secretary had put it into shape, he handed to me, advising me to see the Senators from Indiana. Having met them before, I was glad to do so. They came out of the Senate, and were willing to do what they could, telling me to call in the afternoon and receive what they had written. Then, going to Vice-President Fairbanks' room and finding him in, he soon had a short but full commendation ready for me. After receiving Senator Beveridge's and Senator Hemenway's letters, I returned to the House of Representatives and found James E. Watson, our Representative, and also Joseph Dixon, who had taken a post-graduate course at Earlham. Indeed I had known him from a child in North Carolina. He is now United States Senator from Montana.[176] They both added their endorsement in letters. Armed with all these letters of commendation, I went to the post-office in the building and mailed them, together

---

[176] Charles W. Fairbanks (1852-1918), Senator from Indiana, Vice President under Theodore Roosevelt; Albert Beveridge (1862-1927), Senator from Indiana; James Hemenway (1860-1923), Senator from Indiana; James Eli Watson (1864-1948), Representative from Indiana; Joseph Dixon (1867-1934), Senator from Montana, later Governor of Montana. Note that these officials were all of the next generation after Allen Jay, who was seventy-four at the time. Allen Jay's age and clear, gentle persuasion no doubt had much to do with the success of this effort.

with the application, to Carnegie. Next day I went to New York to see another party, who gave $1,000, and then I came home.

A Gift from Andrew Carnegie

Upon reaching home, the blank applications from Carnegie were there ready to be filled out. President Kelly and I answered the required questions. We asked for the sum of $40,000. In a few days we received word that Andrew Carnegie would be pleased to give us the sum of $30,000 to erect a library on condition that we would raise a like sum, the interest of which was to be used in the upkeep of the library. He also told us where to draw on him for the amount.

This was good news, but at the same time it gave us a serious problem to solve—that of raising $30,000 to endow the library with. It was a time of financial depression, and besides, we had other financial matters upon our hands. We waited that summer, and took no active steps until the next winter. During the winter and spring of 1906 I secured the sum of about $20,000 for the library, and the sum of $25,000 for the Edwin Bundy dormitory building.

Then feeling tired and somewhat worn, I decided to go to California and try to find a little rest, having made such arrangements as I thought would succeed in raising the remaining $10,000. My wife and I obtained a minute liberating us to attend California and Oregon yearly meetings and the meetings composing them so far as the way might open, and to visit the Friends in the State of Washington, especially those who belonged to Indiana Yearly Meeting.

We also had a minute from the evangelistic, pastoral, and church extension board of Indiana Yearly Meeting, requesting us to attend a conference of Friends in the State of Washington, to be held by those belonging to Indiana Yearly Meeting.[177] Two or three years before, Charles Replogle and wife had gone to Everett, in that State, from Muncie Monthly Meeting. Their work had been greatly blessed, and

---

[177] Allen Jay was the clerk of this committee from 1902 until his death in 1910. He had previously served from 1890-96 as superintendent of evangelistic work, visiting and building up the many new meetings in Indiana Yearly Meeting which had sprung up as a result of the revivals.

they had sent a number of names to their monthly meeting of persons who desired to become members of the Society of Friends. Two or three meetings had been established, and Friends in yet other places were holding meetings.

My rest was not to be realized, for when we reached Whittier we found that the trustees of the college had appointed a meeting for that night at the home of our son-in-law to see if they could not get me to assist Rayner Kelsey[178] in raising $100,000 to add to the endowment fund of that institution. Before retiring that night, I had agreed to assist in the effort.

After a few days we went to Imperial City, in the Imperial Valley, where our son-in-law, Stephen Stanton Myrick, and his wife lived, he being the pastor of the Methodist church in that place. They had a child born twenty-four hours before we reached there, whom they named Stephen Stanton Myrick, Jr. I remained there two weeks. Ten days of that time I was engaged in assisting my son-in-law in holding a series of meetings in the church. Several were converted, and a few joined the church. He has since joined Friends and is now pastor of the Friends meeting, Greensboro, N.C.

I then returned to Whittier, and was engaged in soliciting funds for about two weeks, when, to my surprise, I received a letter from the president of Earlham, saying that it looked as though they would fail to secure the $10,000 to make up the necessary amount for the library, and as what had been subscribed was on condition that the remainder be secured, it was the judgment of the board of trustees that I ought to return. After a few hours' thought I filled my valise and started back across the Rocky Mountains, stopping a few days in San José, San Francisco, and Berkeley to secure what I could for Whittier, leaving San Francisco about a week before the great earthquake and

---

[178] Rayner Kelsey (1879-1934) was an Earlham graduate and taught at Whittier College before becoming professor of history at Haverford. He was active for many years with the Associated Committee of Friends on Indian Affairs and edited the bulletin of the Friends Historical Association from 1922-32.

fire which shook the whole country with sorrow.[179]

Reaching home, I commenced to work where I had left off. While asking for the library I found that our dear friends, Zenas and Rachel Bundy, wished to give the $25,000 already mentioned for a dormitory building for boys on the condition that we secure $25,000 more and erect a $50,000 building. Here was another sum to be raised. In prosecuting the work I went to Philadelphia, where I had been so often before on a similar mission.

Here again another subject came to the front. A dear friend, Joseph Elkinton, had lately died and left a large number of Friends books and manuscripts. After consulting with the agent and one or two of the heirs, they agreed that we might have these for $1,500, because we proposed to keep them together at Earlham. I went to work to secure money to pay for the library, and secured all but about $400, which I thought I had the promise of, but it failed, and our librarian, Professor Harlow Lindley, afterwards went out and obtained that amount and had the books shipped, so that they are now in the library. These, with the books we already had, gave Earlham a fine collection of Friends books and writings.[180]

Having spent what time I thought best, I returned to Indiana and continued the work in the two yearly meetings of Indiana and Western, taking subscriptions both for the library and dormitory, but most anxious for the former. I soon had a little over the required amount of $30,000, and having made the library fund safe, I returned to California, where I rode through the country and visited Friends at Pasadena, Los Angeles, Long Beach, and other points. It was slow and arduous work.

---

[179] The San Francisco Earthquake took place on April 18, 1906. Fires broke out after the quake and raged for four days. More than 500 blocks of the city were destroyed, and 500 people were shot by the police and army during the looting and general disorder.

[180] Joseph Elkinton's collection of more than 2,000 books and manuscripts are now cared for in the Friends Collection at Lilly Library, Earlham College.

Raising $50,000 in One Meeting

Yearly meeting came on, and we were still some $50,000 behind. An educational meeting was held one night, much interest created, and a sufficient amount was promised to reduce the required sum down to $30,000. When the final report of the college came before the meeting we were undecided what to do—whether to undertake to raise the balance or not. President Tebbetts, Dr. Coffin, the president of the board, and my associate, Rayner Kelsey, all spoke without making an appeal. Indeed, we all felt that it was useless to make any further effort to raise the amount. It was a serious time, for if we failed, what had been done would be lost. Then I spoke, and as I closed a dear Friend whom I had asked before for $500 rose and said, with much feeling, that he felt he ought to give $500. It broke the spell, and several others followed with liberal subscriptions who had refused before.

Rayner Kelsey then came to the front and made an impassioned appeal; Dr. Coffin and President Tebbetts stood up; and one after another we made remarks. I have seen many interesting scenes where amounts were raised, such as the occasion when Moody raised $60,000 in Providence, Rhode Island, in a short time, and the occasion when the missionary board raised something like $100,000 in two hours, but I never saw a congregation so intensely in earnest as was California Yearly Meeting that afternoon. One after another came forward, and with deep emotion subscribed, until we had only $12,000 left.

Then a proposition was made to raise $5,000 in $1,000 subscriptions. It was soon taken by those who had already done well. The first went to Washington Hadley who had given in the beginning $20,000 on condition that the $100,000 be all raised. Soon all was taken, the president's wife, Imelda Tebbetts, taking the last $1,000. His family had already subscribed something like $4,000. Then it was asked how many would stand good for $50 provided it was all taken. I believe 50 or 60 stood on that call, reducing the amount by about $2,000. That was taken in smaller sums, most of it by young men and young women, and some of it by the children.

Thus, after a session of three or four hours, the announcement was made that all was pledged. I shall never forget the deep feeling of emotion that came over the meeting. Strong men and women stood and wept. There was not much outward excitement. There was a deep feeling of solemnity. Even some who were enemies to the college and had stayed away entered near the close, came under the power that rested over the meeting, and gave of their means. It had a unifying effect.

> It would be good for others of our meetings if they could be brought so under the power of the Lord by giving of their means to build up His Kingdom that they would be melted together in love.

It would be good for others of our meetings if they could be brought so under the power of the Lord by giving of their means to build up His Kingdom that they would be melted together in love. At the close of the yearly meeting the board and faculty of the college gave me an expression of their appreciation for the help I had given, which I found among my papers and which I do not remember having shown to any person, unless it be my wife. It was pleasant to see it, for I had forgotten it.

In Oregon and Washington

In a few days we left for Oregon. We stopped at San José, attended meeting on First-day, and spent a day visiting the ruins of San Francisco, and so on to Oregon, where we made our home with our dear friends, Jesse and Mary Edwards. We had a pleasant time and enjoyed the yearly meeting very much, yet I felt it to be my place to deal rather plainly and to bear my testimony against a spirit of

> How sad it is to see those who make such high claim of being led by the Spirit judging and condemning others in a most un-Christian and bigoted spirit.

judging and fault-finding that was creeping into the Church, especially a dogmatic theology which condemned everyone who did not see things just as others did.

How sad it is to see those who make such high claim of being led by the Spirit judging and condemning others in a most un-Christian and bigoted spirit. You can tell them as soon as they commence. They begin by finding fault. They cannot write an article or preach a sermon without indulging in bitterness, and they may indulge in this until I fear sometimes they verily believe they are doing the Lord service in persecuting others. Indeed, they feel that God has raised them up to save Zion.

It is but just to say that those who indulged in this spirit, with little exception, were those who had come from other yearly meetings and had not resided there long. The body of the meeting labored together in much harmony and love, with a self-sacrificing spirit. Especially were they loyal to the Church and the college under their care, and I feel like saying again what I said in the Five Years' Meeting some years ago when Pacific College was under consideration: "I believe there is not a college in America that has done more good with so small an amount of means. Back there sits a young man who has worn out his life and here by my side sits a woman who is laboring and toiling to build up that institution." We left that yearly meeting with much love for the dear Friends who are doing a noble work on that portion of our Western coast.

In accordance with the request of our committee for evangelistic and pastoral work, and in accordance with a concern which we had before leaving home, my wife and I then proceeded on our way to the State of Washington to attend the conference of Friends in that state. It was called to be held at Everett to consider what they should do about asking for a quarterly meeting, also as to whether they should remain with Indiana Yearly Meeting or turn to Oregon. We felt it would be right to request Oregon Yearly Meeting to appoint two or three delegates to attend the conference with us and assist in coming to the right conclusion. Those who were appointed were a help, and we worked together in much love and unity. Indeed, the conference was a time of much spiritual blessing, and resulted in much good in strengthening the Church and unifying the membership of the various scattered meetings. It culminated in a request for a quarterly meeting to be established in the State of Washington and to be known as Puget Sound Quarterly Meeting, to be opened at Seattle.

My wife and I spent some time in visiting the Friends in the State. We found an earnest little company at Tacoma, likewise at Langley, Seattle, and Everett. The latter was much the largest meeting. Charles and May Replogle were doing a good work in keeping the Friends together in other places. We were much pleased with the result of their labors. At Seattle we found a few earnest Friends, who held their meetings in an old tent on the side of a hill in an out-of-the-way place. It was discouraging. Before leaving home I had thought that it might be right to see Elbridge Stuart, Samuel Hill, and Hervey Lindley,[181] three men who were brought up Friends, whose parents I had known, and whose ancestors came from North Carolina. They had all become rich.

Meeting Elbridge Stuart one day, I told him I would like to meet them the next morning. He made an appointment, and on going to the office I found him and Hervey Lindley there, Samuel Hill being out of the city. I began by telling them about the Friends there and how they were situated, and closed by making an appeal to them for help. I found that they were not entirely ignorant of Friends and their needs, and that they had talked the matter over among themselves.

When I had finished, Elbridge Stuart said something like this: "We knew what thee was coming for, and we have made up our minds to make this proposition: Because of our love for the Society of Friends, and in memory of our parents, we will buy a lot in a suitable part of the city, build a meeting-house on it, furnish it ready for holding meetings in, and turn it over to Indiana Yearly Meeting, on

---

[181] Elbridge Amos Stuart (1856-1944) was the founder of Carnation Condensed Milk, "the milk from contented cows." Samuel Hill (1857-1931) was attorney and executive for the Great Northern Railway, who married the daughter of railroad magnate James J. Hill. Hervey Lindley (1854-1929) was a timberman, railroad man, developer, and president of the Columbia Basin Irrigation League.

two conditions—first, that Indiana Yearly Meeting will select a suitable minister to reside here, and that the yearly meeting will look after the spiritual interest of the Church; and, second, that thee will come out when the house is finished and attend the dedication." With a full heart I accepted the proposition on behalf of the yearly meeting, and agreed to their terms. Returning to the dear Friends, who were gathered at the home of William S. Sinton, I made my report. It was a time of rejoicing, and tears of joy were shed at the thought of having a home to meet in.[182]

These friends bought a first-class lot, built a nice building, costing in all about $12,000, and before the meeting-house was completed they bought a lot adjoining for $3,000 and erected a house on that for a parsonage that cost about $4,000, spending, in all, something like $19,000 before the time came for the dedication. But more about that in the next chapter.

Having visited all the meetings and having become more or less acquainted with the situation of Friends in that State, we returned home with a feeling of love and sympathy for them and with some sense of appreciation of the noble work they were doing. The fields are certainly white unto harvest and the laborers are far too few.[183]

---

[182] Friends Memorial Meeting in Seattle received support for many years from the Elbridge Stuart Trust, and remained a part of Indiana Yearly Meeting until 1948, when they transferred to Oregon Yearly Meeting. They moved to their present location at 7740 24th Ave NE, Seattle, in 1950, and are now known as North Seattle Friends Church.

[183] John 4:35; Matthew 9:37-38; Luke 10:2.

CHAPTER 44

From North Carolina to Puget Sound

Eastern Quarterly Meeting, North Carolina

Upon returning home I found a letter awaiting me, urging that I come to the opening of the new meeting-house at Rich Square, in the limits of Eastern Quarterly Meeting, North Carolina. There had been a separation in this quarterly meeting a few years before, and those who went off were members of the meeting called Cedar Grove, where a new meeting-house had been built, leaving the old house at Rich Square for the Friends who remained loyal to the yearly meeting. The old house was also located to one side of the Friends settlement, so they went to work and built a new house in a suitable location. This left them very much in debt, and they were anxious that I should be with them at the time of the opening of the new house and see if a sufficient amount could not be raised to liquidate the debt.

As they had waited for me to return from the West and had postponed the date until after North Carolina Yearly Meeting, I felt that it would be right to go, for I had much sympathy for them under the circumstances, especially as the quarterly meeting and yearly meeting had come to the Christian conclusion not to take possession by law of the meeting-house and schoolhouse that the Separatists occupied, although the title was in the name of the yearly meeting and in a number of other instances of similar separations Friends in other places had taken possession. But the dear Friends of North Carolina said: "We will not go to law, but let them occupy the property and we will endeavor to get along without it."[184] A beautiful spirit of brotherly love. It might have been well if the same spirit had prevailed in other separations rather than going to war before the world and fighting through the courts, even if they did secure their property. It is better to suffer for Christ's sake. The Master, when reviled, reviled not again.[185]

So, obtaining a minute from our meeting to attend North Carolina Yearly Meeting and for other service within its limits, we were soon on our way. We have always enjoyed meeting with our dear friends of that yearly meeting, but in 1906 we had an unusually good yearly meeting. The subjects coming before the meeting were of great importance. It was largely attended, and many of the young people manifested an interest and took part in the business of the meeting, which is a healthy sign for the future.

After the yearly meeting we visited a few meetings on our way, stopping a few days among the meetings in and around Goldsboro, then going to Rich Square, where we found the house spoken above ready to be opened and set apart for religious service. It was a fine day. We had a large crowd. Near the close of the service I made an appeal for funds, which were subscribed without much trouble, and Friends felt much encouraged because the debt had been met. We held meetings there until after the next First-day morning meeting.

In the afternoon of that day we went over to the other neighborhood and had a very large meeting in the Baptist meeting-house, nearby the meeting-house of the Separatists. The Methodist minister offering their house for a night meeting, we held one there at night, several of the Separatists coming in.

---

[184] cf. 1 Corinthians 6:1-8
[185] 1 Peter 2:23

From there we went on to Belvidere, to the home of our dear friend, Josiah Nicholson, with whom I had made my home, in the same house, nearly forty years before. We attended Piney Wood Meeting on First-day, visited the Upriver Meeting, and held a few meetings in the hall of the academy at Belvidere. It was truly a time of spiritual blessing as we mingled with these Friends once more. Feeling our work done, we returned home in time for our yearly meeting, glad to be settled down in the home again. The year 1906 had been a busy year. I had crossed the Rocky Mountains four times and the Alleghenies six times, attended five yearly meetings, working in all of them more or less. The retrospect was pleasant.

Puget Sound Quarterly Meeting

I have already spoken of the conference held at Everett, in the State of Washington, in 1906, and the decision in regard to requesting a quarterly meeting. It was sent to Winchester Quarter, united with by that meeting, and forwarded to the yearly meeting of 1906, which made the following minute: "Minute 27: Winchester Meeting was united in forwarding to us the following minutes from a conference of Everett, Seattle, and Tacoma monthly meetings in the State of Washington, held Seventh month 22, 1906, also a minute from Everett Monthly Meeting, dated Eighth month 6, requesting a quarterly meeting to be composed of Everett, Seattle, and Tacoma monthly meetings, and to be known as Puget Sound Quarterly Meeting, to be opened at 10:30 A.M. on the first Seventh-day in the First month of 1907, or at such time as meets the approval of the committee appointed to attend the opening."

"Minute 64: The Friends appointed to produce names to attend the opening of Puget Sound Quarterly Meeting propose Allen Jay, Esther Cook, Charles Replogle, and Naomi H. Jay, with whom the meeting unites." As I have already said, our three friends in Seattle,

> The year 1906 had been a busy year. I had crossed the Rocky Mountains four times and the Alleghenies six times, attended five yearly meetings, working in all of them more or less.

who were building a house for the meeting and a parsonage, had not completed their work. Our committee thought it best to wait until the house in Seattle was ready, so we postponed the opening till Ninth month 14, 1907, at Seattle, Washington.

The meeting of ministry and oversight was appointed and held the day before at 3:00 P.M. in a tent, as the meetinghouse was not quite ready. Here I wish to say that our dear friends had done all they could to have everything ready, and the night before the opening Elbridge Stuart, with a number of other men, worked until midnight to have all completed. The meeting-house is a beautiful plain building, Colonial in style, veneered with dark red brick. It is 84 feet long, 42 feet wide, with a porch 9 feet wide across the front. The gable roof extends over the porch and is supported by four large columns. There is a vestibule, with side doors opening into the audience room. The meeting room has a raised floor and fine wainscoting, and is lighted with electricity. There is a nice, good-sized room in the rear for Bible school and other purposes. The building is heated by a furnace, and neatly carpeted.

Of our committee, Charles Replogle, Esther Cook, and myself were present. Oregon Yearly Meeting appointed eight fraternal delegates to attend the meeting, six of whom were present, Jesse Edwards, Mary E.K. Edwards, John Frederick Hanson, S. Alice Hanson, Calva Martin, and Frank Martin; also Francis K. Jones, acting president of Pacific College, was in attendance. The meeting gave to these Friends a warm welcome, asking them to feel at home and take part in the deliberations. Their sympathy and counsel were very helpful and encouraging, expressing, as they did, so much good will and desire for the prosperity of the meeting.

The meeting was opened with a period of silent worship, in which the Lord's presence was graciously manifested. A sermon was preached and several Friends gave brief messages of Gospel love. "Rock of Ages" was sung with much feeling, all hearts being filled with gratitude and praise. The clerk of our committee, Esther Cook, then read Minutes 27 and 64 of the printed minutes of Indiana Yearly Meeting of Friends, held at Richmond, Indiana, Ninth month 2, 1906, authorizing the establishment of the quarterly meeting.

Then a report from a conference of delegates from the three monthly meetings was read, in which they placed in nomination the name of Elmer Harden, of Everett, for presiding clerk, and Sarah Abigail Thomas, of Tacoma, for recording clerk, which was united with, they being appointed and called to the table, taking charge of the business. The three monthly meetings were represented by their delegates, and responded to their names when called. Out of a membership of 290 there were present 212 members. In the afternoon the state of the Society was considered, and the outlook was hopeful. The queries were read and representatives appointed to yearly meeting.

The nominating committee submitted their report as follows: for treasurer, William Swan Sinton; for statistical secretary, May Replogle; for Bible school superintendent, William Brown; temperance, Dorothy Lee; peace, Moses Votaw; foreign missions, Hosetta Sinton; vice-president of Christian Endeavor, Hattie Davey. Puget Sound Quarterly Meeting was now established, and while feeling a sense of added responsibility, we believe they took up the work with a courageous spirit, proposing by the grace and leadership of the great Head of the Church to stand with their sister quarterly meetings and be faithful to their calling, publishing the good tidings of the glorious Gospel of our God, and upholding the standard of Friends in the great Northwest.

First-day morning at 11 o'clock the audience room was well filled. After a time of silence, Edgar Williams with a few appropriate remarks opened the meeting and read the Scriptures, hymns were sung, Charles Replogle offered prayer, and I was led to preach a practical sermon from Romans 1:16, "I am not ashamed of the Gospel of Christ." The people gave close attention and received the message with responsive hearts. A subscription was taken amounting to about $3,000. Then, with solemn, fervent prayer, the house was dedicated to the Lord and His service.

It is proper here to say that the evangelistic committee of Indiana Yearly Meeting nearly a year before this had selected J. Edgar Williams and placed him at Seattle as pastor of the meeting there, and to his energy and devotion to the work was due in great measure the fact that the buildings were ready at the time they were. He had taken a great interest in building up the Church also, and we can but hope that his labors may continue to be blessed to the enlargement of the Church in that place and in gathering a strong and living meeting of those who should believe with us.

At the close of the quarterly meeting I turned my face once more towards home, reaching there in time for the yearly meeting of 1907 and the Five Years' Meeting which was to follow a few days later.

We reached home a few days before yearly meeting, and found Friends looking forward with much interest to what proved to be a very favored yearly meeting. There were present twenty ministering Friends with minutes from other yearly meetings. Among these were Sarah Jane Lurey, from North Somerset and Wiltshire monthly meetings, England; and Elizabeth Beaven Rutter, a minister from Shaftsbury and Sherborne monthly meetings, England; also Bunji Kida, an evangelist from Tsuchiura, Japan. I believe North Carolina, Baltimore, New York, and Canada were the only yearly meetings in America not represented.

The business of the yearly meeting was conducted with much harmony and brotherly love. Our report of the opening of the new quarterly meeting in Seattle, called Puget Sound, was received with much interest. During the course of the meeting we were brought into a feeling of sympathy and love as we listened to a very appropriate memorial of our dear friend, Charles A. Francisco, who had been one of our most efficient reading clerks for a number of years. He held the position of one of the yearly meeting correspondents, and was useful in various departments of Church work. It was also felt that the message from London Yearly Meeting was very fresh and appropriate to our needs. The yearly meeting closed on Second-day, Ninth month 30, 1907.

CHAPTER 45

The Five Years' Meeting of 1907

Much attention was now centered on the convening of the second Five Years' Meeting, which was called to meet Tenth month 15, 1907, at 7:30 P.M. in the yearly meeting-house. It was felt to be an important meeting, and Friends met under a solemn sense of the responsibility that rested upon them. One hundred and ninety-four delegates were sent up by the American yearly meetings, all of them being represented except Ohio and Philadelphia, the latter expressing its deep interest by a number of its members being present, who were warmly welcomed in our midst, it being known that owing to the isolated condition of Philadelphia Yearly Meeting, it could not officially appoint delegates.[186]

Almost all of the delegates were present. The places of the few who were absent were filled by the alternates. It was pleasant to look over the meeting and recognize that I had met them all before in other places, which gave additional pleasure to welcoming them at Richmond. In addition to the above, London Yearly Meeting sent seven, and Dublin Yearly Meeting five fraternal delegates, who added to the usefulness and strength of the Five Years' Meeting.

---

[186] Seeking to avoid yet another division, in 1857 Philadelphia Yearly Meeting compromised by refusing to send or receive epistles to other yearly meetings.

It is not my purpose to give an account of this memorable meeting, for any short account would fail to do the subject justice. Besides, there has been a full and clear account of the proceedings published, and the papers which were read on various subjects that came before the meeting have been put into book form and all published under the title, "Minutes and Proceedings of the Five Years' Meeting, 1907."[187] This book should be read by our members generally, especially our younger members, that they may learn of the work of the Church. They should feel that we are making history, and in order to be able to fill their places, they should be acquainted with what is going forward in the present day.

For the first time the Five Years' Meeting was called upon to consider the propriety of setting up a new yearly meeting, to be known as Nebraska Yearly Meeting, to meet at Central City, in that State, and to be composed of five quarterly meetings belonging to Iowa Yearly Meeting, *i.e.*, Hiawatha, with a membership of 112; Platte Valley, membership, 633; Union, membership, 121; Spring Bank, membership, 336; Mt. Vernon, membership, 108; making the total membership 1,310.

A committee of two from each delegation was appointed to take the matter under consideration and report to a future sitting. This committee, after considering the matter, reported in favor of granting the request, and proposed that Allen Jay, David Hadley, Eliza H. Cary, Eliza C. Armstrong, and John F. Hanson be appointed to attend the opening of this yearly meeting Sixth month 4, 1908.

---

[187] *Minutes and Proceedings of the Five Years Meeting of the American Yearly Meetings of Friends, Held in Richmond, Indiana, Tenth Mo. 15 to Tenth Mo. 21, 1907* (Philadelphia: John C. Winston, 1908). This massive, 545-page book is well worth browsing, partly for the formal reports, but even more for the flavor of the conference, which was very forward-looking and did not attempt to cover up the differences of opinion and religious emphasis among the delegates from the various yearly meetings. The stenographic record of the proceedings shows that Allen Jay spoke several times, and that he was clearly recognized as an elder statesman in the Quaker world.

Another Bereavement

While in common with other Friends our family had looked forward to the time when we would meet our dear friends and have a number of them in our home, yet we were to be disappointed, for on Second-day word came that our son-in-law, A.D. Titsworth, of Canton, Ohio, had died. His remains were brought to our home, and the funeral took place on First-day afternoon, Tenth month 24, 1907, during the time of Five Years' Meeting.[188] It was largely attended. This sad event cast a gloom over our home and prevented us from having many of our friends with us. Yet many of them called, and I was able to attend a number of the sessions. I shall pass over this important occasion by simply saying that whenever present I felt that the Master was with us, and that Friends generally returned to their homes feeling that the Church had been strengthened and unified during the days that were spent together.

Nebraska Yearly Meeting

As the time drew near for the opening of the new yearly meeting in Nebraska, our committee arranged to meet at Central City the day before the opening of said yearly meeting, and on the day appointed the yearly meeting was opened. All the committee were present. We met in the morning before the opening and had a season of prayer, after which the meeting of ministry and oversight was opened. It was interesting to see a number of younger and middle-aged people present.

The next morning, the 4th of Sixth month, the meeting proper was organized in the college chapel, which was on the third floor.[189] It was a pleasant room when reached, but was not large enough. During the season of worship preceding the opening many prayers were offered and words of comfort and encouragement were spoken. The committee then called for nomination of clerks, when Dr. Cyrus W.

---

[188] The sessions of Five Years Meeting ended on the 21st.

[189] The college referred to was Nebraska Central College, which was operated by Friends from 1899 to 1953.

Dixon was nominated for that place. He came forward, the minute of our appointment was then read as a portion of the opening minute, and in a few moments the yearly meeting was ready for business.

A number of Friends who were present had been active members in Iowa Yearly Meeting or others of the older yearly meetings, so that they were soon ready to proceed with the work. It was truly encouraging to see the business conducted with life and inspiration, and it was especially gratifying to see so many young Friends as active members on important committees. Going into one of the class-rooms one day between sessions, I found three young women writing three epistles, one to London, one to Dublin, and the other a general epistle to the American yearly meetings. Upon inquiry I learned that one of the writers was a teacher and the other two were students attending the college.

There was great interest manifested on the subject of education, and much liberality was shown in providing for the needs of the college. The foreign mission work had warm advocates in this yearly meeting. Indeed there were four or five missionaries present who had actually been in the field and who were home for rest who belonged to this new yearly meeting. The missionary meeting was doubly interesting as we listened to those who had been in the field. They spoke but little of their trials or their privations, although one of them had lost one of her legs while in the field. She only spoke, however, of the joy of the work and of the hope that some day she might be able to return. A yearly meeting that has such devoted young people has cause to be thankful, and its light will shine.

> A yearly meeting that has such devoted young people has cause to be thankful, and its light will shine.

After the close of the yearly meeting our committee felt that we should report to the next Five Years' Meeting that we believed it had been opened "in accordance with the mind of truth," and our clerk, Eliza C. Armstrong, was requested to prepare such a report and send it to the clerk of the Five Years' Meeting, to be preserved and presented at that time.

Visit to Puget Sound

During this summer the evangelistic, pastoral, and church extension committee of Indiana Yearly Meeting felt that it might be of advantage to the work if two of our number should visit the meetings of Puget Sound Quarterly Meeting and labor for their help and encouragement, that they might preserve unity and harmony throughout the quarterly meeting. So, soon after returning home from Nebraska, I prepared to take another journey across the Rocky Mountains, our dear friend, Joseph A. Goddard, of Muncie, going with me. It was a long, hot journey.

We worked together in much harmony, visiting all the meetings and helping as the way opened for it. In addition we visited the meetings in Victoria, British Columbia, had a meeting in the afternoon for the older people, and one at night for all classes. After the night meeting we returned to Seattle, some 75 miles. The boat was so crowded that we had to sit up all night. We were present at the opening of Friends new meeting-house in Tacoma. Having done all that we saw the way open for, we returned home by way of the Canadian Pacific Railroad, enjoying the grand scenery very much. It was pleasant to be in the quiet and rest of home once more, where I remained until after yearly meeting.

Central City Meeting-House

Soon after the close of yearly meeting, our Friends of Central City, Nebraska, began to urge me to come to their assistance in raising funds to pay for their new meeting-house. As I have said, the chapel in the college building was unhandy to get to and entirely too small; so, with the zeal that had characterized their efforts, they went to work and rebuilt and enlarged their house in Central City and fixed up a nice parsonage, at a cost of some $4,000 or $5,000. They had selected the last of Second month, 1909, as the time to set the new house apart for religious service.

I went out to them, as they requested. Upon reaching Chicago I found it was raining hard. Next morning when we crossed the Mississippi River it was snowing. It soon turned into a blizzard, which proved to be the worst one I ever saw. We made slow progress. Indeed at times it seemed as though we should not get through. We did not reach our dining car until afternoon. The water pipes froze in the Pullman sleeper and burst, the water running all over the floor. About 11:00 P.M. we reached Omaha, five hours late. The wires were down, and we could not send any word ahead; so when I reached Central City at 3 o'clock in the morning they had given me up, but through the kindness of a stranger I soon found a room.

Next morning a good home was provided for me, and for eight or ten days I was kept busy. On First-day morning, at the time of the dedication, a large crowd was present. They needed about $2,100 to meet the debt on the meeting-house and parsonage. During the day we obtained about $3,100, with the understanding that the extra $1,000 should go to the college debt. It was a great day for the Friends of Central City. But I will not try to describe it, for others have written of it in the *Nebraska Friend* and other Friends papers. The series of meetings did much good. At their close I bade farewell to the dear Friends of Nebraska with a deep appreciation of their devotion to the cause of the Master, and with the belief that a blessing would attend that yearly meeting in coming years.

Conclusion

This brings me to the close, and now, as I have passed my seventy-eighth year, I lay down my pen for younger fingers to take up, and, turning my face towards the western sunset of life, I grasp my staff to continue the journey to the end, leaving that time in the hands of Him who has been with me thus far and who "doeth all things well."[190]

---

[190] "All the Way My Savior Leads Me," hymn, lyrics by Fanny Crosby, music by Robert Lowry (1875).

APPENDIX A

In Memory of Allen Jay

This section is taken from the booklet printed by Allen Jay's children and grandchildren after his death. The booklet contains the full text of the memorial service, which is too long to reprint here. This section is included because of the warm, intimate portrait it gives of Allen Jay on the day before he died.

At the close of the Sabbath day, Fifth month 8, 1910, Allen Jay passed quietly and peacefully into the Great Beyond. After a day of extreme suffering, having dropped for a few moments into a quiet sleep, he passed with only the slightest signs of the change into that Eternal sleep to awaken with the Master for whom he had given a long life of faithful service.

He had often expressed the desire that, as he termed it, "he might die in the harness" and that he should never live to be a care to his friends, but might live only so long as he would be of service to his fellowmen. So it seems that God remembered his desire in permitting him to close his work so soon after a more than usual strenuous campaign in the interests of Earlham College, in connection with useful service at the Friends' conference held during the Laymen's Missionary Conference at Chicago. With his usual haste, after accomplishing a service which required his absence from home, he hastened to return, this time to close his life among loved ones and life-long friends.

The burden of his life for many years had been the welfare of the Church, not for self glorification, but that Christ might be exalted and the sinner redeemed. He believed the hope of the Friends Church lay in the united and concentrated effort of the young ministers.

Nothing pained him more than dissension among Christian leaders and he sought in every proper way to "pour oil on troubled waters." The young ministers believed in him because he loved them and always had a listening ear for their trials and discouragements and pointed them to the Holy Spirit, as their guide. His very presence was a benediction.

It seems fitting that some account of his last words to a group of young ministers at the Friends Conference held in connection with the Laymen's Missionary Congress in Chicago, might form a part of this memorial.

After the conference where Allen Jay had participated with his usual optimistic earnestness, he joined a group of three young ministers, Edgar Stranahan, of Wichita, Kansas; Parvin W. Bond, of Van Wert, Ohio; and Levi Pennington, of Richmond, Indiana; and the four started together to a restaurant some distance from the place in which the conference was held.

On the way, he reviewed his work of the previous day, when in an automobile kindly furnished by Harry C. Starr, formerly of Richmond, he had ridden about the business section of the city soliciting funds for Earlham College. During this walk he gave counsel and encouragement.

At the restaurant a delightful hour was spent by the young men in listening to a wealth of reminiscence, observation, and counsel, regarding the past, present, and future of Quakerism.

The conversation turned to the subject of North Carolina and Allen Jay, at the request of one of the younger men, told of his work in rehabilitating Quakerism in that section after the Civil War.

As he alone could tell them, he recounted incident after incident of labors in that difficult but important field until the work had assumed large proportions, and North Carolina was again a stronghold of Quakerism. During the space of ten years, 1866–76, the Yearly Meeting increased its numbers from 2,200 to 5,500 members.

He continued in this way at some length relating many incidents which help to add interest to those pages of his autobiography which deal principally with his work in North Carolina. He considered his leaving North Carolina Yearly Meeting one of the best moves he ever made for the Church, in as much as just at the time they were learning to depend so much upon him, the burden was thrown on other shoulders and new leaders were brought into the work.

Much more was said on this line, Allen Jay insisting that *the right kind of leadership is that which develops other leaders.*

He admitted that it is not always easy for men to see when they should retire to places of less prominence and power. "One of the hardest things I know of," he said, "is to grow old gracefully. It isn't easy, even when you want to do it, to know just how to get out of the way of younger men."

One of the company observed that he had never been in the way and that nobody wanted him to take a less prominent place in the work of the Church, but he replied: "I know better than anyone else that I can't work and preach as I used to, nor like some of you younger men. I want you boys to be encouraged. I am glad to see you coming on in the work, to take it up when some of us older ones must lay it down. It is not much that I have done; I hope you all may be able to do much more than I have done."

Outside of the restaurant the company separated, and as he turned away, he said: "All right. Good-bye. I will see you again."

Forty-eight hours later he had gone to that other country. The three friends who sat with him at supper that evening saw his face no more in the earthly life, but they are remembering that last interview with joy that they had the privilege of being with him, and with gratitude that in the evening it can be so light. And they are living in the hope of the fulfillment of his last words to them that day: *"All right. Good-bye. I will see you again."*

His service the next day also at Quarterly Meeting is remembered by those who heard him as a most impressive one when he reminded Friends that the Christian life was not only a new life, but an expanding life, and that we are ever learning new lessons and having new experiences, and the deepest experiences and highest life had not yet been reached by anyone. There is always more to follow.

APPENDIX B

Memorial Minute

Memorial of Allen Jay
West Richmond Friends Meeting,
Seventh month 20, 1910

Allen Jay was born in Miami County, Ohio, Fourth month 11, 1831. He was the son of Isaac and Rhoda (Cooper) Jay, members of Mill Creek Monthly Meeting of Friends. In 1850 he removed with his parents to Mississinawa Monthly Meeting, near Marion, Grant County, Indiana. In 1854 he married Martha Ann Sleeper, a member of Greenfield Monthly Meeting, Tippicanoe County, Indiana, and for fourteen years they lived on a farm a few miles from the city of Lafayette, Indiana. He was recorded a minister of the Gospel by Greenfield Monthly Meeting in 1864.

In 1868 he went to North Carolina as superintendent of the work of the "Baltimore Association" of Friends of Baltimore Yearly Meeting, formed to assist Friends in North Carolina after the Civil War and to prevent, if possible, the breaking up of Southern Quakerism through emigration to the West. During the seven years of his service there he had a most remarkable part in the reconstruction of the Society of Friends in the South. His work there distinctly approached the spiritual level and power of early Friends and he will ever be lovingly associated in the minds of North Carolina Friends with the rebuilding of their Yearly Meeting.

He continued this work until 1875, when he went on a religious visit to England, Ireland, Scotland, and Norway. These visits were very helpful to Friends in those parts, especially to the young people.

In 1877 he became treasurer and religious director, in fact if not in name, of New England Yearly Meeting's Boarding School at Providence, Rhode Island.

In 1881 he accepted the position of superintendent of Earlham College. His reputation as a minister and as an educator, an organizer of meetings and of schools, gave him at once a prominent place among the leaders of Indiana Yearly Meeting. In 1885 he was made a member of the Representative Meeting and continued to be a member of it and of the Permanent Board which succeeded it until his death.

He was a delegate to the General Conference of Friends held in Richmond in 1887, and took a prominent part in the discussions, earnestly advocating the proposed Declaration of Faith. He was among the foremost Friends in carrying through the subsequent conferences which prepared the way for the Five Years Meeting, and when the proposal for this central national meeting was made, he threw himself heartily into the plan and helped in every way within his power to make the new organization serviceable to the wider life and work of the society. He was a delegate and chairman of the business committee in the conferences held in 1892 and 1897, and was a delegate to the Five Years Meeting in 1902 and 1907, being made chairman of the business committee in 1902.

In 1887 he became financial agent of Earlham College, and in 1890 he was appointed one of the Trustees of the college. He held both these positions till his death. In 1890 he was appointed a member of the Evangelistic and Pastoral Committee of Indiana Yearly Meeting. He served the committee as its superintendent from 1891 till 1896, and as its chairman from 1902 till his death.

He was a member of the Associated Committee on Indian Affairs continuously from 1891.[191]

He had a life-long interest in Friends Bible Schools, always attending as a teacher or member of a class when possible. He was a promoter of many Bible conferences and was a member of the managing committee of the Bible Institute of Indiana, Western, and Wilmington yearly meetings during its existence from 1897 to 1909. In 1895 he was appointed by the Yearly Meeting to raise the balance of its indebtedness, which he succeeded in doing.

His wife died in the spring of 1899. He was married to Naomi W. Harrison, Eleventh month, 1900, and the following year accompanied by her he made a second visit to Friends in England and Ireland. He died in Richmond, Indiana, Fifth month 8, 1910, after an acute illness of only one day. The funeral services were held in the Yearly Meeting house on the afternoon of Sixth month 12, and the interment was in Earlham Cemetery. The attendance was very large, both sides of the large house being nearly filled. Not only were Friends present from many Quarterly Meetings of Indiana Yearly Meeting, but also from Western, Wilmington, and North Carolina yearly meetings, including the clerks of the two last named. Impressive memorial minutes adopted by the Trustees, faculty, and students of Earlham College, and by the ministerial association of Richmond of which he was a prominent member, were read. The ministers of the city attended in a body, and were seated with the visiting ministers on the raised platform. Besides the principal discourses by Elbert Russell and Robert L. Kelly, more than twenty others in the space of half an hour testified their appreciation of our dear friend.

---

[191] Started in 1867, the Associated Executive Committee on Indian Affairs (Orthodox) was headed in the field by William Nicholson, and had up to eight agents and eighty-five Friends in government service. The work also received visits and support from such prominent British Friends as Stanley Pumphrey, Isaac Sharp, and Henry Stanley Newman.

We insert the following extract from the resolutions of the ministerial association:

> The Ministerial Association of Richmond bears today an unusual loss. Allen Jay, its oldest and one of its most-honored members has been called home. More than of most men it can be said that he went about continually doing good. A devoted lover and most efficient servant of his own church, his broad and intelligent sympathy made him the true and helpful friend of all churches. He was wise in counsel with the wisdom that is from above. His heart seemed ever open to the touch of God, and his spirit ever listening to the still small voice. His simplicity and humility were beautiful to see. Almost four-score [years of age] we never thought of him as old, for his was the eternal youth of the spirit. Our deep sympathy goes out to the Society of Friends in all lands, to Earlham College which has lost a noble friend and spiritual father, and especially to his loved ones at home, so sorely bereaved. By the love of our own hearts for him we measure the sorrow of theirs and pray for them the comfort wherewith we ourselves are comforted of God.

Subsequently, during the Commencement Week of Earlham College, additional memorial services for him were held.

Allen Jay had in a very high degree those personal traits that beget love. He understood with rare insight the problems and difficulties of all kinds of people, and he knew how to speak to all sorts of conditions. Hosts of persons came to him for counsel and help on the most intimate matters of their lives, and found in him the friend they needed in their strait. He did not allow zeal for institutions or causes to blind him to the weal of men, nor allow mere sentiment or sympathy to dim his sense of justice or right.

He was unusually gifted in genuine sympathy. He entered without reserve or restraint into the joy or sorrow of others. He was tender as a mother to anyone passing through losses or suffering, and he knew how to say the right word to help and comfort them. Blessed with the heart of a little child, he understood and loved little children.

His unfailing spirit of youth, his power to keep in touch with the next generation, his gift of discovering what was in young people almost before they knew it themselves, gave him a unique place in the affection of those who came under his influence and made him an ideal elder to whose insight and penetrating counsel a multitude of young Friends owe the discovery and development of their gifts.

All classes of men claimed his sympathy, his love, and his help. The weary, the aged, and forsaken found in him a comforter, who made them feel that age was honorable, life cheerful, and heaven sure.

The erring and sinning found proof of his love in the message of the Savior who loved sinners and died for them. Yet there was no weakness in his love. A discerner of hearts, he knew the obstacles in the way of progress; he put his finger on the sin hidden in the heart; he rebuked that he might bind up and heal by the grace of God.

He gave much time and thought to work for the Indian and the negro and the poor, and it was characteristic of the breadth of his sympathies that the last week of his life was spent at the National Laymen's Missionary Convention in Chicago.

A practical man of affairs with ability to lead and win men such as would have enabled him to succeed as a promoter of great business enterprises or as a political leader, he used these talents to enlarge the Kingdom of God. His heart was not lifted up in pride by his success and popularity. He would not write the story of his own life lest it should seem like boasting, until he saw it could be made the means of a last message to the coming generations of the Society he loved. He had the spiritual insight of a mystic, the self-sacrifice of a saint.

All these characteristics blended in him and permeated his activities. He conducted a revival meeting with a politician's insight into the motives that move men, and a general's knowledge of the means of managing them. He took up a subscription in the spirit of a prayer meeting. He made men feel that giving was worship—a means of serving God to those not gifted to preach and pray. He saw visions and felt ecstasies, but he ever distrusted religious feelings and experiences that were barren of everyday goodness, and resolutely turned away from claims of spirituality that were not fashioned after the pattern of Christ.

His own religious emotions were powerful, but he knew that no church could flourish in the continual whirl of emotion. He knew that the problems of church policy must be solved by statesmanlike wisdom and insight, and he was one of our foremost men in his discernment of what "Israel ought to do."

His character was essentially progressive. He lived in the present age. He kept pace with events and as customs, methods, and ideas changed, he adjusted himself to new conditions, so that he was more used by the church, if possible, in his last years than ever before.

His ministry had the qualities that are necessary for a fruitful and lasting ministry. His early religious experiences had been vivid and clear-cut, so that his religious thinking was free from vagueness and doubt. He knew the power of God unto salvation in the Gospel, and the need of men to be born from above. He had a clear and vivid vision of Jesus Christ, who was for him no mere theory or part of speculative theology, but a most real person. To him, his faith clung with simple trust to the end, and he was able to make others see Christ as he himself knew Him. He knew his Bible in a vital way and had always upon his tongue the passages needed for instruction, or reproof, or rebuke, or comfort. He was rich in material for illustration, and his examples were often homely but effective.

His strong common sense and fine sense of humor prevented his religious seriousness from becoming harsh or morose. He knew human nature so that he was able to touch the springs of the human heart; was intensely evangelistic in his Christ-like desire for men's salvation, and withal had a genuine appreciation of the intellectual side of life and sympathy with its development. Above all he had an anointing from above, and revealed a Power above his own powers. His ministry was an all-around ministry and met the many-sided needs of those to whom he ministered.

In his early ministry he was highly favored in family visiting or in public meetings, to speak to individual needs and conditions. At the acme of his power he was an effective and successful evangelist. In later life his message became more and more the message of brotherhood and unity. In face of rancor and division he grew like a second beloved disciple whose constant exhortation was, "Little children, love one another." [192]

His power as a minister and his gift for raising money caused him to be widely sought for to dedicate new meeting-houses. His spirituality and loving sympathy made him in great demand both by Friends and others for funeral services. We shall never know how many were turned by him from an old life to the new, from a thin, passive, and formal religion to a positive, vital Christian life, but it was a great harvest.

We cannot realize the greatness of his sacrifices for the gospel of Christ. He wore no outward marks of sorrow or sadness. He knew the meaning of that wonderful phrase, "the joy of the cross."[193] As a young man he shrank from the public ministry as only a keen and sensitive nature can, because of the impediment in his speech. He suffered much from painful operations undergone in the hope of being able to speak more plainly the gospel of Christ. He endured the hardships of travel, the separation from those he loved, and the bitterness of controversy. Like the Apostle Paul, he counted not his life dear unto himself if only he might fulfill his ministry;[194] and in accordance with his wish he was permitted to be useful to the Church until the very end.

---

[192] 1 John 3:18, 4:7

[193] Hebrews 12:2

[194] Acts 20:24

His most concrete service and the one for which he will be longest-remembered is probably that which he rendered to education. In this particular, his service is without parallel in the history of our Society. His own education was limited, but he realized most keenly the deficiency and desired that others might not be handicapped in the same way. To his rare natural endowments he added the influence of wide reading and extensive travel and close association with men and women of culture both in America and England.

With sublime faith that truth is always valuable and endless, he worked for education and was not disturbed when others went beyond him. He trusted the reverent spirit of scholars when he could no longer understand, nor judge of their teaching; and he feared not that any discoveries in God's world would cause men to lose faith in Christ, nor that devout thinking would lead away from God. His interest in education soon outran his ability as a teacher, but he continued to foster it as superintendent, promoter, and director.

He was in a very real sense one of the makers of at least five of our colleges. He put his rare ability for raising money and enlisting tangible support for educational work at the service, at critical times, of Earlham, Guilford, Whittier, Penn, and Pacific colleges. Back and forth across the continent and up and down its coasts he went repeatedly, pleading for education and taking upon himself the drudgery necessary to raise funds to realize his ideals.

During his last years he bore the brunt of much opposition to the pursuit of truth and the development of the intellect, but he took it patiently, and went ahead in the sure faith that "truth is mighty and will prevail."[195] He had a deep conviction that most of the excesses committed in the name of religion could be prevented by the proper fostering of educational work. He recognized that the processes of education are slow and he had the true teacher's patience for the weaker ones.

---

[195] "Truth is mighty and will prevail"; "Magna est veritas et praevalebit"—quoting Puritan preacher, Thomas Brooks (1608-1684).

He fought a good fight; he kept a great faith;[196] he left us the legacy of the achievements and examples of a noble life. He loved the church better than his own life and did his part to save and advance it. He was ever full of hope and cheer, with large visions of future advances of the Lord's work, and his face was always toward the dawn. Memorial minute prepared by:

Mahalah Jay
Hannah D. Francisco
Harlow Lindley
Elbert Russell

---

[196] 1 Timothy 4:7

APPENDIX C

Dr. Nereus Mendenhall and Delphina Mendenhall

The following section appeared as chapters 24 and 25 in the original edition of Allen Jay's Autobiography. *They have been moved to an appendix, because they break up the narrative of his work in the South, and have little mention of what Allen Jay was doing. However, these chapters shed interesting light on two important figures in North Carolina Yearly Meeting, and on some of the conditions facing Friends before, during, and after the Civil War.*

Dr. Nereus Mendenhall

Allusion has been made in these pages while speaking of the Baltimore Association work to Dr. Nereus Mendenhall and Delphina E. Mendenhall. Each of these persons was of such prominence in the affairs of North Carolina Yearly Meeting and the surrounding country that I have thought a little further account of their lives would be of interest and not out of place in the history of the period which is under consideration.[197]

---

[197] A copy of Allen Jay's *Autobiography*, in the collection of Guilford College, contains a note dictated by Lewis Lyndon Hobbs, saying that his wife, Mary Mendenhall Hobbs, wrote the chapters on Nereus Mendenhall and Delphina Mendenhall, but asked to be anonymous at the time. Mary Mendenhall Hobbs was the daughter of Nereus Mendenhall and the great-niece of Delphina Mendenhall. Special thanks to Gwen Erickson, Librarian and College Archivist at Guilford, for sharing this information.

Dr. Nereus Mendenhall, the third child of Richard and Mary Pegg Mendenhall, was born at the old homestead in Jamestown, North Carolina, on the 14th of August, 1819. Early in life he manifested a decided interest in literary and religious matters. His studies were watchfully encouraged by his father, who was himself a fine classical scholar. At the age of thirteen Nereus entered a printing office in Greensboro and in this congenial occupation furthered his love of learning, and at the same time saved money to enable him to enter Haverford School, now Haverford College, which he did in 1837. By earnest application he was enabled to graduate in 1839, thus crowding a four years' course into two years, a very unwise procedure which doubtless bore fruit in after years.

That the spiritual vision was cleared as well as the intellectual life invigorated is shown by the following little testimony given by him near the close of his life to his dear friend and classmate, Dr. Richard Randolph, of Philadelphia.

It will be noted that in this, as in many other instances, the enlightenment came through the devoted study of the Holy Scriptures, of which to his dying day he was a tireless student. His little Greek Testament lying on the stand beside his bed was one of the few books read during his last illness.

"The revelation which in my little dormitory at Haverford came to me as alone by the narrow window I read Psalm 34:10, 'The young lions do lack and suffer hunger, but they that seek the Lord shall now want any good thing'; however unable at some time to see how it is true, for that time to the present I have never relinquished nor ceased to cherish."

Upon his graduation from Haverford he took the place as principal of Friends Boarding-school at New Garden. The life was arduous, for in those days the boards had the idea, not yet wholly outgrown, that the fiber of teachers was rubber and steel and that the occupation of teaching was such an easy task that the more work which could be piled on the better. Notwithstanding his multifarious duties, which lasted from early morning until the students were in bed asleep, he prepared himself to enter Jefferson Medical College, Philadelphia, from which institution he graduated in 1845.

Although he practiced medicine successfully for several years, the strain was too severe for one of his sensitive and sympathetic nature, and he retired permanently from the profession after five or six years.

In a letter to a friend written about this time he said that he believed teaching to be his God-given calling and that he always felt as if he were wasting his time when he was otherwise employed. During the years in which he was practicing medicine he was issuing a small educational paper and doing all he could to promote public education.

In 1851 he married Oriana Wilson, an own cousin of Delphina Mendenhall, who had for several years lived in her home and been one of her chief aids in the management of her affairs. She was a very energetic, capable woman with a well-balanced mind and sterling character.

Dr. Mendenhall had been almost continuously connected with the boarding-school either as teacher, superintendent, or trustee. His always delicate health would not permit of several consecutive years in the schoolroom, and he varied his employment from time to time by engaging in civil engineering, the outdoor exercise and tent life being the best tonic available. He was thus occupied during the years immediately preceding the Civil War, his home being in the pleasant little village of Florence, North Carolina, one mile from Deep River Meeting-house.

In the confusion and distress incident to the outbreak of the war, the boarding-school was left without a teacher. Numbers of Friends had already gone West and others were going, and the whole country was in a turmoil. The trustees appealed to Dr. Mendenhall to again take charge of the school. He consented to do so and moved his family into the farmhouse, the first house built upon what is now the college property.

The war cloud gathered with alarming velocity, and as many of the Friends and relatives of the family were joining the general migration, the question as to what was his duty in the matter became a pressing one.

In the West was freedom from the ever-pressing burdens which all antislavery men were compelled to bear in slave communities. He was very averse to bringing up his daughters in the midst of slavery. The prospect for lucrative employment was alluring and the great claims of those he had known and loved from childhood beckoned him away.

In the South [were] war, trial and sacrifice, hardship and an uncertain subsistence for him and his. The furniture was sold, the boxes packed and at the station, and the family ready to leave on the morrow, when the responsibility of abandoning the school which would be left without a teacher and must of necessity be closed so oppressed him that in earnest prayer he laid the matter before the Lord and was fully convinced that it was the will of God for him to remain and face the consequences, be they what they might.

His wife was perfectly willing to abandon the undertaking and return to the old farmhouse with her little flock and again gather such household goods as were indispensable in the effort to make a home which would live in the minds of her children while life lasted.

As a result of his action the school was never closed but continued in operation through the Civil War, the only educational institution in the State which was able to breast the storms of that terrific time.

During this period Dr. Mendenhall was active in behalf of Friends who were either drafted or conscripted and went several times to Richmond to interview the Confederate authorities. He appealed to Jefferson Davis in person and was most kindly received and courteously listened to by him. While he was unable to secure relief which was perfectly satisfactory, the Friends were granted the privilege of buying their freedom from military service by the payment of $500 in Confederate money. At one time when addressing a committee to whom the matter was referred, it was said Dr. Mendenhall made a most remarkable speech, which held the Confederate legislators spellbound by the force of its argument against war. During these years and several succeeding years he was clerk of the yearly meeting.

Soon after the close of the war he bought a farm near Deep River Meeting-house and removed to that place. For two or three years he conducted a monthly meeting school and then again engaged in civil engineering, an occupation which always brought renewed health and vigor.

His political affiliations had always been "union" and antislavery, but during the terrible reconstruction period he allied himself with that party which alone cared whether the South sank and went to ruin or survived as a part of the national life. He was elected several times to the Legislature of the State and while there served faithfully the interests of the people. Now he and his friend, Dr. William Nicholson, who was also a member of the Legislature, were on the committee to write the new constitution for the State and did much towards giving the State the constitution that it now has. Particularly did Dr. Mendenhall labor in the cause of education and for the improvement in the care for the insane, which latter class were in a most pitiable condition, confined in jails and county houses without proper care or right medical attention.

When the State decided to provide additional room by the erection of a new hospital at Morganton, Dr. Mendenhall insisted that it be called a hospital and not an asylum, insanity being a disease and not a possession.

He was made a member of the very important committee to whom the erection and equipment of this building was entrusted. His services on this board were of the greatest importance, both in the arrangement of the hospital and in the thoroughness of its construction. He was very watchful that no ill-made bricks or inferior material should have a place in the building.

After he retired from all other outside employment he still served on the Educational Board of Guilford County and interested himself in the public schools. No one was more interested in the work of the Baltimore Association than he. Francis T. King often sought his counsel and advice in the inception of the work. His interest and delight in the normal schools inaugurated and was an inspiration to those in charge. From time to time as invited he was willing to assist by lectures, readings, or impromptu speeches. In later life he was for a time connected with Penn Charter School of Philadelphia and then as instructor and superintendent of Haverford College. Three years he enjoyed greatly in the renewal of old friendships, and the formation of many new and congenial ones.

His interest in religious matters strengthened as the years went by and his whole nature mellowed and ripened. The Society of Friends was always one of his chief concerns.

With very much of what was introduced after the war he had no sympathy. The crude religious instruction, coupled with the uncultured expressions which came in various emotional groans and gestures, did not appeal to one who had not only experienced the deep things of God personally, but had made himself acquainted with the breadth of human history and the development of the mind of man.

His last years were spent at Guilford College, where he bought a cottage home for himself and wife that they might be near their daughters, four of whom were living in or near the College. These three years he greatly enjoyed. Frequently he lectured to the students, and his little library was a rendezvous for any who wished to consult the doctor on literary or religious subjects. After the death of his wife in 1890 his own health steadily declined until his death in October of 1893.

His influence in North Carolina Yearly Meeting can scarcely be estimated, and many are still living who rejoiced to call him teacher.

Delphina E. Mendenhall

Delphina E. Mendenhall, at the time I knew her, was a widow living on the large estate bequeathed to her by her husband, George C. Mendenhall, a distinguished lawyer and legislator of the State.

[George] was a birthright member of the Society of Friends, but was disowned, as were hundreds of others, by the suicidal policy of the stringent marriage rules of the day. His first wife [Eliza], besides not being a Friend, was the owner of a large number of slaves. She was a kindly, sensitive woman and was strangely attached to and influenced by the elder brother of her husband, Richard Mendenhall, who was all of his mature years a leader in the yearly meeting and one of the very first to express openly antislavery views and labor for the manumission of slaves. Eliza Dunn Mendenhall sympathized with these views and wished her own slaves liberated, and, had it not been for the hasty, injudicious action of Friends in disowning her husband, would have most likely become a Friend herself.

Her early death left George Mendenhall with an infant son and a colony of negroes. His home was a plantation which had been deeded to his grandfather by the Earl of Granville, to whom Carolina had been ceded by the English Crown. A grist mill, a sawmill, a blacksmith shop, a carpenter shop, and a large farm could not give employment to all of his negroes and he was obliged to send many of them from home to labor for others, a thing he very much deprecated. Such were looked after closely and if abused brought home. The negroes were often bought by him because they begged him to become their master, but not one was ever sold. To this home he brought as his second wife one of the loveliest women who has ever graced the Quaker garb or adorned the high seat in a Friends meeting-house. Why she was not disowned was a wonder, but she was not, and from that time until the day of her death that home was a retreat and a refreshment for Friends from far and near.

The most generous and even lavish hospitality was dispensed to the equal enjoyment of husband and wife. The coaches and barouches were always ready to take either the ministers or the guests to whatever Friends meeting was in progress, the master himself often occupying the seat with the coachman if the inside were full of plain bonnets and broad brimmed hats.

The maiden name of Delphina Mendenhall was Gardner. Her father, Barzilla Gardner, had died while the children were very small and in after years her mother married William Long, a lawyer of prominence, who beautifully filled the place of father to her two daughters. When George Mendenhall asked Mary Wilson Long for her consent to the marriage, she replied that her only objection was the fact that he owned slaves. To this he replied that he regretted this fact as much as she could and that he intended to liberate them as rapidly as he could settle them comfortably upon the free soil of Ohio. This then became the combined effort of these two congenial spirits.

The way was difficult and very much more care was necessary than many antislavery people in the North realized. These people were children in their experiences; unaccustomed to provide for themselves, it was necessary to train them to some useful handicraft and fit them to lead independent lives. They could not be liberated in the South, and careful conduct was necessary to bring them safely to Ohio. Once there, it would be cruelty to leave them to the haphazard arrangements of their own devising. Group by group, as fast as they could be made ready and be removed without breaking up families and the master could find time for the undertaking, the slaves were being taken to freedom. Both master and mistress accompanied them and remained with them in Ohio until all were secured in some sustaining situation, then back again to prepare others for the journey.

George Mendenhall had an extensive law practice in the State, and the education of his wife had been so broad and thorough that she became of the greatest assistance to him in his work at a time when stenographers and typewriters were unknown. It was said of her in after years that she knew as much law as he did. With all these duties and the management of the immense household and ceaseless entertainment of the lawyers, judges, and governors, which were as frequent guests as the "visiting Friends," she still found time not only to attend Deep River Meeting regularly and participate in the business and burden bearing of the Church, but to keep herself well informed upon the topics of the day and, better still, to study the best literature of the world, including a loving, reverent study of the Bible.

She was a poet herself of no mean order and many of her poems may be found in the volumes of the *Friends Review*, signed D. or D.E.M. These are full of the keen appreciation of the beautiful in nature and in human life, which was one of her most striking characteristics.

With now and then a visit to Philadelphia or some other point in the North and West, and frequent journeys with her husband on legal business through the surrounding counties of their native State, many fruitful, beneficent years glided by. The war cloud began to gather and they were eager to get the remainder of their slaves to Ohio, but before the cloud burst in fury and bloodshed, George Mendenhall was gone—drowned, on his way to a distant court, in the swollen waters of the treacherous Uwhwuaria.[198] Stunned beyond all telling, stricken to the heart over her personal loss and loneliness, Delphina endeavored to execute her husband's will in regard to the slaves and started the last band on the journey towards freedom. They did not reach the Ohio River, but were met by hostile officers in Virginia and compelled to return to their old home.

Then the war closed her in. The son of George Mendenhall became her most bitter antagonist, because he regarded the negroes as his property and disregarded the expressed desire of his father that they should be freed. Under all of these difficulties she bore herself as a prophetess of old might have done and was supported by the clearest sense of the divine presence. The care of such a household during the perilous days of the war was a burden great enough to tax the powers of the strongest men, but she patiently met the days as best she could and cared lovingly and tenderly for every one and all loved her.

Property depreciated, state bonds became just so much paper, horses died and there was no money with which to purchase new ones. Many mouths were to be filled, many persons to be clothed. Her native resources were great and she managed to control matters until relief came at the surrender.

Although at the close of the war her mode of life was almost entirely changed and she was reduced to one small carriage, one horse, and a little negro for driver, she never slackened her attendance from

---

[198] The Uwharrie River, now included in Uwharrie National Forest, flows roughly sixty miles from near High Point, N.C., through Montgomery County until it joins the Pee Dee River near Albemarle, N.C. The river has been known by several names, including Uwhwuaria.

meeting and her saintly face in the gallery of the old Deep River Meeting-house is one of the most precious memories to many a young man and woman in the body of the meeting.

Her influence over the young people was unbounded, because they all knew that she loved them and sympathized with their feelings. She was always ready to join in the meeting of their literary clubs and to encourage them to go forward in their educational efforts. No one could so entertain a roomful of young people with charming reminiscences or recite verses or exhibit quick repartee or sweet-spirited jest.

Her face and form were as beautiful as her character and her bearing as queenly as Elizabeth Fry's must have been if the portraits are a correct representation. The Friends dress was wonderfully becoming and the soft material and shining silk worn in antebellum days adorned her person without attracting the thoughts from herself to her clothes.

She was very averse to contention in a Friends meeting and seldom participated in a debate. Once when such had been rather more heated than loving, after meeting she remarked, "It worried me. I wished that I were out of the gallery and sitting down there between M.W. and his wife." These persons had been married but a few days and no doubt were very happy and contented with themselves, and their company would have been more to her taste than that of wrangling elders. She abhorred "tale-bearing and detraction" and some of her most forceful expressions were directed against this sin.

For years she was clerk of North Carolina Yearly Meeting and a most competent one. Afterwards during the remainder of her life she sat at the head of the women's meeting. Her expressions were full and clear, for she had the mind of Christ and clothed her thoughts in perfect English.

Her interest in the work of the Baltimore Association and her enthusiasm over its progress were unbounded, and in every way possible she aided in advancing the cause. As Ezra Meader was leaving his New England home to come South and engage in the work of teaching in the schools of the Association and had told John G. Whittier, an old friend of his family, that he intended first to go to the home of

Delphina Mendenhall, Whittier said, "Delphina—why, she is a whole quarterly meeting in herself."

When the summons came to come up higher she was so ready and willing to go as to almost hurt those who loved her. Not a shadow in her way, not a wish in her mind to linger, ready, willing, almost jubilant, she entered into her rest with the request that her dear nephew, Nereus Mendenhall, who had loyally stood by her in every emergency, should close her peaceful eyes.

At the funeral a near relative was heard to say, "I do not feel that we have any more right to be seated near her than any one else in this room, for all are chief mourners."

The household is scattered, the old home place sold and in the possession of strangers, but her influence and the benediction of her love and life live on and can never perish.

Timeline of Events in the Life of Allen Jay

1831   Born in Miami County, Ohio, eldest son of Isaac Jay and Rhoda Cooper Jay

1841   Moved to Randolph Meeting, six miles north of Dayton, Ohio

1843   Conversion experience; active in the Underground Railroad; worried by the Millerite (Adventist) prediction of the second coming of Christ

1845   Allen Jay's father becomes active as a Friends minister

1850   Allen Jay's father recorded as a Friends minister; family moves to Mississinawa Meeting in Marion, Indiana

1851   Studied at Friends Boarding School in Richmond, Indiana (now Earlham College)

1852   Studied at Farmers Institute, near Lafayette, Indiana, and at Antioch College, Ohio

1854   Married to Martha Sleeper

1855   Settled near Farmers Institute and worked as a teacher; organized First-day school classes

1859   First spoke in Meeting for Worship

1860   Allen and Martha Jay appointed as elders at Greenfield Meeting; Allen Jay appointed by Western Yearly Meeting to visit local meetings

1864   Recorded as a Friends minister; first minute as a traveling minister

1866   First visit to North Carolina after the Civil War; attended Baltimore Friends Peace Conference

1868   Start of work with Baltimore Association of Friends and North Carolina Yearly Meeting

1875   Visited Friends in Ireland, Great Britain, Scotland, and Norway

1876   Visited meetings in North Carolina and Tennessee

1877   Called to serve as treasurer of Providence Friends School (later Moses Brown School) in Providence, Rhode Island

1880   Death of Allen Jay's father

1881   Called to serve as superintendent and treasurer of Earlham College

1885   Fundraising trip to England for Earlham College

1886   Appointed by Indiana Yearly Meeting to the committee to explore a joint Friends foreign mission board

1887   Appointed fund-raiser for Earlham College; Richmond Conference leading to the Richmond Declaration of Faith (which was written at Allen Jay's desk)

1892	Served as superintendent of Indiana Yearly Meeting; attended General Conference of Friends which urged the creation of a united missions board
1894	American Friends Board of Foreign Missions launched; death of Allen Jay's mother
1898	Death of son William
1899	Death of wife Martha
1900	Marriage to Naomi Harrison; visit to England and Ireland
1904	Fundraising for Guilford College which left it debt-free
1905	Fundraising to build a library for Earlham College, plus fundraising for Bundy Hall and Lindley Hall; fundraising for Whittier College
1909	Founding member of West Richmond Friends Meeting
1910	Allen Jay died in Richmond, Indiana
1915	West Richmond Friends Meeting moves to new site (now the Community Building/Richmond Friends School) which was a farmhouse belonging to the family of Naomi Harrison Jay
1916	Present West Richmond Friends meetinghouse dedicated in memory of Allen Jay

Index

Aareg, Torbjorn 228
Ackworth Boarding-School, England 232
Albright, Arthur 202, 208
Allen, Stafford 202
Allen, Hanna Stafford 202
Alsop, Christine 202
American Friends Board of Foreign Missions 240, 242–53, 299–300, 381
Amesbury, Massachusetts 3, 320–1
Andrews, Frederick 232
Antioch College 43–4, 54–5, 379
Archdale Monthly Meeting - *see* Bush Hill
Archdale, John 136
Armstrong, Eliza C. 348, 350
Back Creek Monthly Meeting 49, 163, 191, 246
Backhouse, Jonathan and Hannah 240
Backhouse, Edward 202
Bailey, James E. 108, 111
Baily, Joshua L. 330
Baldwin, Mary E. (Jay) 4, 34
Baldwin, Isaac 79
Bales, Eleazar 79
Bales, Joseph 119
Baltimore Association 73, 118, 121–5, 127, 135–6, 139, 141–72, 180, 183, 185–90, 245, 357, 367, 371, 376, 380
Baltimore Yearly Meeting 40, 103, 107, 112, 146, 148, 188, 241, 307, 357
Barker, Seth 113, 166
Barker, Daniel 110
Barton, Daniel D. 111
Bean, Hannah 123, 243

Bean, Joel 123, 243–4
Bean, John 108
Bear Creek Quarterly Meeting, Iowa 95
Beard, Elkanah and Irene S. 244–5
Beard, William 108, 111
Bedford Institute, England 205
Beecher, Henry Ward 209–10
Bellefonte 107
Belvidere, North Carolina 114, 180, 343
Benbow, Thomas J. 139, 149, 166
Bentonsville, North Carolina 115
Berkeley, California 310, 334
Beveridge, Albert 332
Bewley, Samuel 186, 198
Bible Institute, Indiana Yearly Meeting 303–5, 359
Birmingham, England 236, 327
Black Creek Monthly Meeting, North Carolina 110
Blair, Franklin S. 149, 166
Bloomingdale Quarterly Meeting, Indiana 59
Blue River Seminary, Indiana 150
Blue River Monthly Meeting, Indiana 63
Boyce, Samuel 113
Bradfield, Margaret M. (Newsome) 79–80
Brady, Charles 202
Braithwaite, Joseph Bevan 201–2, 205, 215, 240, 299–300, 326
Braithwaite, Martha 202
Bright, John 25, 202, 207–14
Bristol, England 235
Brown, Asher 13
Brown, Isaac 202, 216–7, 233, 235
Brown, Moses 256–7
Brown, Obadiah 257
Brown University 256, 258
Brown, William 345
Bryn Mawr College 13, 147, 258
Bryne, Thorstein 225
Bulla, J.R. 178
Bundy, Zenas and Rachel 277, 335
Bunhill Field, England 205
Bush Hill Monthly Meeting (Archdale), North Carolina 118, 124–5, 148, 157
Bush River Quarterly Meeting 1–2, 39

Butler, John 113
Cadbury Cocoa Company 236
Cadbury, George 327
California Yearly Meeting 291, 307–10, 333, 336
Canada Yearly Meeting 32, 291, 294, 296, 307, 346
Cane Creek, North Carolina 149, 160, 163
Cannon, Joseph G. 332
Caraway, North Carolina 174
Carey, James 113, 144, 187, 300
Carnegie, Andrew 277, 331–3
Carpenter, Walter T. 267–8, 281
Carter, John 149
Cartland, Abby 180
Cartland, Fernando 180
Cartland, Joseph 113
Cartland, Mary 180
Cary, Eliza H. 348
Case, William H. 113
Catell, Ezra 113
Centennial Exposition, Philadelphia 255
Central City Monthly Meeting, Nebraska 348–9, 351–2
Centre, North Carolina 149, 163
Chester Monthly Meeting, Pennsylvania 40
Christian Endeavor 63, 199, 251, 290, 295, 303, 345
Christiansand, Norway 230
Clark, Asenath 98, 233
Clark, Dougan 98, 113, 233, 288, 299
Clark, Sarah S.B. 202, 240
Clark, William 124
Clay, Henry 85
Cobden, Richard 209
Coffin, Charles F. 113, 246
Collins, Samuel 161
Concord Meeting, Pennsylvania 40, 59, 70
Congdon, Ellen 163
Conservative (Wilburite) separation, Western Yearly Meeting 79–96
Contentnea Quarterly Meeting, North Carolina 100, 136
Cook, Esther 343–4
Cooper, Joseph B. 187
Cork Monthly Meeting, Ireland 195–7, 325
Cornell, Eliza P. 259
Cox, Elwood 330

Cox, Isham 113, 119, 139, 166
Cox, Jonathan 131–2
Cox, William 115
Craven, Braxton 161
Crenshaw, John B. 108, 110, 113, 133
Crosfield, Joseph 202
Cuba 250–1, 253
Curwensville, Pennsylvania 107
Dahl, Endre 219–21
Darlington, England 233, 327
Davey, Hattie 345
Davis, Jefferson 109, 370
Day, Mary 79
Deep River Monthly Meeting, North Carolina 2, 98, 110, 132, 136, 160, 163, 331, 369–70, 374, 376
Deer Creek Monthly Meeting, Indiana 85, 87, 113
DeVol, Jonathan 113
Dick, Robert P. 161
Dillwyn, William 83
Dixon, Cyrus W. 349–50
Dixon, George 241
Dixon, Joseph 332
Doan, Joseph 13
Doeg, Robert 216, 219–21, 225, 227, 230
Doncaster, England 325
Dorland, Seaburn 88
Douglas, Cornelius 274
Dow, Neal 261
Dublin Yearly Meeting 144, 148, 189, 192, 197, 199, 216, 286, 298, 319, 323–4, 329, 347, 350
Dunkard Church 108
Earlham College 44, 50, 53, 88, 121, 124, 150–1, 153, 161, 167, 169, 183, 211, 262, 265–94, 305, 319, 329–40, 353–4, 358–60, 364, 379–81
Eastern Quarterly Meeting, North Carolina 341–3
Edinburgh, Scotland 233
Edmundson, William 147
Edwards, Jesse 337, 344
Edwards, Mary E.K. 337, 344
Elkinton, Joseph 335
Elliott, Catherine 79
Elliott, Joseph 144

Elliott, John B. 108
Elliott, Nathan 79
Estes, Lewis A. 274
Evangelistic and Pastoral Committee, Indiana 292–3, 303, 305, 333, 338, 346, 351, 358
Evans, Thomas 13
Everett, Washington 333, 338–9, 343, 345
Evergreen, Alabama 311–14, 316
Fairbanks, Charles W. 332
Farmers Institute 44, 51, 53–4, 59, 88, 183, 379
Five Years Meeting/Friends United Meeting 27, 101, 112, 114, 202, 240, 251–2, 294–301, 338, 346–9, 358
Flint Creek Preparative Meeting, Indiana 58
Flint Hill Academy, North Carolina 132
Florence, North Carolina 132, 369
Flounders Institute, England 216, 233
Forbush, North Carolina 149
Forster, William 118
Fort Sill, Oklahoma 44
Foster, Josiah 240
Fountain City, Indiana 85
Fox, George 6, 25–7, 82–3, 90, 92, 143, 147, 205, 212, 217
Francisco, Hannah D. 365
Friends Academy, Belvidere, North Carolina 180
Friends Boarding-School, Providence, Rhode Island 53, 255–63, 289
Friends Memorial Meeting, Seattle 340
Friendsville Monthly Meeting, Tennessee 118, 124, 167
Fry, Elizabeth 376
Fry, Joseph Storrs 202, 235
Fry, Theodore 233
Gardner, Barzilla 373
Garrett, John B. 239
General Conference of Friends, 1892 .... 248–9, 381
Gillett, George 202
Goddard, Mary A. 291
Godlee, Mary Jane 326
Goldsboro, North Carolina 115–6, 342
Graham, William Alexander 137
Grant County, Indiana 4, 32, 39, 85, 87, 357
Grave, Jacob 84
Green, Harriet 240–1
Green, Jesse 108, 112–3

387

Green Mount Boarding School..53
Green, William..196
Greenfield Monthly Meeting, Indiana............44, 51, 54–5, 57–8, 67, 69, 357, 380
Greensboro, North Carolina........115, 125, 149, 157, 160, 163, 334, 368
Gregg, Smith..31
Grinnell, Jeremiah A. 58, 63, 65, 88, 113
Grubb, George..196
Guilford College 98, 111, 124, 134, 147, 188–9, 241, 319, 329–40, 364, 367, 372, 381
Gurney, Eliza P. 239
Gurney, Joseph John....................................100, 146, 201, 238, 240, 276
Hack, Daniel Pryor 235
Hackney, Francis 119
Hadley, David 348
Hadley, Washington 336
Haines, Jesse P. 113
Haines, Mary R. 215
Haines, Robert B. 239
Hampton, Virginia..241
Hanson, John Frederick..223–5, 344, 348
Hanson, S. Alice..344
Hardee, Harry..161
Harden, Elmer 345
Harris, Jonathan..110
Harrison, George...83
Harrison, Miriam A. 324, 327
Harrison, Naomi W. 323–4, 359, 381
Harvey, Thomas 202
Haughton, Benjamin..195, 325
Haughton, Benjamin Jr. 195, 325
Haverford College 124, 258, 334, 368, 372
Hazard, Seneca..108, 111
Heaton, Samuel..108, 113
Hemenway, James 332
Hiatt, Sarah...79, 99
Hiawatha Monthly Meeting, Nebraska..348
Hickory Valley Monthly Meeting, Tennessee..119
High Point, North Carolina 176–7, 246, 375
Hill, Daniel..108, 113
Hill, Nathan B. 132
Hill, Samuel 331, 339

Hoag, Huldah C. 274
Hoag, Joseph D. 14, 92, 113
Hoare, Samuel.. 83
Hobbs, Barnabas C. 50, 113, 150, 274, 295, 297
Hobbs, Lewis Lyndon 330, 367
Hobbs, Mary Mendenhall 125, 127, 141, 367
Hockett, Mahlon.. 124
Hodgkin, John 91
Hodson, Robert W. 79
Honey Creek Quarterly Meeting.. 59, 79
Honolulu, Hawaii 244
Hoover, John Y. 180
Hopewell Monthly Meeting, Virginia... 2, 40
Howell, Samuel... 124
Hubbard, Charles S. 276
Huff, Miriam 111
Hunt, Nathan 97–101, 124, 186, 233
Hunt, Thomas.. 98
Hunting Creek, North Carolina 149
Hutchins, Daniel H. 31, 108
Indiana Association for Foreign Missions 247
Indiana Yearly Meeting.................... 29, 39, 49, 57, 65, 79, 84–7, 106–7,
    121, 175, 191, 243–6, 248, 265, 269, 271, 274, 291–3, 296–8, 303,
    307, 324, 333, 338–40, 344, 346, 351, 358–9, 380–1
Iowa Conservative Yearly Meeting 95
Iowa Yearly Meeting 79, 91, 122–3, 248, 250, 307, 348, 350
Jamaica... 253
Jamestown, North Carolina... 110, 132, 368
Janney, Richard M. 107, 113, 118, 149
Jay, Charles A. 58
Jay, Eli and Mahalah...................................... 42–5, 54, 57, 161, 248–9, 365
Jay, Esther Furnace 35
Jay, Milton 4, 49
Jay, Rhoda E. 58
Jay, Thomas... 35, 104–8, 111–12
Jay, Walter D. 33
Jay, William.. 2, 35
Jay, William C. 318
Jessup, Levi.. 113
Johns Hopkins Hospital 147
Johns Hopkins University.. 147
Johnson, Levi 248

Johnson, William B. 106
Jones, Abijah 31
Jones, Augustine 261–2
Jones, Eli and Sybil 98, 108, 111, 233, 245, 261, 294
Jones, Elisha 32
Jones, Francis K. 344
Jones, James 32, 180
Jones, John B. 119
Jordans, England 231
Kansas Yearly Meeting 79, 300
Kelly, Robert 359
Kelsey, Rayner 334, 336
Kemp, Caleb 202
Kendal, England 216, 218, 327
Kenworthy, Murray 282
Kersey, James 113
Kida, Bunji 346
King, Francis T. 113, 121–2, 135, 143–4, 146–7, 161, 186–8,
   192, 371
King, John 92
King, Joseph 146
Kinnesdal, Norway 228
Knoles, Thomas 83
Ladd, Thomas W. 163
Ladd, William H. 113
Lafayette, Indiana 5, 44, 51–3, 76–7, 357, 379
Lake Mohonk 257, 259–61
Langley, Washington 339
Lawton, Isaac 257
Lean, William Scarnell 233
Lee, Dorothy 345
Leinster Quarterly Meeting, Ireland 197, 325
Leominster, England 324–5
Liberia 245
Lindley, Alfred and Eliza 289
Lindley, Harlow 335, 365
Lindley, Hervey 339
Lindley, Joshua 149
Lindley, Myra 150
Lisburn, Ireland 197, 201, 325
Liverpool, England 195, 213, 232, 236–7, 324
Lloyd, John 83

Locke, William 84
London Yearly Meeting 27, 85, 99, 118, 189, 199, 201–5, 207,
    215, 218–9, 236–7, 287, 299, 325–6, 346–7
London Yearly Meeting (women's meeting) 25, 204, 326
Long Beach, California 335
Long, Mary Wilson 373
Long, William 373
Los Angeles, California 335
Lost Creek Monthly Meeting, Tennessee 118, 136
Lurey, Sarah Jane 346
Macy, Thomas 2–3, 321
Macy, Uriah 149
Madagascar 244–5
Manchester, England 207, 209, 214, 325
Mann, Horace 44, 54
Marion, Indiana 4, 32, 34, 39, 49, 51, 265, 357, 379
Marlboro, North Carolina 149, 163
Martin, Calva 344
Martin, Frank 344
Martin, Zenas L. 250
Maryland Bible Society 147
Maxfield, Daniel 320
Meader, John and Elizabeth 14, 166
Melbourne, Florida 317
Mendenhall, Alpheus L. 149
Mendenhall, Delphina 130, 367, 369, 372–7
Mendenhall, Elihu E. 329–30
Mendenhall, Eliza Dunn 372–3
Mendenhall, George C. 372–5
Mendenhall, Mary Pegg 368
Mendenhall, Nereus 111, 125, 143, 161, 367–72, 377
Mendenhall, Richard 373
Mennonite Church 108
Mexico 245–7, 253, 283
Miami Monthly Meeting, Ohio 40
Miami Quarterly Meeting 13
Mill Creek Monthly Meeting 9, 32, 357
Miller, Ellen Clare 233
Miller, William 17, 233
Mills, J.J. 288
Minnewaska 259–60
Mississinawa Monthly Meeting 32, 48–9, 87, 357, 379

Mitchel, Maria 320
Mitchel, Peleg.. 92
Model farm, North Carolina 143, 161, 185–7, 189
Monktown, Ireland 201
Moon, Enoch 59
Moon, Mary (Meredith).. 180
Moore, Joseph 45, 118–9, 121, 140, 149–52, 155, 159, 161, 266, 276
Morgan, William B. 150
Morland, John.. 326
Morris, William E. 70
Morton, Oliver.. 77
Moses Brown School - *see* also Providence School..................... 255–7, 380
Mountmellick Boarding-School, Ireland.. 201
Mountmellick, Ireland.. 197
Mt. Vernon Monthly Meeting, Nebraska.. 348
Mt. Pleasant, Ohio.. 65
Muncie Monthly Meeting 333
Munster Quarterly Meeting, Ireland.. 197, 325
Murray, Robert Lindley 113, 163
Murray, Ruth 163
Myrick, Stephen Stanton 334
Naerstrand, Norway 226
Nantucket Historical Association 92
National Road 48, 329
Neave, Joseph... 133
Nebraska Central College 349
Nebraska Yearly Meeting 348–9
New England Yearly Meeting 32–4, 99–100, 189, 238, 245, 256, 261–3, 265, 297, 319, 358
New Garden Boarding School 98, 111, 124, 131, 142, 165, 180, 270, 368
New Garden Monthly Meeting, Pennsylvania 40
New Garden Quarterly Meeting, North Carolina........... 49, 98, 110, 112, 136, 142, 149, 163
New Hope Monthly Meeting, Tennessee... 118
New London Monthly Meeting, Indiana... 59
New York Yearly Meeting 32–4, 113, 163, 189, 255, 297, 319, 329, 346
Newark Monthly Meeting, Pennsylvania 1, 40
Newberg, Oregon 310
Newcastle-on-Tyne, England 233

Newhall, William O. 297
Newman, Henry Stanley 240, 242, 248, 324, 359
Newtown Boarding-School, Ireland.. 201
Nicholson, Josiah 343
Nicholson, Timothy 248, 295, 297
Nicholson, William 113–4, 166, 300–1, 359, 371
Norfolk, Virginia 114
Normal Schools............... 44, 50, 151, 159, 161–3, 165, 190–1, 258, 371
North Carolina Yearly Meeting........... 32–5, 39–40, 73, 83, 98–101, 104, 106, 108–12, 119, 125, 144, 147–8, 156, 160, 165–7, 170–2, 180, 188, 190, 236, 241, 329–30, 341–2, 346, 355, 359, 367, 372, 376, 380
Northern Quarterly Meeting... 32, 49, 191
Nottingham Monthly Meeting, Maryland... 40
Oak Forest, North Carolina... 149
Oberlin College.. 43
Ohio Yearly Meeting 33, 65, 112, 216, 248, 299
Olsen, Soren... 224, 227
Oregon Yearly Meeting....................... 291, 307, 310, 333, 338, 340, 344
Osborn, Peter 111
Osborne, Charles 84
Otis, Job... 92
Overman, Eli... 57
Owen, James 113, 123
Pacific College... 291, 310, 338, 344, 364
Page, John 113
Palestine 245, 283
Parker, John.. 113
Parker, Joseph R. 139
Parry, Mordecai 289
Pasadena, California 308, 335
Peace Association of Friends of America 112, 292
Pearsall, Robert... 235
Pearson, Thomas 139
Pearson, William L. 297
Pease, Arthur 202
Pease, John 233
Peele, Albert 166, 180
Penn Charter School 259, 372
Petersburg, Virginia.. 108
Philadelphia, Pennsylvania 83, 192, 195, 210, 215, 232, 235, 237, 239, 255, 330–1, 335, 375
Pickett, Nathan 268

Pike, Ebenezer 196
Pike, Lydia 196
Pine Creek Preparative Meeting, Indiana 58–9
Piney Woods, North Carolina 149
Pinkham, William P. 249
Plainfield Meeting, Indiana 90, 104
Platte Valley Monthly Meeting, Nebraska 348
Pomona College 258
Posey, John B. 273, 275
Pray, Enos G. 32, 99
Providence, North Carolina 163
Providence School 53, 255–63, 265, 270, 289, 320, 358, 380
Puget Sound Quarterly Meeting 339, 341, 343–6, 351
Pumphrey, Stanley 215–6, 237–42, 247–8, 359
Purdie, Samuel A. 245–7
Purdue University 53
Pym, Anna 325
Queen Victoria 210–11, 234
Queenstown, Ireland (Cobh) 195
Randolph Meeting 9, 23–9, 272, 379
Randolph, Richard 368
Redstone Monthly Meeting, Pennsylvania 40
Replogle, Charles 333, 339, 343–5
Replogle, May 339, 345
Rhoads, James E. 300
Rich Square Monthly Meeting, Indiana 44
Rich Square, North Carolina 112, 163, 341–2
Richardson, Henry and Marla 235
Richardson, Joseph 197
Richmond, Indiana 39, 44, 49, 51, 53, 106, 112,
    114, 196, 202, 224, 244, 246, 252–3, 266, 298, 345, 347–8, 354,
    358–60, 379–81
Robinson, Isaac 218
Robinson, William 3, 321
Rochdale, England 207–8, 213
Roisland, Tollag 228–9
Rowntree Company 236
Rowntree, John Wilhelm 240, 327–8
Russell, Elbert 24, 89, 101, 288, 305, 359, 365
Rutter, Elizabeth Beaven 346
Sampson, William A. 163, 186
San Francisco, California 244, 334–5, 337

San José, California 334, 337
Sand, Norway.. 224, 226
Sandwich Islands, Hawaii 243
Santiago, Cuba (Oriente) 250
Scattergood, Thomas 330
Scipio Yearly Meeting 92
Scott, John 113, 118, 148–9
Seattle, Washington 339–40, 343–4, 346, 351
Seebohm, Benjamin 14
Sharp, Isaac 202, 208, 216, 218–20, 223–5, 227, 230, 359
Sharpless, Charles L. 187
Sharpless, Isaac 330
Shawnee Prairie, Indiana 54
Sheffield, England 325
Shipley, Murray 113
Sims, W.D. 236
Sinton, Hosetta 345
Sinton, William S. 340, 345
Slade, Sarah 289
Sleeper, Buddell 52
Sleeper, Chloe A. 55
Sleeper, Martha 55, 357, 379
Slogvig, Anders and Berta 227
Smiley, Albert K. 255–7, 259, 261
Smiley, Alfred H. 256
Smiley, Daniel 259
Smiley, Eliza P. 256, 259
Smiley, Sarah F. 110, 118, 149
Smith, Hannah Whitall 235
Somerton Monthly Meeting, North Carolina 110
Southern Friend, The 109, 133
Southern Quarterly Meeting, North Carolina 136, 331
Sovde, Norway 224, 226
Spencer, Nathan F. 139
Spiceland, Indiana 44
Spring Bank Monthly Meeting, Nebraska 348
Spring, North Carolina 149, 163
Springfield Monthly Meeting, North Carolina 118, 124, 149, 157,
159–63, 186, 256
Spurgeon, Charles 27, 203
Stakland, Elias 227
Stakland, Norway 227

Stanley, Matthew 79
Stanton, Benjamin 84
Starbuck, Lewis 149
Stavanger, Norway 219, 224–5
Steddom, Samuel 13
Steere, Deborah 124
Stevens, Moses C. 53
Stevenson, Marmaduke 3, 321
Stoke Newington, England 326
Street, Louis and Sarah 244–5
Stuart, Elbridge 339, 344
Sturge, Joseph 205
Suffolk, North Carolina 114
Sugar Grove Christian Church 35
Sugar River Monthly Meeting, Indiana 59
Swan Sisters 262
Swarthmore Farm 187
Swarthmore Hall, England 217
Syria 245
Tabor, Sarah 163
Tabor, William C. 113
Tacoma, Washington 339, 343, 345, 351
Talbot, Caroline E. 216
Tatham, Benjamin 113
Tatum, Anna 163
Tatum, David 68
Tatum, Hannah B. 79
Taylor, Abram 13
Taylor, Ann 65
Taylor, George W. 113
Taylor, James 187
Taylor, Joseph 13
Taylor, Phoebe G. 79
Teague, Prudence 31
Tebbetts, Charles E. 252, 336
Tebbetts, Imelda 336
Tedneland, Cecilia 226
Test, Zaccheus 150
Thomas, Deborah 215
Thomas, Francis W. 113, 297–8
Thomas, James Carey 113, 143–4, 300
Thomas, John Charles 144, 146, 188

Thomas, Sarah Abigail 345
Thorne, Mary 151
Thorntown Quarterly Meeting 59
Tippicanoe City, Ohio 44
Titsworth, A.D. 349
Tobey, Samuel Boyd 100
Tomlinson, Allen U. 113, 124, 139, 149, 176
Tomlinson, Andrew D. 79
Toms, Pharaba 111
Trinity College, North Carolina 173
Tyler, Charles 202
Tyson, Jesse 113, 144, 188
Ulster Quarterly Meeting, Ireland 197, 325
Underhill, Mary 297
Uniform Discipline 100–1, 250–1, 295, 298–300
Union Monthly Meeting, Nebraska 348
Updegraff, David B. 65, 299
Upriver Monthly Meeting, North Carolina 343
Victoria, British Columbia, Canada 351
Virginia Half-Yearly Meeting 110
Votaw, Moses 345
Wabash, Indiana 49, 51–2
Walker, Susan 167
Walls, Alson R. 111
Walnut Ridge Monthly Meeting, Indiana 88–9
Warder, Robert 319
Wasson, Calvin 79–80, 89
Waterford Monthly Meeting, Ireland 197, 201
Watson, James E. 332
W.C.T.U. 26, 235
Wea Plain, Indiana 5, 52, 54
Welch, Turner 52
Wernle Orphans Home 53
West Branch, Ohio 39, 47, 104
West Branch Quarterly Meeting 10, 13, 32, 39–45
West Milton, Ohio 36, 39, 104, 107
Western Literary Union 65
Western Quarterly Meeting, North Carolina 136, 331
Western Yearly Meeting 53, 79–82, 88–9, 91, 96–7, 113, 189, 191, 196, 268, 286, 291, 295–8, 305, 307, 309, 335, 359, 380
Westland Monthly Meeting, Pennsylvania 40
Whitall, James M. 192, 195

White, Francis 144, 147, 331
White, John 163
White Lick Quarterly Meeting, Indiana 104
White, Lilburn 248
Whitewater Quarterly Meeting, Indiana 269
Whitlock, Jane 110
Whittier, California 307–8, 310
Whittier College 252, 291, 310, 329, 331, 334, 364, 381
Whittier, John Greenleaf 210, 257, 261, 320, 376–7
Wilbur, John 100, 238
Wiley, Calvin H. 161
Williams, J. Edgar 345–6
Wilmington, Ohio 79, 249
Wilmington Yearly Meeting 79, 136, 170, 249, 251, 291, 305, 307, 359
Wilson, Drusilla 79–80
Wilson, Henry 79, 202
Wilson, Martha 79
Wilson, Oriana 369
Wing, Asa 330
Winslow, Caleb 144
Winston, Pleasant A. 55
Winthrop, Maine 294
Wood, Marcus L. 161
Wood, William 155
Woodard, Rachel H. 79
Woodbrooke Movement 327
Woods, Adam 197, 326
Woods, Joseph 83
Woody, Mary 180
Woolman, John 82, 295
Wooton, Isom P. 297
Worth, Jonathan 161
Wright, Ellen C. 248–9
Yadkin Valley Quarterly Meeting, North Carolina 331
Y.M.C.A. 147, 282
York, England 234–6
Young Friends Association, Indiana 273
Young Friends Christian Fellowship Union 199, 205
Y.W.C.A. 282

www.ingramcontent.com/pod-product-compliance
Lightning Source LLC
Chambersburg PA
CBHW022046160426
43198CB00008B/139